Gabriel Fauré

Gabriel Fauré

Portrait by John Singer Sargent
Fogg Art Museum
Bequest of Grenville L. Winthrop

Gabriel Fauré

by Émile Vuillermoz

TRANSLATED BY

KENNETH SCHAPIN

CHILTON BOOK COMPANY

PHILADELPHIA   NEW YORK   LONDON

To my dear Joseph Benvenuti,
a Fauréan by race
with much affection.

E. V.

Contents

✼ Chronology

Gabriel Urbain Fauré born in Pamiers, Ariège, France, on May 12th, the sixth child of Toussaint-Honoré Fauré, a school teacher. His first four years were spent in the home of a foster-mother in Verniolles.

1849

The Fauré family, with Gabriel, moved to Montgauzy, near Foix.

1853

It is unclear how Fauré developed his musical talent, but in this year he was already able to play the village harmonium and improvised with ease.

1854

Louis Niedermeyer, the distinguished music pedagogue, heard Fauré and was so impressed with the child's talents that he offered to teach him on a tuition-free basis.

1855

Fauré entered the École Niedermeyer in Paris, where he studied for the next ten years.

1861

Camille Saint-Saëns joined the faculty of the École Niedermeyer and befriended the fifteen-year-old Fauré.

1863

Fauré's *Trois Romances sans paroles, Op. 17,* his first work for piano, was published. He gave the set a high opus number so that buyers of music would not recognize it as an early effort.

1865

Fauré graduated from the École Niedermeyer.

1866

He was appointed organist of the Saint-Sauveur Church in Rennes, a town in Brittany.

1868

Marie Miolan-Carvalho, a well-known singer, visited Rennes and sang Fauré's *Le Papillon et la fleur* as a part of her recital.

1870

He was dismissed from his position in Rennes for playing a morning service in dinner dress. He returned to Paris and was appointed organist of Notre-Dame de Clignancourt. With the outbreak of the Franco-Prussian War later that year, he joined a regiment of light infantry.

1871

Fauré returned to Paris after the war and became organist at

Saint-Honoré d'Eylau. He was also assistant to Widor at Saint-Sulpice and periodically substituted for Saint-Saëns at the Madeleine.

1872

He joined the faculty of the École Niedermeyer.

1873

He entered the circle of the famous singer Pauline Viardot-Garcia and, later, fell deeply in love with her daughter, Marianne Viardot.

1877

Fauré became engaged to Marianne Viardot but she broke the engagement shortly thereafter. The composer was deeply hurt by this incident. During this year he was named assistant organist and choirmaster of the Madeleine and Saint-Saëns introduced him to Liszt in Weimar.

1878

The *Sonata No. 1 for Violin and Piano in A Major, Op. 13* is performed in Paris.

1879

Returned to Germany where he heard Wagner's *Ring* cycle in Munich. It impressed him deeply but he did not fall under Wagner's musical spell. The first movement of his *Violin Concerto, Op. 14,* which was not completed, was performed in Paris.

1883

Visited Bayreuth and married Marie Frémiet, daughter of the sculptor Emmanuel Frémiet. Besides providing a comfortable home for the composer, she did not affect his career or his musical style.

1885

His *Symphony in D Minor, Op. 40* received its world premiere performance under the direction of Edouard Colonne in Paris. Fauré's father died.

1886

He began to compose the *Messe de Requiem, Op. 48* in memory of his father.

1887

Fauré completed the *Requiem.*

1889

The *Requiem* received its world premiere performance at the Madeleine in Paris.

1890

He visited Venice and composed *Cinq Mélodies, Op. 58* to poems by Verlaine.

1891

Began *La Bonne Chanson, Op. 61,* again setting poems by Verlaine.

1892

Completed *La Bonne Chanson* and was appointed inspector of music of state-aided conservatories.

1896

Named chief organist at the Madeleine and professor of composition at the Conservatoire in Paris.

1898

Visited London for a production of Maurice Maeterlinck's play *Pelléas et Mélisande* for which he composed incidental music.

1901

Prométhée, Op. 82, a "lyric tragedy," received its world premiere performance at Beziers and was repeated the following year.

1903

Fauré appointed music critic of *Le Figaro.* At this time he realized that he was losing his hearing.

1905

Appointed Director of the Conservatoire.

1907

Lucienne Breval, the dramatic soprano, suggested that he compose an opera for her based on the story of Penelope.

1909

Fauré elected a member of the Académie des Beaux-Arts.

1910

Fauré was further honored by his country with the rank of Commander of the Légion d'Honneur.

1913

The lyric drama *Pénélope* (no opus number) received its world premiere performance in Monte Carlo.

1920

Resigned from the Conservatoire due to deafness. Further honored with the *grand cordon* of the Légion d'Honneur.

1924

Fauré completed the *String Quartet in E Minor, Op. 121.* A short time afterwards, he died in Paris on November 4th at the age of eighty.

Gabriel Fauré

"Vuillermoz is a great critic and a thoroughbred musician."
—Gabriel Fauré

❧ His Life

To honor Gabriel Fauré's memory with the respect and affection it deserves is to fulfill a mission in which melancholy is mingled with fervor. The joy with which one approaches the study of his chief works is quickly counterbalanced by the irritation caused by the indifference from which they still suffer and the mediocre destiny reserved for this precursor of genius. The more one penetrates into the intimate details of Fauré's life, the more one is pained by the injustice of his fate. As I am writing these lines much over a century after his birth, only a very choice few are interested in the treasures with which he has enriched us.

Certainly, one can easily guess at what might be disturbing to foreign ears in his highly personal music which would prevent it from easily crossing France's borders. This art is, as a matter of fact, representative of the most subtle and expressive elements of French culture, traditions, customs and emotions. For this reason, Fauré will undoubtedly remain too reserved and a bit enigmatic for other peoples.

It would be of no use to search among the supposed imperatives of heredity for an explanation of the exceptional gifts of so consummate a composer In his country ancestry, consisting of butchers and blacksmiths, not one was involved with music. Like so many special artists, Gabriel Fauré represented a phenomenon of "aristocratic spontaneity."

His son, Philippe Fauré-Frémiet, has left us a striking description of his rustic Ariégeois ancestors which, however, does not explain how an ordinary citizen could create the most distinguished "sweet patrician harmony" of his time; but never-

1

theless hints at many of the traits of his character. "The men of this country," Fauré-Frémiet said, "were robust, amiable and tenacious. Deeply tanned, with a bold nose, lively eyes, stern jaw, and small chin, with a wise heart and a *wanderlust*, they seem to carry within themselves some trace of nomadic and Saracen blood. They have the toughness of a mountain dweller who knows that in winter man is completely subject to the will of a savage nature, and the indulgence of the Toulousian who knows that in summer sun and earth will be reconciled in order to please him. They deserve the name of 'Magnagues,' which is a strain of gentry which means 'he who is agreeable, kind and honorable.' What they possess is not great, but honestly acquired. And their wives, those women always dressed in black, are their coworkers. Their tasks are the feminine counterparts of those of the men. If sometimes the man softens, if he is more the Toulousian than the Montagnard, the wife is there to prevent the home from disintegrating."

Because of his smiling affability, his noble profile, his swarthy complexion like that of an Arab nobleman, the obstinacy of his will and the penchant for travel, Gabriel Fauré showed the distinctive and most characteristic traits of his ancestors in certain ways.

In the realm of intellect, Fauré, by being born in Pamiers, had the good fortune to find himself in an environment which had already evolved. His father, the son of a Foix butcher, had pursued his studies seriously in order to become a teacher, and the child did not have to contend with any naive indignation when he showed the first signs of his artistic vocation. Quite to the contrary, his family, whose income was too modest to sustain the expenses of a musical education, went about obtaining a stipend which permitted him to enter the École Niedermeyer in Paris as a boarder when he was nine years old.

This venerable music institution offered its students a complete scholarly education, but it groomed them as a matter of course for honorable positions as organists and choirmasters. It was, in short, really a conservatory of religious art.

Its austerity must have shaken the sensibilities of the small Ariégeois. Until his ninth year, he had lived in an atmosphere of maternal care close to nature, first at his nurse's home, then in the lovely garden which surrounded his parents' house when they settled in Montgauzy. Here his only friends and confidants were the trees, flowers and birds. His delicate constitution agreed with this solitary, poetic and meditative existence which had initiated him into the pleasures of silence and dreams. Uprooted from this naturalistic existence and brusquely thrown into a commonplace Parisian suburb among wild companions who did not spare the new arrival from their hazing, this transplanted country boy must have experienced cruel moments.

But this sweet and rational child, raised to a great extent by parental discipline, courageously accepted the servitudes of his new life and submitted without grumbling to the house rules. This submission imbued his character early in life with a philosophy which was to stand him in good stead during the course of a career fraught with injustice and deception. In a letter he wrote to his wife three years before his death, moving because of its simplicity and frankness, one can read these touching words: "Grant me at least one quality among so many defaults, that of never complaining about anything."

For eleven years he studied at the École Niedermeyer. He found the school's severe director to be sympathetic. Niedermeyer had immediately discerned the remarkable gifts of his new boarder and took it upon himself to personally make sure that these gifts would have a solid technical basis. Thanks to him, when Fauré ended his course of study at twenty, he possessed a "profession" based on a firm foundation and a secure, but flexible, musical style acquired by daily association with the masterpieces of the great German composers. This basic foundation soon allowed him to create a style and vocabulary which were completely his own, without betraying the essential dogmas of the most orthodox musical gospels.

Moreover, this quiet boy was going to discover in boarding-

3

house life the pure joys of friendship. It was at the École Niedermeyer that he pledged to a friend, Eugène Gigout, to the youngest of his teachers, Camille Saint-Saëns, and later to his disciple, André Messager, a consistent and irreproachable loyalty which was to become one of the solaces of his life.

During this period he modestly applied himself to composition, producing several efforts whose vigor, clarity, elegance of form and distinctiveness of conception are astonishing. He was only fifteen when he wrote a graceful song, *Le Papillon et la fleur, Op. 1, No. 1.* The piece was so successful that it immediately received its due reward. Saint-Saëns, who was not able on a particular day to leave Paris to accompany a recital by Mme. Miolan-Carvalho in the suburbs, sent his student Gabriel Fauré as his replacement, at the same time asking the eminent singer to include in her program an unpublished song by the young man. The artiste accepted and enjoyed such success with this charming creation that she soon added it to her repertoire and asked that it be dedicated to her.

Fauré was no more than eighteen years old when he composed his *Cantique de Racine, Op. 11,* for four-part chorus with instrumental accompaniment, and one continues to be amazed at the serenity, nobility and balance which is evidence of an unexpected maturity and a musical inspiration whose purity of elocution was worthy of that of a poet.

The first of the three song collections by Gabriel Fauré brings together his first twenty compositions dating from his youth. One has not been able to fix with precision each one's birthdate. According to an indication by the composer, all seem to have been conceived during his stay at school. And, when one observes that there are pages in this album as accomplished as *Lydia, Op. 4, No. 2; Chanson du pêcheur, Op. 4, No. 1; Sérénade toscane, Op. 3, No. 2; Dans les ruines d'une abbaye, Op. 2, No. 1; Après un rêve, Op. 7, No. 1,* one has an idea of the extraordinary precocity of this schoolboy who never had a career as a child prodigy but who, nevertheless, at the most

4

tender age, manifested a taste, a critical faculty, and a lucidity which astound the imagination.

It is not surprising to learn that this student left the École Niedermeyer bent over with the weight of all of the first prizes from all of his classes, and that soon he was engaged as the organist at the Saint-Sauveur Church in Rennes where, for four years, he was to lead a simple but peaceful existence.

At this point we can already observe some striking aspects of his character, in particular that tranquil independence which was always so dear to him and with which he learned how to defend himself with resolute obstinacy, an inheritance from his distant ancestors. Educated by the disciplines of a religious school of music, professionally destined by his duties as an organist to live in constant contact with an ecclesiastical structure, Fauré, who was neither a believer nor a practitioner, thanks to his perfect manners, learned to hold the esteem of the clergymen with whom he worked without renouncing the freedom of his own convictions.

However, despite his total disinterest, he never hesitated to rebuff parish curates who would ask him to introduce works in the service which inspired in them a naive admiration but whose banality or bad taste were anathema to the composer of the *Cantique de Racine*. It was in the same spirit of mild but inflexible tenacity that, as the head organist, he refused the venerable curate of the Madeleine the satisfaction of using, in the Pentecost Mass, that gross stop, labeled "thunder," which has the effect of evoking to the astonishment of unsophisticated parishioners the spectacular descent of fiery tongues on the foreheads of the twelve apostles.

There was also a similar incident at Rennes where he could not be cured of his habit of going out for a smoke under the church entrance whenever a sermon came along which did not require his services. But his good nature, his charm and talent forgave him everything.

5

However, one day he went too far. The young organist of the Saint-Sauveur having left a dance at dawn and not having had the time to return home to change his clothes, conducted the first morning mass in evening dress, wearing brightly polished shoes and a white tie. Traditionally this was the regulation dress of a keyboard virtuoso and this unintentional dandyism created a scandal, putting an end to his career as a provincial organist.

He returned to Paris and was hired at Notre-Dame de Clignancourt, but soon had to leave this position for one in a military regiment, for the Franco-Prussian War of 1870 had just broken out and his sense of duty did not permit him to stand by as a spectator. He handled himself valiantly in the battle of Champigny, but as soon as the news of the armistice was proclaimed, he hastened back to more peaceful pursuits. We soon find him installed at the great organ at Saint-Honoré d'Eylau, then at the choir organ at Saint-Sulpice, and finally the grand organ loft of the Madeleine where he was to terminate his career as an organist.

That career, lasting for thirty years of his life, was marked by a dilettante-like quality which one must not think of hiding. It was not an enthusiasm for the faith which drew him to these religious duties. The organ was, as far as the students of the École Niedermeyer were concerned, the logical and usual goal of their musical studies. It was also the customary means of earning a livelihood for these artists. By going from one church to another, Fauré was only following the regular channels of his profession, each one of these stopping places representing a gratifying advancement. Only, he was never to consider this kind of activity as an end in itself, but as a means of survival.

He needed to support himself and, unfortunately, the only work which he loved—composing—was not remunerative. The need to give piano lessons, to play for processions and recessionals during High Mass, to write articles, to teach a class, to go on tours of inspection of music institutions or administer examinations, represented for him an uninterrupted succession of necessary duties that he accepted with his customary air of resignation. But Fauré found them irksome for they prevented him from devoting precious time to thought and creation and he suffered seeing himself thus deprived.

While he was very conscientious in the duties he had to perform, he was eager to seize upon all possible avenues of escape which his imagination suggested. The sweet compensations which he had learned to extract from his organist's job were those liberating moments during the course of the service when he improvised. This was for him a projection onto a higher and more spiritual plane of the clandestine cigarette smoking in the Church of the Saint-Sauveur. With sensual pleasure he made the supple, opaline scrollwork of his modulations and his undulating and florid melodic arabesques rise heavenward! Fauré's improvisations quickly became famous among his friends and early admirers and they drew for the eleven o'clock Sunday mass at the Madeleine a small group of the faithful whose assiduousness and fervor were perhaps more musical than religious, but who came, notwithstanding, to hear him play the organ.

Another benefit which Gabriel Fauré derived from this lengthy familiarity with the organ repertory and the liturgical antiphons was a thorough knowledge of the ancient modes which were to enrich his technical vocabulary and make it flexible by freeing it from the traditional and arbitrary dictates of Major and Minor keys. Without employing them for archaic effects, he learned tastefully and with wonderful feeling how to utilize in an extraordinarily subtle manner the Greek scales by fashioning from them passages of an unusual and nuanced flavor. Never has one seen a more eloquent example of the exquisite transmutation of values which can be operative in a musician of genius by borrowing the boldest and most effective elements of an entirely novel grammar and syntax from the oral heritage of the distant past.

7

The inner feelings of an artist as discrete and secretive as Gabriel Fauré are not easy to define or to classify. Outwardly, his life unfolded without any major jolts or spectacular catastrophes. To any observer his destiny was a happy one. This young provincial of modest origin was able to conquer Paris with apparent ease. What beginning artist without means does not envy the fate of this village scholar who knew how to climb slowly but surely to the highest echelons of fame by effortlessly charming the Parisian salons and successively becoming organist at the Madeleine, inspector of musical instruction of the Administration des Beaux-Arts, professor of composition at the Conservatoire, music critic of *Le Figaro*, Director of the Conservatoire, member of the Institut, recipient of the Légion d'honneur cross, and the supreme honor awarded by his country of a national burial? Had he not traversed with a firm and sure step the whole cycle of official honors and professional canonizations?

But, the other side of this lovely picture was less brilliant. Fauré was a modest and wise man who remained utterly indifferent to the vain satisfactions which his career could bring him. "You possess every quality," Saint-Saëns told him, "but you lack one fault which is indispensable to an artist: ambition. . . ." All of his positions represented only economic security for him. Moreover, despite appearances, they were not very remunerative. They devoured his time and exiled him from that "secret garden" of his dreams and had no other purpose than to sentence him to a mediocre existence which was disheartening.

But still he was sensitive, emotional and sensual, wonderfully constituted to gather and savor the pleasures of life as a connoisseur and consequently more apt to suffer from being deprived of them. His private correspondence, in which one can find candid reflections as he relates the most humble daily events, shows him to be as happy as a child over some little satisfaction resulting from pure chance. During his vacations, the discovery of an agreeable hotel accommodation, the pleasure of having a balcony, the view from a terrace overlooking a lake or a well-ordered countryside would overcome him with delight. It was as a gourmet that he appreciated these niceties. One's heart misses a beat when he is seen leaving, with a courageous good humor which fools nobody, a delightful Swiss pension which enchanted him and where he worked so well, but whose room and board went beyond his budget. And it is a bit sad to hear this supremely unselfish being exclaim brightly, after having treated himself to the rare luxury of some modest comfort, "All the same, it's nice to be wealthy! . . ."

The deep-rooted pessimism which characterized this "smiling" philosophy has often been the subject for discussion. The term seems to me to be badly out of place. He should have had the right to express this feeling considering his disadvantaged financial condition together with the prospect of growing old without resources. But in reality, his clarity of mind and lack of illusions did not deprive him of his forebearance and confident equanimity. He wrote to his wife: "I have a naivete which has always led me to believe in good rather than in evil. . . . You speak to me of your love for God and your scorn for his creatures. Are you being fair? The universe is order; man is disorder. But, is this his fault? He was cast upon this earth where everything seems to be harmonious, and yet he staggers and stumbles from the day of his birth to the day of his death. He was put on this earth burdened with such a magnitude of physical and moral afflictions that it was necessary to invent the original sin in order to explain this phenomenon! . . . No, this little package of evils which is man, this being condemned to struggle for life and whose first and most awful task is to devour another in order not to be devoured himself, is worthy of more leniency."

Is this the language of a pessimist? Moreover, who would dare apply this word to the musician who wrote the tenderest and most compassionate of requiems? Fauré was a melancholy and resigned observer of the human condition, but, as he said himself, he possessed the capacity to "never complain about anything."

Concluding his difficult internship, the young organist of the Saint-Sauveur made contact with Rennes society under quite favorable circumstances. The small town welcomed him congenially. Several middle-class salons opened their doors to him and he was received with open arms by local singers who sight-read his first songs.

The *mélodie,* the *lied* and the *romance* are genres eminently suitable for fostering a close relationship between composer and listener. Their modest dimensions, which do not curtail conversation for long, their pleasant melodic lines and occasionally the charms of their interpreters, are all in their favor. It is probable that *Le Papillon et la fleur* ruffled the heart of more than one romantically inclined female. The same social phenomenon recurred in Paris and Fauré had no difficulty in being admitted to those cultivated circles interested in his distinguished music.

One of the households which he found exceptionally attractive belonged to the famous singer Pauline Viardot, where composers such as Saint-Saëns and Gounod socialized with such authors as Flaubert and Turgenev. The family was gracious and Fauré was intoxicated by the artistic and stimulating atmosphere.

He was passionately taken with one of the hostess' daughters, the distracting Marianne, asked for her hand and received her family's permission. But after several months, the young girl, for reasons no one really knows, broke off the engagement and sent the unfortunate Fauré away. This was a very severe blow to the young, emotional artist and it wounded him deeply; the scar healed slowly. As always, with delicacy and discretion, he kept his sorrow to himself and tried to excuse her for her ungratefulness, but his sensitive nature had been touched to the quick with a red-hot poker by this, the first of his life's cruelties. Chopin, with whom Fauré has more than a spiritual affinity, harbored the same secret melancholy all of his life after Maria Wodzinska left him.

Too reserved to expose his grief in his works—the moving

andante from his *Piano Quartet No. 1 in C Minor, Op. 15* has been considered a confession a bit too often—the young composer manfully returned to work. And it is in this incident that one can clearly observe the prerogative exercised by Fauré's musical genius to escape from any threatening force alien to his art. In a similar way, a Beethoven and a Berlioz "orchestrated" their despair and forced their cellos and clarinets to express their deepest emotions. With Fauré, this did not take place. His inspiration did not allow itself to become sidetracked from the internal logic and dignity of pure music by any external influences, even if they were of the most demanding nature. If his heart was broken, he still wrote with a lucid and free hand the dazzling *scherzo* and *finale* of his first *Piano Quartet,* his graceful *Berceuse, Op. 16* for violin, songs such as *Nell, Op. 18, No. 1; Le Voyageur, Op. 18, No. 2; Automne, Op. 18, No. 3; Les Berceaux, Op. 23, No. 1; Le Secret, Op. 23, No. 3,* and he concluded the exquisite *Ballade, Op. 19* for piano and orchestra with the rustling of a thousand small voices in an enchanted forest.

Thus it can be observed that in the realm of expression he does not want to be descriptive. Like Chopin, Fauré refused to give titles to his works (painters would call them "symbols"). His scores can be deeply impregnated with emotions or secret thoughts, but they have to be content with bearing the most impersonal titles like prélude, impromptu, nocturne, ballade, barcarolle, valse-caprice or fantaisie. And often the suggestive element in a title like "nocturne," for example, is not honored in the piece which has this title, because the discipline of mental transposition that the composer imposes upon himself is so inflexible. For Fauré, music is a direct and complete language which needs no outside assistance in order to find its way to the heart.

Approaching forty, the ex-fiancé of Marianne Viardot found in the family of the famous sculptor Frémiet an affectionate environment which offered him the comforts of happiness.

Frémiet, a friend of Saint-Saëns, sincerely admired Gabriel Fauré's genius, and he took it upon himself to pledge his support and help him in his difficult career. He was, therefore, particularly happy to see his intelligent and artistic daughter, Marie, succumbing to the charms of this elegant musician and accepting his offer of marriage. Two sons were to be born as a result of this union which, despite the thirst for independence and the taste for travel of this descendant of the Ariégois, insured the protection of his family life and offered him benefits that he enjoyed until his last breath.

The young family struggled courageously to survive. Marie Frémiet painted fans tastefully while her husband gave music lessons and, with difficulty, arranged for performances of his works. Moreover, he composed with greater regularity. He was no longer content with charming songs. Fauré's songs were being transformed. He had come in contact with the major works of Wagner. While admiring their grandeur and nobility, he very quickly came to understand, just as Debussy was to later realize, how dangerous a fascination Wagnerian music-drama could be for French composers. But he did not condemn the composer of *Tristan* with the brutal intolerance of the exasperated Claude de France who wanted Wagner excommunicated.

Fauré learned something useful from the Bayreuth master. The discovery of continuous melody and the loosening of formal boundaries in musical composition made him finally abandon the use of couplets in his first collection of songs and in his subsequent vocal works. The romances became melodic, and the striking harmonic discoveries of the second collection of songs became more numerous. He employed other formal schemes in his aristocratic *Pavane, Op. 50* for chorus and orchestra, his *Madrigal, Op. 35, Concerto for Violin and Orchestra, Op. 14, Symphony in D Minor, Op. 40,* and a *Suite d'orchestre, Op. 20* (three pieces that he withdrew after their first performances), his noble *Élégie, Op. 24* for cello, his *Piano Quartet No. 2 in G Minor, Op. 45,* and his *Requiem, Op.*

48, his incidental music for *Caligula, Op. 52,* and *Shylock, Op. 57,* and above all, the flowering of admirable pianistic works: barcarolles, impromptus, nocturnes, valses-caprices, a *Mazurka, Op. 32,* and the delightful *Dolly, Op. 56.* And, if one wants to understand that secret sadness which sometimes hovers like a light mist over Fauré's inner life, one must remember the distressing material conditions under which this industrious man was creating this catalogue of masterpieces. How does one measure the energy that he expended in order to resist the discouragement his job continually brought him? "I am forever going to the Madeleine and giving lessons. My students are in Versailles, in Ville-d'Avray, in Saint-Germain, in Louveciennes. It takes me, on the average, three hours a day travelling on the train. I should really like, even for just ten days, to forget about everything, and see some other people and places rather than that everlasting Saint-Lazare station, and not have to listen to any more sonatas, to have a change of atmosphere."

A third family was to play an important role in Gabriel Fauré's professional and emotional life, that of the celebrated harpist Alphonse Hasselmans, composer and virtuoso, who trained the most illustrious French harpists of the time. Fauré had had the opportunity to be associated with him at the Conservatoire in the intense struggle that the advocates of the pedal harp had undertaken against the partisans of the chromatic harp, just invented by Gustave Lyon. This tireless and vital man had discovered an ingenious simplification of the instrument's mechanism and had created a special class at the Conservatoire for the propagation of his method. Those loyal to the classic harp held that, among other faults, the new disposition of the strings did not preserve their characteristic sonority. They did not accept the middle position between the two rival instruments officially taken by the Office of Instruction. A protest group was organized, and Fauré, clearly taking up the defense of the pedal harp and opposing Lyon's chromatic harp, was brought forth to support Alphonse Hasselmans, the brilliant professor of that class at the Conservatoire. He succeeded in having the chromatic harp class dropped, and everything returned to normal.

Frequently seeing Hasselmans, Fauré became interested in his two children, both musicians. There was Louis, a cellist for whom the two sonatas for cello were composed, and subsequently a conductor, and Marguerite, an excellent pianist who was passionately interested in Fauré's music. He found amongst them a wonderful musical atmosphere and sincere affection whose intensity and fidelity were particularly touching and which helped him to the end of his days to bear many an ordeal.

Continually concerned whether he could snatch a few precious hours that he wanted to devote to composing from those jobs which sustained him economically, Fauré periodically tried to escape the responsibilities which lay upon him. Unfortunately, his hopes for liberation were always disappointed because the official positions he filled were not very remunerative.

Let me give a small but very characteristic example of what I am talking about, if I may, drawn from my personal memory. When I was at the Conservatoire, in this incomparable master's composition class, I had to fulfill the requirements for my admission to the Society of Authors and Composers. I was asked, according to regulations, to provide two sponsors. With his customary goodwill toward young people, Fauré allowed me to choose him. Georges Hüe, then at the height of his career, completed my grand patronage.

Immensely proud to possess an application form signed by two such illustrious composers, I confidently presented it to the office of the S.A.C.E.M. However, the employee who took it did not appear to be as astonished as I had hoped. Quite the contrary. He scowled and said to me, "Fauré? . . . . Fauré, Gabriel? . . . . We don't have anyone here with that name." And he leafed through his registration book with a suspicious expression on his face.

14

Angered with the impetuous indignation of youth, I severely reprimanded the impertinence of this petty official by reminding him that Gabriel Fauré was a professor of composition at the Conservatoire, that he was world famous and had composed numerous masterworks. "That's quite possible, young man," he calmly retorted, "only, you see, in the Society of Authors, in order to be a sponsor, after all one must be first a member, and in order to be a member, a composer must receive from his performances a minimum of 200 francs in royalties a month. And, your Gabriel Fauré has never earned such a sum!"

And it was true. The composers of little popular ditties were already making astronomical amounts of money at that time but, incomprehensibly, the composer of the *La Bonne Chanson* was classified among the obscure and itinerant workers, the "economically unemployable," unworthy of taking his place next to the powerful magnates of the variety halls. I had to find another sponsor, all the while bitterly deploring such a monstrous social structure which passed judgment on people, on an era, and on an entire civilization.

My indignation was all the more sincere because the circumstances under which I had met my teacher had instilled in me a lasting gratitude. I regret introducing in this study a small personal recollection which, in itself, has no interest for the reader, but it does show Gabriel Fauré's kindness and natural goodness that I must publicly acknowledge after having benefited so much from it.

My first meeting with this rare being took place in Lyons, in the austere main city of the Rhône, where my parents, who had discovered with trepidation my dangerous inclination for music sent me, after finishing high school, to prepare simultaneously for two licenses, one in the liberal arts and the other in law. This double task, it seemed to them, would be absorbing enough to leave me no spare time for my perverse dreams. But the germ of an artistic vocation is so virile and so active that it will resist the strongest antibiotics administered by prudent families. I was observed attending jurist and philology courses with an air of resignation, but no one suspected that at the same time I had secretly enrolled at the Lyons Conservatoire where I studied organ and harmony under the direction of Daniel Fleuret, that remarkable musician who was organist at the Church of the Redemption.

I was thus, for better or for worse, drawn by three steeds harnessed to the chariot which was my destiny, when it was announced one fine day that an inspector of music education from Paris was going to visit the classes at the Lyons Conservatoire and question the pupils. His name, we were told, was Gabriel Fauré. The mere mention of this name caused great confusion among us. We were only slightly reassured when he was introduced to our harmony class, this "special envoy" of the Administration des Beaux-Arts who was making a tour of the provinces.

He walked in, and when I had the courage to lift my eyes toward his face, I was immediately won over and charmed by the august visitor. I saw before me a smallish man, somewhat stout, dressed without studied elegance, but possessing a fascinating physiognomy. Framed by a beautiful head of prematurely silver hair, whose waves were like a halo, this well-shaped face was instantaneously and for all time engraved on my mind. The color of this Ariégeois was somewhat amber, like an Indian sultan. A trim mustache, slightly yellowed from constant contact with a cigarette, hid a smile which hovered between indulgence and malice. His voice was veiled and had the delicate and compelling inflection of a violin string which had been muted. One could not resist its persuasive softness.

However, the most irresistible feature of his attractive head was his eyes, which had the tenderness and the languidness of a gazelle. Those eyes did not look upon the commonplace or the sordidness of life. They were created for dreaming. The direction of their gaze was beyond mankind and material things. They looked on an enchanted universe where a composer's thoughts could develop with ease. From this first contact, I sensed that this inspired person dwelled partly on this earth and that the unreal and invisible fairyland was more familiar to him than his day-to-day existence. Paul Valéry admired the life of the dancer who "spends half of his life up in the air." Fauré spent half of his life in a mysterious stratosphere where his masterpieces flowered one by one. And that is the reason why he was so often thought of as distant and indifferent, when he was only distracted by his compelling inner thoughts.

The director of the Lyons Conservatoire, Aimé Gros, presented our small group. We were polite but a bit unsettled in the presence of this Grand Inquisitor who seated himself comfortably at the piano and asked to see some samples of our student efforts. He carefully examined our "basses" and our "given melodies," made some technical observations whose novelty and correctness impressed us. Then, as I later saw him do in his class in Paris, he pushed aside these academic exercises and asked with a smile if some of us had not made some attempts in the realm of composition. Our teacher, Daniel Fleuret, who was fond of me and had picked me as his assistant at the organ of the Church of the Redemption, had two or three of my timid attempts. To my horror, I saw him place one of my more recent efforts on the piano and I felt my blood turning to ice when Fauré began to play. And it was during my extreme embarrassment and confusion that I vaguely heard the few words of encouragement addressed to me after closing my score. Then he vanished like some supernatural being.

A year later, I had succeeded in overcoming my family's opposition to a musical career. They allowed me, at my own expense, to settle in Paris in order to devote myself entirely to music. However, before resigning himself to such a misfortune, my father, who had a practical nature, wanted to assure himself with some tangible guarantees and decided to put me through a preliminary examination by a panel of experts, very much like a health examination by a board of medical specialists.

One fine day I was put in a room with a double lock. There was a piano and a supply of blank music paper. I was, like a candidate for the Prix de Rome, told to instantaneously produce a masterpiece! A Parisian music critic, Georges Street, hired by my family and, supposedly, a natural son of Liszt, had organized the whole thing and had taken it upon himself—the traitor!—to submit the manuscript wormed out of me to Massenet and to Gabriel Fauré.

My anger and humiliation were complete. I completely sensed the childishness of such an examination, and I was disheartened to have my future depend on this absurd experiment. However, having been forced into a corner, I could not escape the challenge. Gritting my teeth, I began the task and paid the price required by my executioners.

The results were soon forthcoming. Massenet got rid of any troublesome person who brought him a manuscript by killing him with kindness. He stated that my genius seemed to be on a level with that of Bach and Beethoven, which favorably impressed my parents. As for Fauré, he answered courteously that he had remembered seeing one of my student works the year before at the Lyons Conservatory and had a good impression of it. My new work was of modest ability and indicated that it would not be unwise to allow me to undertake serious music studies in Paris, where Fauré would willingly accept me in his composition class after a period of one or two years with Tandou, who was, in his opinion, the best teacher of harmony in the school. I had thus beat them at their own game, thanks to the professional conscience of that so-called dilettante who did not consider it unworthy of himself to take an interest in the fate of an obscure provincial student.

If I cite this anecdote, it is because Gabriel Fauré has too often been described as a frivolous and thoughtless person, an egotist, a salon composer, and a simple and spoiled child. His success with women, his easy-going nonchalance and his indulgent scepticism had earned for him this false reputation furthered by rivals jealous of his superlative grace. Austere pedagogues detested him and could not accept the fact that he was an admirable composition teacher, in spite of the fact that he did not adhere to strict dogmatism.

He seemed to have adopted for rules of conduct those very wise philosophical maxims that later a mock moralist was to formulate for the use of an imaginary son: "Take seriously only those people who know how to smile, and beware of all the others. People who speak too seriously are usually rather ordinary. And, since they take themselves so seriously, you will be quickly dispensed with." Fauré detested bondage, routine and constraints, but his good humor, his simplicity, and his complete absence of pedantry did not prevent him from being a secure and enlightened leader who exposed his disciples to the most marvelous instruction.

Gabriel Fauré's presence in the composition class at the Conservatoire, where he succeeded Massenet, revealed a few of the more attractive features of his personality. He entered the venerated Faculté de Musique of the Poissonnière District, whose director at that time was the academician Théodore Dubois, where his appointment was preceded by some suspicion. He was not part of the "establishment." He was going to teach in a system whose doctrines and traditions he did not know. He possessed no degree from any official course of study. He was considered flighty, frivolous, nonchalant and quite the dilettante. What kind of authority could a teacher command who was not licensed? Wasn't it absurd to entrust the fate of an entire generation of young composers to someone who did not even have credentials?

Assuredly, Gabriel Fauré did not have the outward appearance of a teacher. Unpretentious, cordial, pleasant toward students, he did not try to assume a haughty domineering attitude. He treated his students in a friendly manner, like an older brother. But, he had a mysterious element of authority which was irresistibly effective—his genius. No pedagogue with a degree ever held sway over his students with a magic equal to this smiling educator who was completely devoid of arrogance. He dominated them and subjugated them by reason of his staggering musical superiority which the least gifted of his students, even those who were incapable of attaining his goals, came to be aware of without understanding its nature.

There emanated from him, unconsciously, a kind of flowing mastery which was captivating. I have always wondered how those students whose names were not Schmitt, Ravel, Enesco, Casella, Louis Aubert or Koechlin had the audacity to show him their manuscripts that he read or played at the piano so obligingly. Personally, when my turn had come to be presumptuous, I felt a real uneasiness, as if I had been guilty of an act of megalomania and disrespect.

And yet, we were not unaware of the friendliness and indulgence of our teacher who sustained an atmosphere of cordiality to make us feel comfortable in his class. He knew how to criticize in an affable tone which never wounded our egos too cruelly and did not leave us with any bitterness. He would seat himself at the piano and we crowded about him. He quickly corrected our counterpoint exercises and with a more marked interest turned to our original efforts which drew extraordinarily perceptive comments from him. And when a piece seemed mediocre to him, he would simply say to the composer, "Have you brought along something else?"

At that time he did not yet suffer from the arterial sclerosis which was to torture him, and his fingers were visibly magnetized by the keyboard. Instinctively, between two manuscript readings, he would brush the keys nonchalantly, trying out a melody or a series of chords which came into his mind and which he seemed to put hastily away in some remote corner of his memory where they would wait until he had the opportunity to use them. It was only a brief glimpse at a book quickly opened and closed for him alone. It was a means of furtively appeasing the thirst to create which tormented him continually. But he soon regained his composure and affably started playing the sonata fragment, the scherzo or the theme that the next student had given him.

And then, suddenly, as if he had exhausted his usual amount of politeness and patience, he would get up, close the piano, stretch, and mutter pleasantly, "I think I'll go. . . ." Then he made his farewells and went quietly away, his head certainly buzzing with themes, harmonic discoveries and bold modulations which fermented within him whenever he was about to gain his freedom.

On this subject, I should like to clarify a misunderstanding arising from an incorrect interpretation of a bit of information from Philippe Fauré-Frémiet, who told us that as Director of the Conservatoire his father had been given the name of "Robespierre" when he became the director, because of the ruthless "executions" he delighted in issuing. "He ordered a head to roll every day." Let me say that no student was ever tempted to call him such a name for we all had a passionate liking for him. But it is accurate that upon entering our Faculté de Musique, Fauré had to get rid of some undesirable parasites who were jeopardizing the school's good reputation and this he had to accomplish more or less forcefully.

The juries, in particular, had been sometimes overrun by unscrupulous "opportunists" who cashed in on their duties or indirectly drew unlawful benefits from them. Too many candidates, in order to gain their support, understandably asked them for lessons during the year preceding the examination. Moreover, certain teachers at the Conservatoire who got their jobs through intrigue and politics were deservedly excluded from the juries. Conscious of his responsibilities, the new director wanted to stop these scandals immediately and despite the violent opposition that his decisions aroused, he was unmerciful toward these instructors. It was for this, not because of strict disciplinary rules, that he was called "incorruptible." And it is only in this sense that the nickname should be under-

21

stood because it does the greatest honor to his honesty and courage.

Fauré naturally was a good person and I am going to take the liberty to give additional evidence, proudly, for his conduct in my opinion was in the nature of a test. I related with what kindness he treated me and helped me at the start of my studies. When I entered his class, he greeted me in a most affectionate manner and never ceased to be interested in my future from that time on. However, I did not represent for him, professionally speaking, a disciple, who could possibly do him honor. From the beginning I had not hidden any of my plans or objectives from him. Basic good sense had taught me that, unless one hears within oneself the imperious call of genius, one has to be quite pretentious in order to claim a place in the sun during a period as exceptional as the one in which fate decreed my birth.

An apprentice composer in 1900 would be literally inundated by the abundance of masterpieces which were being created daily around him. At no other time was the beautiful tree of French music covered with so much fruit. Not being presumptuous enough to believe I could augment this magnificent harvest, and realizing on the other hand that the revolution I was witnessing was producing a quantity of exciting esthetic problems, I persuaded myself that by studying them I would find a less congested battleground where I would perhaps have a chance to be of some service.

Already dangerous misunderstandings were beginning to be discernible and public opinion was bewildered. One had to fight to support the efforts of a Fauré, a Debussy and, before long, a Ravel, whom the public fearfully avoided when all three had their arms full of incomparable treasures. To defend them, to clarify their still unformulated gospel, to open up a path for them in the hostile crowd, to support and order all of the divergent ideas which were circulating, to identify the imposters and to focus on the musicians of good intent, seemed to me to be an exciting mission.

But in order to accomplish it effectively, one had to thoroughly know music, to have the advantage of an authority and competence which could not be questioned. That is why I was anxious to conscientiously learn my "profession" as a composer, to speak and write fluently in the language of music and to prove myself in this direction before turning to music criticism, which had always secretly attracted me. It was then agreed that I would not prepare myself for the Prix de Rome competition and that no purely scholastic ambition would deter me from my plans.

Any teacher other than Gabriel Fauré would have been offended by such a decision, but this understanding person did not pressure me to change my direction even when he was given the directorship of the Conservatoire. Though his duties separated him from his students, he always assured me of his artistic sympathy for my goal. He would call me to sit on Conservatoire juries and kept in regular contact with me. I have a vivid memory of friendly and lively conversations with him around a table at the Mollard restaurant where we used to lunch, *tête-à-tête*, between two sessions when the Conservatoire was on the Rue Madrid. It was there, and in another restaurant that he loved in the Malesherbes district, that I can still see him relaxed, serene and carefree while I was enjoying the charm of his voice and his conversation. He was gifted with a nature rarely accorded an artist.

I can't count the number of times he confided in me. When he composed some rather delectable incidental music for a play by Clemenceau, *Le Voile du Bonheur* (*Op. 88*), created for the Théâtre de la Porte-Saint-Martin, it was I whom he chose to conduct the small instrumental and vocal ensemble from the wings. In the confusion which followed a sudden cancellation of the play some weeks later, the score and parts for this embarrassingly grotesque farce disappeared and were never found.

When Fauré left his post as music critic of *Le Figaro*, he thought of me as his successor. He was also anxious to write a preface for one of my books, a collection of some of my musical

23

writings for *Le Temps*. Some time later, learning that one of his friends, a wealthy industrialist, was going to found a newspaper refusing all advertising in order to remain totally independent, it was again Fauré who offered me the position of music critic with all of the intoxicating freedom that went along with it. This was one of the most curious journalistic experiments in the history of the press, but its basic concepts could not survive the caprices of a patron and it inevitably died with him. Beyond the precious lessons I got out of this amazing adventure, it afforded me the opportunity to journey frequently to Nice where Gabriel Fauré, because of his health, had accepted the hospitality of the daring founder of *L'Impartial Française*, in his beautiful home on the Promenade des Anglais, where we spent, with André Messager, wonderful winter evenings.

To conclude this sketch of the so-called "Robespierre," I should like to show, by means of a final anecdote, the extents to which his affectionate generosity, complete integrity and artistic scruples would go. In the old Salle Erard I was sitting next to my teacher at the first performance of Ravel's *Histoires Naturelles* sung by Jane Bathori and accompanied by the composer. The audience was excited, and one could sense a storm brewing. It was known that Ravel, anxious to capture the incisive prose of Jules Renard, had attempted a revolutionary treatment of musical meter in this work. He had wanted to preserve the sound and rhythms of daily conversation, and in order to facilitate the melodic transference, had omitted the mute syllables on which the music, putting one note to each syllable, produced a strongly accented chord. Instead of the following proper division: "Il ap-pel-le sa fi-an-cée, el-le n'est pas ve-nu-e," he notated the words this way: "Il ap-pel'-sa-fian-cé', ell'-n'est pas-v'nu'." Thus he saved six syllables and consequently six notes out of sixteen.

The lyricists of café concerts have for a long time adopted this simplification, but at this concert there was trouble, be-

24

cause this innovation was not to everybody's taste. It was shocking to hear a serious composer introduce elements of musical diction in his music borrowed from music hall revues. The greeting extended to this charming collection of songs was clearly hostile and there were slight riots in the hall.

Fauré said nothing, but the vulgar and common prose visibly annoyed him. For the first time, his favorite student had wounded him and he was suffering because of it. He rapidly left the hall at the end of the concert, asking me to drive him home.

On the way, he did not hide his irritation and sharply criticized this stupidity. After arguing his point and noticing that I did not seem as outraged as he, he said to me, with a certain bitterness, "Did you like that, you of all people?" With caution and respect, I began a timid defense of Ravel's intention. He had, in my opinion, tried to bring across by that free elocution the ironic and sarcastic aspects of the author's tongue-in-cheek style. Didn't the music reflect faithfully the characteristics and exact mood of the text's humor? Didn't the rapid declamation curiously reproduce familiar intonations, as in relating a pleasant story, when a person would let his voice fall at the end of a sentence and put his hand on his hip while pirouetting on his feet? I even mentioned the official sanction that French classic prosody grants to the systematic elision of mute syllables when they end a line. All lines which have a feminine rhyme scheme should have, in reality, a foot too much if the prosody laws did not require suppressing their final syllables.

Fauré listened to me attentively and I really felt that he would have loved to have allowed himself to be convinced because he held Ravel in such affectionate esteem, but his bad mood was stronger. However, when I took leave of him, on the porch of his home, he said to me, "After all, you might be right. One must not trust first impressions. Tell Ravel to come tomorrow and play his score for me again, so that I will not be committing an injustice!"

Fauré required that student composers who were assigned to him already possess a basic technique. He was particularly insistent on this point. He did not consider it his duty to teach them the rules of the road at the moment when he gave them control of the wheel. That is why he always considered it an error to teach counterpoint, fugue and composition in the same class. Counterpoint and fugue are, for the future composer, indispensable tools. They are comparable to gymnastic exercises and the daily routines of physical culture without which no true athlete can succeed. They are to composition what solfeggio is to harmony. They should be taught in a special class which would constitute the first step in the science of musical composition.

Fauré did not underestimate the technical benefits derived from fugue and counterpoint. His course of study at the École Niedermeyer and his thorough knowledge of the works of Bach reveal his orthodox views on this subject. But, just as one does not take a harmony class at the Conservatoire without having proved himself capable of harmonizing a given bass and melody, he should not become a composition student before concluding his studies in fugue and counterpoint. These are the concrete, unchanging requirements for the composer. Not until these skills are mastered does composition become an entirely different thing.

The creative act calls upon areas which escape classification in scholarly texts. That is why Fauré believed his true task consisted of discovering, even in the most modestly gifted of his pupils, the mysterious sparkle of life, the interior throbbing, the minor miracle which, by the juxtaposition of three notes or two chords, produces a novel, fresh effect or a powerful emotion proclaiming an authentic musician and a sound poet. That is also why he often entrusted the strongest technicians of the class, especially Charles Koechlin, with the task of correcting our counterpoint exercises, while he would scrutinize a piano piece, a melody, or a sonata movement which told him a lot more about the weaknesses and strengths of their composers.

26

The teacher who has the job of forming the hand, the mind and the heart of a young artist at the time when his sensitivity is still malleable, like the warm wax of a record before it is pressed, is too often inclined to impose the seal of his own personality upon this tractable material. He can conclude that the beginner will save precious time by being told the solutions to the problems which are causing him difficulty by the professor who has discovered the answers in the course of his own career. In such a manner dogmatic instruction, uncompromising theories, and what one might call "totalitarian esthetics" are born.

Such was not Gabriel Faure's aim. His principal concern was, on the contrary, to allow the individual qualities of the young creators under his care to develop freely. He helped them when they were in trouble, but allowed their personal temperaments to assert themselves. And it was thus, while endowing his students with a very solid basic technique and with an astonishing facility, that he was able to safeguard the precious individuality of a Maurice Ravel, a Florent Schmitt, an Alfredo Casella, or a Georges Enesco, and to protect the gifts of a colorist such as Laparra, the elegance of a Louis Aubert, the pedagogical mind of a Nadia Boulanger, the warm lyricism of a Henri Février, the dramatic sense of a Mazellier, or the encyclopedic curiosity of a Charles Koechlin. That was a unique tour de force in the history of the teaching of composition.

Gabriel Fauré's great attribute was to have understood that the musical language can progress only by the development and enrichment of harmony. Counterpoint had been brought to a point of perfection by Bach. No step forward had been made in harmony since the death of the great Cantor and nothing since has shown that it could go further. Fauré was formed at the École Niedermeyer among a stable of organists and choirmasters who thoroughly knew the secrets of this style of writing, but used it for a technical exercise and not as a means of expression. Fauré knew that harmonic discoveries—the annex-

27

ation of a new chord, of an unexpected relationship between superimposed sound—make for the life and energy of our art. All of the conquests of Wagner, Liszt, Chopin, Gounod, Lalo, Moussorgsky, Chabrier and, naturally Fauré, Debussy and Ravel, were realized solely in the domain of harmony. Counterpoint had no part in it. To have had the courage to base one's teaching on that axiom denotes a singular clairvoyance and true courage.

But courage was a natural virtue of this would-be philosopher who was both nonchalant and a sceptic. He knew how to defend his pupils. When the Institut, bringing ridicule on itself, refused to allow Maurice Ravel—who had already shown at that time the extent of his talent with his *Sonatine, Shéhérazade, Miroirs, Pavane pour une infante défunte,* the dazzling *Jeux d'eau* and the masterful *String Quartet in F Major*—to compete for the Prix de Rome in 1905, Fauré publicly defended his student so vehemently that there was a scandal and the official jury got what it deserved.

Several years later, he was to show his noble character again. The Société Nationale de Musique, founded after the war of 1870 by Saint-Saëns and Raymond Bussine in order to protect the rights of French composers, was then the only outlet for the young composers of France. For many years, it rendered the most invaluable service for music, and it deserves much praise for the generous hospitality it accorded Gabriel Fauré's works (he was briefly its secretary). But the infiltration of the most active members of Vincent d'Indy's Schola Cantorum into its committee progressively modified its musical atmosphere. Vincent d'Indy, who possesed the ardent soul of an apostle and a preacher of crusades, had communicated to the members of his clique his uncompromising zeal for pedantry. Legitimately concerned in having his esthetic theories win out by opposing those of the Conservatoire, he had assumed the directorship of the Schola in the spirit of a missionary ready for a fight. The Scholists systematically blacklisted concert programs which featured heretical works by students enrolled in the official courses of instruction, and in particular those who admired Fauré and Debussy. This strategy was logical. Without a doubt this deprived the Société Nationale of its impartiality and its reputation as a friendly host. But could crusaders filled with a faith which heroically drove back the unfaithful be stopped by such scruples? They continued their "cleanup" and remained in control of the battlefield on which they had solidly entrenched themselves.

They eliminated all scores that were "suspected of heresy" while their products manufactured on the Rue Saint-Jacques were shown off to advantage in shop windows. This was so annoying to good sense and justice that a violent reaction set in. The young musicians who were ousted joined together and decided to establish a concert society which would be called Société Musicale Indépendante. My friends appointed me to organize this movement and assemble a committee. The only disconcerting problem was that of choice, for among the victims of the Scholists were Maurice Ravel, Florent Schmitt, Charles Koechlin, Jean Huré, Louis Aubert, Roger Ducasse—all students of Fauré—and D. E. Inghelbrecht, who put his baton in our service. The publisher A. Z. Mathot, who had been interested in us for some time, agreed to house the Société on his premises in the Rue Bergère, in immediate proximity to the Conservatoire which had not yet moved from Rue Madrid. Mathot took charge of our general office and administrative functions. And then the uproar began.

Until then, there was nothing unusual in all of this. Every generation has known impassioned differences of opinion. The era of 1900, which witnessed the appearance of *Louise, Pelléas, Ariane et Barbe Bleue* and so many other shocking works, was particularly ripe for guerrilla tactics indispensable to the life blood of the arts. The disappearance of this in our present day society is very regrettable. Now music lovers remain passive and reactionless in the presence of the most stupefying musical events which ought to provoke their enthusiasm or their indignation. The counterattack that we were preparing was then very legitimate, but our audacity was to ask Gabriel Fauré to take over the presidency of our group. To invite a high official, a member of the Institut and a director of a state organization like the Conservatoire to take command of a battalion of revolutionists, represented an action whose impertinence we were incapable of measuring. But we were right to count on the bravura and independence of our teacher, because he gave his immediate approval to our plan.

His value was limitless. While professing in music very different opinions from those proclaimed by the Schola, he was on friendly terms with Vincent d'Indy, whose cordiality was certainly going to be compromised by this open act of opposition. On the other hand, he knew the sullen conservatism of his teacher Saint-Saëns, who unpityingly condemned "Debusssy-ism" and the audacious staking out of the claims of "prospecting" young composers whose language differed from his own, and he could, with good reason fear the reaction to this coup d'état. It was not long in coming. Fauré received from the composer of *Samson* a letter which shook the foundations of the new temple by ordering his former pupil to break immediately with those "little anarchists" who were compromising him by having him play such a dangerous role.

Fauré had a fervent and respectful tenderness toward his celebrated teacher which never flagged. He must have assuredly suffered from this "fault," but when it came to art, his honesty was firm and unshakeable. He had the courage to answer Saint-Saëns' criticism by saying that those "little anarchists" had talent, that they were unjustly bullied by mediocre people, that most of them were his favorite pupils, that they brought honor to him and that in view of these things, his duty as an artist was to support them and to help them defend their place in the sun. This he did with the greatest zeal.

The "concert without the names of the composers" was one of the most spectacular and instructive achievements of the young S.M.I. For a long time I had dreamt of denouncing the abusive role which the association of ideas, the directions of snobbery, the strength of suggestion of a title, of a form, or a signature, had played in forming public taste. I succeeded in getting permission from our committee to put on a public experiment.

With several trustworthy comrades, we organized a concert of classical, romantic and contemporary works presented strictly in anonymous fashion. We wanted to put the public face to face with unpublished or unknown scores in order to oblige our audiences to be honest with themselves by avoiding all extraneous conditioning which might influence their judgment. And we distributed to each of them leaflets on which they were requested to write the names of the composers to whom they attributed the compositions, or name the probable period, school or nationality of the composer.

The result of this unexpected poll went beyond our wildest expectations. The collection of leaflets contained a storehouse of startling surprises. The public very honestly had fulfilled its mission. Not one of the numerous critics in the Salle Gaveau had dared to commit himself!

The variety and the unexpectedness of the diagnoses were fascinating. A work by Gluck had been attributed to Mozart, an aria of Handel to Wagner, a Renaissance work to Stravinsky. We were able to establish that our audience, which did not represent the public at large but a group which regularly frequented concerts, did not possess, as a body, any notion of the particulars of style, vocabulary or syntax which separate the various chapters of our musical heritage and usually betray immediately the supposed period of a composition. The organized language of music remained completely unintelligible to them.

What most people look for at a concert is only aural satisfaction, to have their ears caressed by the sonorities of an orchestra, to be charmed by the sound of a flute, interested in the oboe timbre, moved by the cello, and disconcerted by the horn. It is touching and sad at the same time. Most listeners come away from the performance of a symphony or a sonata with only a physical pleasure, analogous to that which an illiterate Chinese would feel listening to the poetry of Racine recited by a harmonious voice. Its sonority would please him, but he would not understand a single word. Such frightful misunderstandings form the basis for a public success!

In the hall a drama was unfolding. Ravel was in a box surrounded by several distinguished amateurs whose salons he frequented and who gloried in being among his fervent admirers. Having taken the vow of secrecy, the composer of *Jeux d'eau* had hidden from them the fact that an unpublished work of his was part of the program—the delightful *Valses nobles et sentimentales*, that no one knew existed.

From the very first measure, everyone pricked up his ear. "What's that dance music doing with all those sour notes?" "What kind of a bad joke is this?" "A hoax by the management?" And as, on stage, the two pianists, one of whom was Louis Aubert, continued playing unperturbedly this four-hand arrangement, the hall began to resound with chuckles and hisses. Ravel's elegant entourage quickly joined in, protesting indignantly over the presentation of such mediocre buffoonery by loud jeering aimed at the composer of such a "horror." Ravel stoically kept his sarcasm bottled up and remained faithful to his promise by remaining quiet.

At the end of the concert a very cruel deception awaited him. A celebrated critic, very well known because of his uncompromising support of Ravel came up to him and speaking loudly, ex cathedra, literally said the following in my presence: "You are mistaken in trying to dupe us by putting such a 'lemon' on this program. Nobody has been fooled. It is obviously the work of an amateur who has heard some waltzes by Chopin and intended imitating them. But the total absence of craftsmanship is too evident. It shows itself so clearly! He is a shabby fellow, this composer! We shouldn't be taken for imbeciles, you know!" And he went off, happy to have had his perspicacity admired.

Needless to say, this curious experiment, as successful a demonstration as it was, was never again repeated. It would be decidedly too dangerous to confront, in such a situation, society and professionals with another unmerciful "moment of truth."

Four years after the founding of the S.M.I., the First World War began to disperse the composers who could no longer take an interest in such quarrels. Moreover, the aim of the society had been attained. The group of imprisoned composers had been set free and had henceforth thrust themselves upon the public. Employing an armored tank was no longer necessary. Thus, when peace was declared, the Société Nationale, much weakened by the schism, had great difficulty convincing its adversaries to lay down their arms and resume friendly relations.

But the hour of exalted combat had passed and musical life had lost much of its vigor. New generations of composers were lacking adolescent geniuses; new methods of communication— records and radio—were soon to be of greater help to these composers than the private soirées of the Nationale. The latter now played an eclipsed role in the musical history of our times, and it is only out of faithfulness to its glorious past that it is still in existence, running through, courageously, in private, the scores which humble candidates for glory bring it.

This characteristic episode in the musical career of Gabriel Fauré posed a small psychological problem for his admirers that has not been seriously considered until now: What effect did the rapid evolution of classical musical vocabulary at the beginning of this century have upon him? What did the prudent disciple of the École Niedermeyer, the good student nourished on the marrow of Johann Sebastian Bach, think of this revolution in grammar and syntax?

The character of his music answers this question. No composer was more able than he to move about in the most subtle and mysterious regions of sounds. One finds harmonic aggregations of paradoxical freshness in his works. Even before Debussy and Ravel, he had utilized with astonishing facility all the daring language whose paternity was much later attributed to these two composers. The most audacious chord progressions, unresolved appoggiaturas, exceptional resolutions, retards, modal alterations, ambiguous tonalities, and even the whole-tone scale, were customarily used by him. But he did not use them in the same way or in the same spirit as the others.

In Debussy's music, these verbal conquests are exploited mainly because of their mysterious sensuality, for the purely auditory voluptuousness with which they titillate the ear beyond any literary or visual connotation they might have. In themselves, they possess a strength of seduction and of magical charm that the composer can adroitly put into the service of a word, story or a picture, but which has no need whatsoever of his collaboration in order to affect our nervous system.

The Fathers of the Church formerly condemned, in religious music, the interval of the tritone because of the tension it produced on the senses. It was thought to possess in itself something voluptuous and of the flesh. These stern defenders of public morality were not mistaken. As a matter of fact, in the course of centuries, the auricular caress of the tritone which was to give birth to the provocative family of chords of the seventh did threaten morality. The lascivious interval of the ninth was no less guilty. In that culture of sound for its own sensual sake, the rigorous theologians had caught a whiff of the odor of sin. One could say as much for certain of Debussy's tonal combinations whose refined perversity intoxicates us. And I need only cite for proof the guileless remark of Vincent d'Indy, a religious mind par excellence, who, after having heard *Pelléas*, said that this music was "inferior" because its purely harmonic and orchestral sensualism was related to the gross sensualism of a Rossini searching in the *bel canto* style for damnable pleasures. Happier than this shameless Venetian marquis, who was sorry that the taste of sherbert was not sinful, the Debussyists were thus able to spice their delights with a vague threat of damnation.

For Ravel, an unusual dissonance had another function. It formed part of the stylistic elegance of a virtuoso who used it with the precision of a Swiss clock. Its effect is a lot more consciously calculated. It obeys more confining, formal disciplines and more thought-out stylistic requirements. It had the value of a brilliantly successful laboratory experiment. When it is used, it represents an enriching of the musical vocabulary. In short, when Ravel uses a new dissonance, we can consider it almost as a scientific discovery. It functions in all of his works in a clearly defined role under the most diversified circumstances.

The expressive discoveries of Gabriel Fauré have a quite different character. With him, neologism is never spectacular. It exists very naturally in the course of a phrase because it is placed there by the logic of inner necessity. It becomes part of the discourse so easily that one is not aware of its entrance. And that is why, for such a long time, its existence was not even noticed. Since Fauré is not a programmatic composer, his most striking harmonic discoveries do not serve to underline any picturesque detail, but content themselves with creating a musical mood evocative of a sensation or a feeling. Such harmonies impregnate a melodic phrase with an imperishable perfume, color and light. It never has the effect of appearing thought out, affected or laboriously invented.

Fauré, the most profound and most specifically "musical" of all composers speaks a musical language of prodigious richness instinctively. He discretely slips in his dissonances, taking constant care to melt them harmoniously with an eloquence stemming from that noble and purified traditional style which forbids any clashing or indiscrete interruptions in the musical discourse. It is known that he worked slowly and many times with almost paralyzing qualms. The care he took not to parade his jewels like a nouveau riche surely accounted in some part for the frequent hesitations of his pen.

Considering these conditions, what are we to imagine were his feelings about the new generation of composers whose defense he had so courageously taken? It is quite evident that, by accepting the presidency of the S.M.I., he was not working for himself and for his personal ideals. Neither was he only looking out for the students in his class. He knew very well that the principal beneficiaries of his gesture would be the impassioned initiates of the newly-born cult of Debussyism. The fact that he had consented to patronize them on the strength of his name is again proof of his complete objectivity and his exemplary artistic integrity.

No one was ignorant of the fact that Fauré and Debussy were not exactly friends. Certain circumstantial opinions and feelings in their private lives had created a wide gap between them. But, even though the ill-natured composer of *Pelléas* made violent imprecations against the composer of *Pénélope*, whose talent he refused to acknowledge, Fauré did not hide his admiration for his enemy's genius. It was thanks to measures Fauré took that Debussy's *Cinq Mélodies de Baudelaire*, scorned everywhere, finally found a publisher. Never did I hear him expressing the least reservation about any score of Debussy. It was because of his principles that he chose to hold himself aloof from Debussyism.

Personally, he had a very different conception of the art of music. Fauré sensed in the fascination for Debussyism something too direct, and too shocking, since he cultivated a less obvious and more discrete charm which was more intimate and spiritualized. Where Debussy confounds us with magic and sorcery, Fauré insinuates with slow persuasion. Fauré is said to have declared, "You must never speak to me about Debussy. If I were to love Debussy, I would no longer love Fauré. Why be Fauré, then?" This statement, which is so just and shrewd, summarizes the state of mind of the president of the S.M.I. at the time when, by his courageous attitude, he demonstrated to his friends and enemies such a marvelous lesson in impartiality and independence.

A new source of income was soon made available to him— the directorship of the Conservatoire. This spectacular promotion caused a sensation. The quiet and regular progression along the road of fame and fortune that this solitary individual, this free-shooter of the musical army, was making shocked some and delighted others. Fauré accepted with frank satisfaction for he was neither vain nor ambitious, but he did harbor illusions about the "liberation" his new job might bring him. "I will have things to do, but I won't have any other job! No more classes and no more Madeleine! That will leave a clear field. And especially no more 'matinées' to honor my works, good or bad; I won't have the time." And because of this solid reasoning, he already imagined making his dear music paper the beneficiary of this honor. "I am in a hurry to organize this life, because a thousand things are rushing about in my head that I should like to put on paper. . . ."

Without losing any of his introspective behavior, or his absent air, without extinguishing his constant cigarette in a temple where smoking was forbidden, Fauré brought to his new position the same artistic conscientiousness and the same intelligence that he had demonstrated in his composition class. Unfortunately, his new job carried with it duties which were a lot more oppressive than his previous commitments and were progressively to consume all of the free time he longed to give to composition.

His job imposed on him absorbing administrative tasks, and his music paper was quickly buried under a mass of bureaucratic red tape. The task of devoting the greatest part of his time to the study of irrelevant problems in music seemed to him terribly tedious. The visits of the parents of students, the uninterrupted requests for recommendations, the enormous amount of correspondence that his job entailed, the official functions inflicted on him added to his discouragement. The interminable entrance examination sessions, judging competitions and the year end public and private competitive examinations imposed a harassing fatigue on him. He was, of all the tenants of that honored house, the one who most impatiently counted the days until vacation time. Even the vacations were unceasingly interrupted by late official business or advance meetings which disrupted all of his travel plans.

In spite of everything, he did accomplish a great deal. It was his heart's desire to restore to the classroom a respect for music per se, whose prestige had been weakened by abuse. Tiresome practice routines had, in effect, sacrificed the delights of music too often to those of pure technique.

The Conservatoire is justly proud of always having upheld the highest standards of virtuosity among its students. Without renouncing this brilliant professional preparation, the new director greatly modified the study programs. He required that young artists work on masterpieces which would educate their taste at the same time as their fingers, their breathing, or their vocal cords. The esthetic climate of the competition and the significance of the prizes were changed. At the same time, he judiciously lowered the age of the jury members and decreed that henceforth they were to be chosen from among artists of proven abilities and of unquestionable artistic authority. All this did not come about without tears or the grinding of teeth. Fauré removed a number of worthless teachers in order to loosen the influence of arrogant *"seigneurs"* who were in favor and believed to be impregnable. He replaced them with young *"chevaliers"* whose present was the future. The calm obstinacy of this likeable director was naturally met with every resistance.

His main concern in teaching was to safeguard the rights of pure music which, in his eyes, constituted the necessary basis of any serious composer's education. Faithfully reflecting the taste and the fashion of an era when only successes in the theater assured the reputation of a composer, the Conservatoire had become a preparatory school for composers and performers destined to stock official state theaters. The course of study for singers dealt only with the repertory of the Paris Opéra and the Opéra-Comique, and the artist's compensation was a definite engagement in one of the subsidized theaters. As for the composers, they were only considered if they could, when locked up by themselves, turn out a small operetta in no time flat for a specific occasion. This would open the doors of the Villa Medicis, the Palais Garnier and the Salle Favart for them.

Fauré understood the injustice of this method of selection. The examination for the cantata prize exasperated him, and he didn't bother telling those of us in his class what he thought of this absurd enterprise and its consequences. He could not resign himself to seeing the future of a young symphonic composer of genius or a lover of chamber music sacrificed in such a manner by submitting to the uninspiring and insignificant doggerel of the Concours de Rome, or that of a talented singer lacking dramatic vocation and taste for the stage. Chamber music, song, oratorio, the innumerable instrumental works of unadulterated pure music seemed to him as respectable as the repertoire of the lyric stage. This system would have excommunicated a new Chopin.

He demanded, therefore, a more comprehensive classification of students, permitting no exceptions among the future servants of the muses. In the realm of interpretation, definite progress had been made, but the composer's cantata competition had a difficult existence and the Institut continued to use this derisive thermometer mainly to gauge the artistic temperature of the aspiring candidate who presented himself for their evaluation. Although this was the case, Gabriel Fauré's promotion to the captain's bridge of the old naval school was to be extremely beneficial for it permitted him not only to effect important reforms, but to give timely impetus and direction which would one day make the laws of logic, good sense and fairness triumph.

Honors attract more honors. Shortly after he had assumed the directorship, Fauré was offered the position of music critic on *Le Figaro*. He was not terribly enthusiastic about this. He considered himself as having been born to write music, not articles. His friends had to pressure him to accept this new job in which, they told him, his influence would serve his art. He did his job without pleasure, but with complete integrity.

In temperament, he was more inclined to be indulgent rather than severe. His natural affability stood him well under the circumstances. Moreover, the journalistic climate of *Le Figaro* required discretion, for its clientele would not have permitted judgments which did not conform in a certain manner. Fauré's difficulty consisted then in observing a great courtesy while allowing his feelings to be guessed at whenever his artistic judgment would condemn a work submitted to his department. Some of his articles are masterpieces of diplomacy, and at the same time testify to his scrupulous artistic honesty.

This job, moreover, was not without profit. It obliged him to study at close range many things with which he was not too well acquainted, and to alter his opinions about musicians and works that he had formed too hastily. Educated in a religious school where the musical life of Paris was considered to be frivolous and contemptible, and later as a faculty member of the Conservatoire, a "place of musical debauchery," for a long time he had an instinctive horror of the idols of the crowds, and in particular of theater composers who flattered the lazy ears of the public. Not yet having attempted anything for the lyric stage, he was indignant over the easy success enjoyed by works whose musical substance seemed to be of inferior quality.

For Fauré, his passionate love for chamber music threw a curse on the repertoire of the French musical theater. In his letters, one is surprised and slightly taken aback when he denounces *Tosca, Manon,* and *La Bohème* as typical examples of "atrocious" scores. He was at a loss to cite works more worthy of the pillory. But, it was in having to dutifully attend the Salle Favart and the Palais Garnier, that his profession as a critic did him service by obliging him to analyze carefully these faulty works. He then understood that he had been unjust toward Massenet and Puccini. He realized that they were real composers who knew their craft thoroughly and possessed remarkable lyrical and dramatic gifts. At times he deplored their tendency to indulge in facile effects conducive to success but he did do justice to their musical qualities and to their technical mastery with a perspicacity and a relevance which at the same time were proof of the lucidity of his critical faculties and his honesty.

For ten years he kept his position at *Le Figaro*. His kind and perceptive reportage, written simply and sincerely without literary affectation or the least trace of dogmatism, produced a great many interesting subjects and he was read profitably. Incapable of following the examples of unscrupulous critics who looked for ways to shine at the expense of the artists they judged, or attract the attention of ninnies by systematically writing savage reviews or exploiting the bad taste of the masses, Fauré spoke to musicians in the language of one who was talking to his elders, to his equals, and to his charges by using a familiar and rational tone of voice. This concept of criticism was evidently not understood by everyone, but it has left us with a sterling example of what musical criticism can be.

What had become of the creative activity of this imprisoned magician during these various changes in his situation? When he was working as organist at the Madeleine and as inspector of the provincial conservatories he found time to compose— between two trains or two marriage ceremonies—works as important as *La Bonne Chanson, Op. 61* and the *Nocturne No. 6 in D flat Major, Op. 63,* whose quality of supreme detachment and heavenly peace proved how quickly this inspired being could escape from daily cares into the refuge of dreams. Freed from his church duties, he constructed that noble pianistic edifice of eleven stories which he called *Thème et variations in C sharp Minor, Op. 73* and sculpted his ravishing *Dolly, Op. 56.*

He exchanged his job as inspector for that of professor of composition at the Paris Conservatoire. It was at this time that we gather the enervating emanations from his *Parfum impérissable, Op. 76, No. 1*, when he composed the incidental music for *Pelléas et Mélisande, Op. 80*, that he traveled to London to conduct at the Prince of Wales Theater and when, on command of a patron of the arts from Béziers, he began his *Prométhée, Op. 82*, with that sublime theme conceived for the amphitheater of Béziers that met with the greatest success. Masterworks of sadness, of tenderness and compassion such as *Soir, Op. 83, No. 2* and *Prison, Op. 83, No. 1*, also date from this period and parallel a series of religious works in the same vein and the new approaches which enriched his series of nocturnes, barcarolles and valses-caprices.

But there he was, imprisoned in the director's office at the Conservatoire. The chains which immobilized him were to become heavier. But still he found a way to write his *Piano Quintet No. 1 in D Minor, Op. 89*, his *Neuf Préludes, Op. 103* for piano, his *Sonata No. 1 for Cello and Piano in D Minor, Op. 109*, and once again, attracted to the song cycle, he composed *Le Chanson d'Ève, Op. 95, Le Jardin clos, Op. 106* and *Mirages, Op. 113*. He completed his collections of impromptus, barcarolles and nocturnes as well.

Thus we arrive at that painful period when the state, noticing that its prisoner, weakened by age and infirmities, could no longer perform as many duties for it, brutally notified him of his dismissal and cast him, almost without funds, into the Parisian jungle. Fauré thus regained his liberty at that moment when his health no longer allowed him to gather its benefits. Now he was only to compose, but under harrowing circumstances, *L'Horizon chimérique, Op. 118*, the *Piano Quintet No. 2 in C Minor, Op. 115*, the *Sonata No. 2 for Cello and Piano, in G Minor, Op. 117*, the *Trio in D Minor, Op. 120* for piano, violin and cello, and the *String Quartet in E Minor, Op. 121*, his last composition.

In order to allow him to receive the care which his illness required and to assure him an income to the end of his days, a benefit evening party was officially organized at the Sorbonne, a humiliating act of charity that an enlightened republic should have spared an artist who had so magnificently brought honor to his country. He lived out his days in the serenity and resignation which were habitual with him, preserving until the end his reasoning power and his philosophical composure. And he would have been the first to be surprised, and perhaps a bit sadly amused, if he had been able to find out that, giving in to some vague feeling of remorse, the government which had so shamefully disregarded the fate of this great Frenchman was to give him a national burial. This ostentatious generosity which could have been put to better use came too late.

Despite the devotedness and affection of a few family friends who tried to sweeten the bitterness of the final years of his existence, the slow twilight of Gabriel Fauré was characterized by an inexpressible sadness. This poet who had loved the joy and beauty of life so much and knew so well how to gather the flowers which grew along the rough paths he followed, needed music, that singular source of strength for the soul, in order to accept the ordeals which were reserved for him and in order to accept the inexorable progress of the illnesses which were going to crush him over a long period of years.

This man who possessed such subtle and refined senses was struck a blow in his sensory perception. The sense of sight had to be carefully guarded as it was cruelly limiting his reading and writing and was making the daily work, which was the only consolation of his old age, painful.

But one single loss was going to be the most painful to him—that of his hearing. No crueler blow can befall a musician. As early as 1903, he experienced disquieting auditory difficulties which were to resist all treatment and to worsen until his death. Imagine, for more than twenty years he was the attentive onlooker of the regular progress of the sickness which tortured him. Arteriosclerosis was slowly destroying that organism which once had been a happy and robust man of irresistible charm.

He did not become deaf in the usual sense of the word. His fate was much worse. A deaf musician can compose without having all of his hearing intact. Beethoven is proof of this. Deafness isolates a composer from the outside world and maintains a silence which might help his internal perception of those sound relationships that he collects, arranges on the staff and hears very well in his mind. Doubtlessly, the cooperation of a musical instrument offers an irreplaceable service to someone searching for new sonorities. A Chopin, a Liszt, or a Debussy would never have been able to write certain of their piano works if their ability as pianists had not allowed them to extract their most mysterious secrets from the strings and felt hammers. But, again, a composer can silently imagine, while seated at a table, a complex score without any aural verification.

Fauré's infirmity was a lot more depressing. He heard sounds, but with hellish distortions. He perceived the middle register as if from a distance and almost in tune, but as soon as he would attempt the treble or bass, the pitch in his mind no longer corresponded to the sounds emitted. They shifted to an interval which reached and sometimes went beyond a third away from the actual tone. Hearing a piece whose medium range was normal but whose extremities were completely altered produced an indescribable cacophony for him.

Certain well-intentioned biographers thought it charitable to cover up Fauré's bad fortune. Alas, how can we question it when we read this passage from one of his letters written from Monte Carlo in 1919: "Last evening I went to hear a comic opera by Verdi. I heard sounds which were so insanely confused that it was enough to make me believe I was crazy. This proves that in connection with the spoken word, to be deaf is to hear very indistinctly, but in connection with music, I notice this unfortunate phenomenon. The intervals of the low register change as they become lower in pitch, and the intervals of the high register as they become higher. So, you can imagine what the result of this difficulty of association is! It is awful. And it was as if in the midst of that horrible conglomeration of sounds that I heard *Pénélope!* The least painful thing for me to listen to is the voice of a singer, but an instrumental group is chaotic. What anguish!" And, in 1922, he confesses: "With my wretched hearing, there are moments when I could not tell what passage in my music someone was playing. . . I have never played, either for myself or anybody else, a single note from *Pénélope* since it was first written in Lausanne in 1907. If I'm not mistaken, even then I was not hearing things on pitch when my fingers pressed down the keys. I heard different notes!" Fauré died without having been able to "hear" a single measure, other than in his mind.

We have just seen the paradoxical conditions under which Gabriel Fauré wrote his masterpieces. He often complained of composing slowly and with difficulty. He spoke incessantly of the "blocks" against which his creative spirit was powerless, or of the "knot" he had not succeeded in unraveling. One can scarcely believe that this composer, whose leisure time was so minimal, left us a body of works the last of which bears the opus number 121.

This productivity is quite exceptional for an artist of our time, especially when one thinks about the wonderful refinement of modern styles of composition. At an earlier time, when the vocabulary of a musician was limited to a half dozen strictly regulated chords and to a few modulations to neighboring keys, lengthy catalogues of a composer's works were common. Simplicity of means in instrumentation and agreed-upon usage of structured, commonplace and stereotyped cadences explain why it was child's play for a Haydn to write so many trios, string quartets, operas and symphonies. But when you hold between your hands the finely chiseled jewel represented by the shortest of Faure's songs, you wonder how his scores, whose minute workmanship is comparable to that of a gold-smith, could have been composed in so short a time span.

The precarious state of health of the composer of *Pénélope* periodically required that he leave Paris, even for a few days, in order to breathe pure air and enjoy a milder climate. His vacations were spent in regions conducive to rest and medita-tion. The names of the places where he vacationed give us an indication of his taste. He loved the poetic quality of lakes. The serenity of those beautifully glistening mirrors framed by mountains agreed with his musical feeling. It was on the shores of Lakes Zurich, Maggiore, Thoune, de Garde, Como, du Bourget, Annecy and the Lake of the Four Cantons that he found the meditative tempos for his andantes. His letters are postmarked from Lausanne, Ouchy, Zurich, Lucerne, Vitznau, Aix-les-Bains, Divonne-les-Bains, Stresa, Pallanza and Lugano. It was in hotel rooms overlooking peaceful landscapes that his most moving scores were created. This tone poet, who was not inclined toward program music, had musical feelings deeply impregnated with the laws of nature's harmony and the sover-eign rhythm of the elements.

To the very end of his life, he tried to keep in close contact with the great mirrors of water, in which heaven and the stars confided their most precious secrets and which, for centuries, have heard the thoughts of men. He was on the shores of Annecy at the home of his friends, the Maillots, who saw after his every need, when he became aware of the approach of death. Wanting to receive him in his own home, he begged his son Philippe to take him to Paris. When his train, upon leaving Aix, went along the Lac du Bourget, Fauré, his head pressed against the window of the coach, watched the setting sun play on the waters. "That was," his son tells us, "his last sunset, for he was no longer able to see anything from then on but overcast skies and gray days."

❧ His Work

The inventory of the magnificent heritage of beauty that Fauré
has left us is astonishing, not only because of its abundance, but
by the variety of its riches. The highest forms of chamber
music—the sonata, trio, quartet, quintet, song, the piano piece
—religious and secular choral music; music for the theater and
opera in turn engaged his attention and allowed him to affirm
in very different styles his own encompassing mastery.

He only made one excursion in the domain of the symphony.
This attempt did not please him and he abandoned this form of
expression for it did not satisfy the demands of his nature. One
can easily assume that the techniques of writing a symphony
did not intimidate him. His chamber music has shown us the
ease with which he practiced the art of symphonic development.
However, the many colors of orchestral writing held little attraction for an engraver who only needed his magic pen to
express the most subtle shadings of his imagination. The or-
chestrations that he did himself, such as those for the *Ballade
for Piano and Orchestra, Op. 19,* the *Requiem, Op. 48,* or the
first act of *Pénélope,* are characterized by a reserve which is
revealing. It is known that in spite of the pleasure he admitted
taking in this work requiring patience and cleverness, he often
entrusted this task to his best students or to certain composer
friends because he considered it too demanding for the little
time he had at his disposal. He thought, doubtlessly, and not
without reason, that being naturally endowed with a particular
vocabulary and style, orchestration did not merit the major role
for him that it necessarily played in the works of other composers.

It will suffice to contrast his situation with Berlioz' to understand this phenomenon. Play a page from *Les Troyens* on the piano. Its lack of musical substance and its contrived, weak invention prevent it from passing the test of the piano reduction. In order to come alive, it cannot do without the help of the orchestral palette. To the contrary, any work of Fauré, even if it is operatic, will preserve its power to charm and its purely musical values in piano reduction. That is why the orchestration of his chief works was only of relative importance to him. If a work had an agreeable "attire" no further ornaments were necessary. Let us not forget what Ravel said when asked to orchestrate a work of his teacher: "Nothing Fauré has written can be orchestrated." That remark was, on the part of an orchestrator of Ravel's stature, a singularly respectable honor.

Fauré reigns supreme over a world of sounds, where everything is ordered, beautiful, rich, peaceful and pleasurable. The natural refinement of his temperament turned him away from violent emotions. But do not conclude that his art is therefore affected and lacking in virility. Notice with what very simple means, devoid of pomposity and noisy gestures, he is able to rise to the highest summits of nobility and grandeur.

This charm, which is one of the most characteristic traits of his artistic physiognomy, revealed itself early. One can clearly see its manifestations from his first work. Fauré entered the earthly paradise of composition through the door of melody. He was a well-behaved student of fifteen who lived in the austere boarding school of the École Niedermeyer and was subject to religious and pedagogical disciplines. But as soon as he dared steal some time from his counterpoint and fugue assignments, he wrote, based on a Victor Hugo poem, his song *Le Papillon et la fleur, Op. 1, No. 1,* which is as moving as one could wish. This was a symbolistic attempt at escape by a captive child who already imagined the sights and fragrances of the outside world. This unpretentious piece, very much influenced by the style of writing and singing in vogue in the 1860's, today still contains a lot of promise. I mention it now because it foretells many things that came to full realization in the course of Fauré's career.

In beginning the study of Fauré's vocal works, we immediately come up against a misunderstanding. It is currently quite the fashion to look ashamed when discussing the "inept" or "abominable" poetry that this refined composer chose to set to music. His blindness is deplored and his collaborators scornfully criticized. Many people are shocked to learn that Fauré had a strong taste for doggerel verse. Let us try to reassure them, by presenting the complete list of poets chosen by the composer. The list includes Jean Racine, Victor Hugo, Théophile Gautier, Leconte de Lisle, Armand Sully-Prudhomme, Villiers de l'Isle-Adam, Victor Wilder, Catulle Mendès, Romain Bussine, Jean Richepin, Marc Monnier, Armand Silvestre, Charles Grandmougin, Charles Baudelaire, Louis Pommey, Paul de Choudens, Albert Samain, Henri de Régnier, Paul Verlaine, Jean Dominique, Charles van Lerberghe, Baronne de Brimont, Jean de la Ville de Mirmont, Stéphane Bordèse and Georgette Debladis.

Does this choice really seem disgraceful? Certainly, one finds here the names of some minor poets, poets who were in good repute at the time. What strikes us about these scornful condemnations is their pretense in making the literary snobbism of the present judge the past. Nothing is more ephemeral in literature than the discrediting of a fashion or taste. Is it right, or even honest, to reproach a composer for not having studied, before 1900, a poll of current taste which would only be outdated a half century later? In my opinion, even when it is pointed out that the authors of 1880 ornamented their verse with texts of this sort, I must humbly admit that I do not blame these writers for having exposed Gabriel Fauré to the poetry for *Soir* (Samain), *Nell, La Rose, Lydia, Le Parfum impérissable* and *Les Roses d'Ispahan* (all by Leconte de Lisle) for they resulted in six tantalizing masterpieces of song.

For, in my opinion, the question is not if such and such a

text was, in itself, part of an anthology before becoming the basis of a song. The rank it occupies later in the list of honors of literary criticism is only of secondary importance. What matters is what the composer can draw from this collection of words, syllabic impulses, vague and mysterious suggestions which emanate from an adjective or a rhyme scheme. His job consists in distilling the verbal material in order to ascend to higher regions where it will escape the confining rules to which it had to submit before being disembodied and then clothed in glorious garments.

Fauré excelled more than anyone in this kind of miracle work. From a simple poem by Armand Silvestre—which would seem prosaic to us if recited aloud—he found a means of extracting inexhaustible reservoirs of enchantment. He has the ability of so deeply imprinting a poem by having the music rethink and rewrite each verse that henceforth one can no longer accept it in any other musical setting but his. Even the best ones will always seem to be false to the poetry and deformed as well. For here is the secret of Fauré's music. While closely respecting the idea of inspiration, he is never the menial slave of the words and does not blindly obey the minor demands of the poetry which would break the impetus of his melodic arabesques and compromise the music's unity. No line-by-line translation takes place here, but rather a subtle transposition. This technique is inadequately defined by saying that he exteriorizes a text. Fauré has a means of dissolving his poem in the music which internalizes it so that it makes the poet as much a composer as the composer himself. In working out this fusion, Fauré gives us, really, something beyond the words of the poet's idea which is more intimate, more secret and, consequently, more profoundly convincing. A good piece of advice is when one becomes well acquainted with a Fauré song, one never separates the poetry from the music. The song is only weakened by doing so.

Fauré's first twenty-four compositions are vocal works: twenty songs, two duos, and two choruses. From his fifteenth to his twenty-fifth year, this young man did not seek any other means of expression but the human voice, specifically the female voice. The titles of his early works reveal the romantic nature of his daydreams. He took seven poems by Victor Hugo, four by Théophile Gautier, three by Baudelaire, two by Armand Sully-Prudhomme, two by Romain Bussine, two by Marc Monnier, and one each from Jean Racine, Leconte de Lisle, Louis Pommey and Paul de Choudens.

This important group of works in which can easily be found the subject matter for the first of his three collections of single songs, poses a delicate problem for the musicologist. When we talk of a composer's catalogue, we have immediate recourse to the "three style periods." There is not always a consensus about the length of these periods, but with a little ingenuity one can successfully reach an agreement and can compartmentalize the composer's works.

The first period of a composer is the one during which he searches for his style. The second is when he has discovered his path and produces his most glorious works, the third is the one in which, moved by some grace from above, he devotes his genius to reexamining the old and exploring the new, he "sheds his skin" so that his music, like Istar, may return to its original state on the threshold of the beyond.

Reread the biographies of the most celebrated composers and you will notice that their entire output can be divided into these three compartments. In France, it has been used successfully with Debussy and, naturally, it has been applied to Fauré's works. Both composers searched to discover their originality during their first period, found it during the second, and disowned it during the third period. The parallelism is perfect.

Florent Schmitt, who did not waste words, put himself out on a limb when, one day, he declared that he found it quite easy to find three characteristic style periods for the works of Fauré, but that they paralleled the most different periods of his life. As a matter of fact, as early as his so-called first period, Fauré, on occasion, utilized the daring vocabulary he didn't have the right to use before his second period, and at the end of his life, he did not hesitate to speak in the blandly charming language of his youth. Musicology finds it difficult to forgive him for these indiscretions.

Certainly, these three stages in the development of genius and the creative force can be observed among most great artists. However, isn't it arbitrary and isn't there a tendency to attribute to them moral meanings and, above all, to have the heroic will of an author interpose its authority in the "shedding skin process" which signals the end of his career? Debussy himself condemned in terms which leave no room for doubt that what certain esthetes show us as the fruit of ambrosia today unexpectedly turns into the hypothetical road to Damascus. Fauré was so little convinced of the value of his last works, conceived when he was ill, that he asked several trusted friends to destroy his *String Quartet in E Minor, Op. 121* if, in view of his past efforts, they thought it unworthy upon his death.

Couldn't one accept, in good faith, the fact that the "trois manières" of creative artists have a basis which is not psychological, intellectual, or spiritual, but simply biological? It is the science of biology which imposes on universal life the great ternary rhythms of growth, flowering and decline. Man must, quite simply, obey the same laws as the tree which does not excuse itself from spring and summer and which, after the two successive conquests of flowers and fruits, is obliged to "shed" its leaves, see its branches wither and sap run dry with winter's approach.

That is why, while sincerely admiring the penetrating finesse of his enthusiastic poetical analyses, it seems to me difficult to go along with Vladimir Jankélévitch in the reverent description he gives of Fauré's twilight years by praising the composer of *Soir* for having had the courage to disown his past. Jankélévitch said, "He who naturally possessed an inexhaustible melodic gift henceforth turned his back on all the simple pleasures, accepted being sealed off and revoked the concessions to where, at another time, a legitimate desire to please had led him. His greatness was in abstaining. Isn't that will to be ungracious, difficult and disconcerting one of the traits of reservedness which describes better than any definition the composer of *Le Secret?*"

What impertinence! Besides, such a burning thirst for asceticism appears quite unreasonable to those who understood the philosophy that lasted until the last breath of this sensual man so enamored of beauty. Isn't it unpleasant and even somewhat offensive to summarize the whole career of Gabriel Fauré as the simple opposition of two periods the first of which was to have been devoted to musical delights, to the privileges and affabilities for one's self, and the second to the wish to be cut off, unyielding, difficult and disconcerting? Those who consider Fauré as having no reason to be ashamed about his past and to have no need to atone for it publicly by self-humiliation will not willingly accept the sad short cut this dual synthesis indicates.

Florent Schmitt was not mistaken. Fauré's first attempts were masterly. As soon as the candid, but fresh and graceful, *Papillon et la fleur, Op. 1, No. 1* was concluded in a respectful climate of conformity, the song entitled *Mai, Op. 1, No. 2,* came forward with more assurance. This song already contained, in essence, two major traits of Fauré's style: the flavorful use of modulation, and the expressivity of the accompanimental pattern. It no longer is a question of a timid try at independence. These have become definite characteristics.

One of the most personal and attractive elements of Fauré's compositional style is assuredly his artistry in modulating. His conception of modulation is very much removed from that of César Franck, who does not change the key because he enjoys it, but because he has to. To modulate was for Fauré the fulfillment of a purely architectural requirement. It was like putting a girder, a rafter, or a crossbeam into position according to a prefabricated plan of a building. We are acquainted with the naive pride with which he announced to his intimate friends that an entire modulatory scheme had definitely ended up as an important symphonic composition, for which he had not yet begun to look for the thematic materials. Modulation for him does not represent a solely constructional element. It modifies either greatly or gradually the color or the shading of a phrase and intensifies its expressive character upon occasion.

It plays yet another more subtle role, that of cunningly tricking with inimitable skill the natural urges of classical tonality. We are in the key of C Major. We travel confidently along a broad road which will lead us infallibly to a final chord of C Major. The way is long and would be monotonous if we could not, from time to time, leave it and turn off onto little shaded paths which run off the main road and follow them momentarily without straying too far from the main tonality. This is what is called modulating to neighboring keys—the dominant, subdominant, or other closely-related tonalities.

Fauré was not content with such a simple conception. What interested him was reaching, in one jump, a distant road which went off toward quite another point on the horizon. He starts off, turning deviously to the left, then to the right. In a sometimes abrupt manner he modulates to distant keys but always reveals scenery of unexpected beauty.

But C Major is far away. We lost sight of it a long time ago. How can we find it again and reach our destination? Fauré, who never showed any apparent uneasiness, has a surprise planned for us. Just when it seems impossible to ever reach that final C, the wizard draws the one remaining natural from his pocket, and miraculously, contrary to all probability, the final chord of C Major appears before our eyes. The sensation of arriving at the end so effortlessly after having traversed this labyrinth has something intoxicating about it.

If the modulations in the song *Mai, Op. 1, No. 2* do not yet have this audaciousness, it is still interesting to note that, from his very first steps on the road of tonality, Fauré was already thinking of avoiding the usual routes.

In the same song, a second sign indicative of his avocation as an explorer appears in the way in which he treats his accompanimental formulas. It is possible to speak of a "formula" at the time when the international influence of the *Lieder* of Schubert and Schumann had popularized in French song an accompaniment of stereotyped arpeggios and of repeated chords which swallowed up the vocal line. Fauré could not permit himself, at his age, to suddenly break with such a solidly established tradition. However, observe the effect which he alone produced to give more elegance and grace to the shape of these architectural designs.

The disconcerting appearance of a characteristic Fauréism shows up in the first group of twenty songs in a totally novel way. Naturally one discovers melodic lines whose graceful contours reveal the natural admiration the young man had for Mendelssohn, Gounod and Schumann. But what a striking testimonial to his budding originality and the precocious acquisition of the essential elements of his future style! The theoreticians most bound by the convention of the "three periods" were visibly disturbed to see that the charming *Lydia*—with its calmly melodic stepwise movement, its well-balanced, essentially Fauréan elegance, its use of the Hypolydian mode, its chaste "Hellenic nudity" and its rarified style (which presages the ascetic themes of *Inscription sur le sable, Op. 106, No. 8*)—obliged them to recognize its close relationship with *Pénélope, Le Jardin clos, Op. 106* and even with the *String Quartet in E Minor, Op. 121* which contradicted their theory of a voluntarily penitential old man! They are no less embarrassed when they see in *L'Absent, Op. 5, No. 3* inflexions from the *Nocturne No. 13 in B Minor, Op. 119* and in the *Barcarolle No. 9 in A Minor, Op. 101* new examples of that supreme simplicity which used to be ascribed exclusively to Fauré's last works.

What can one say about the prodigious melodic liberty with which *Après un rêve, Op. 7, No. 1* is treated? Casting aside all the usual symmetry created by the division of a melody in strophes, couplets and refrains, this neophyte invented a long, lyric and tender phrase which is carried along on one breath without repetition, without turning back. It is this strength that his pupil Maurice Ravel, sixty years later, wanted to revive in composing the celebrated *andante* of his *Concerto for Piano and Orchestra in G.*

Is it necessary to draw attention to the very personal anguish or nostalgic touches of such a precocious maturity that one finds in *Seule!, Op. 3, No. 1,* in *La Rançon, Op. 8, No. 2,* in the moving *Chanson du Pêcheur, Op. 4, No. 1,* in *Chant d'automne, Op. 5, No. 1,* and even in *Ici-bas, Op. 8, No. 3?* Did we not already discover in the *Sérénade toscane, Op. 3, No. 2,* in the *Barcarolle, Op. 7, No. 3* and in the *Tarentelle, Op. 10, No. 2* this sensuality of a make-believe Italy whose atmosphere is created from lullabies, the odor of wandering perfumes and floating caresses which were to inspire in Fauré so many charming works for the piano?

Finally, isn't it exciting to observe, after *Mai, Op. 1, No. 2* and *Les Matelots, Op. 2, No. 2* the rapid development of the famous Fauré arpeggio which was to play such an important and novel role in his most diverse works? The accompanimental arpeggio was a slave which owes its freedom to Fauré. Condemned for centuries to utilitarian tasks, it was used from time to time only to replace the small groups of repeated chords in closed position which geometrically punctuated a sung phrase. It was, quite simply, a spread-out chord, unstringing its notes one after the other to avoid the hammering monotony of their vertical alignment. This oversimplified formula, borrowed from the lute and guitar by keyboard composers, sufficed for the needs of our ancestors, from Beethoven's *Piano Sonata in C sharp Minor, Op. 27, No. 2, "Moonlight"* to the songs of Loïsa Puget.

Chopin and Liszt tried to variate the scroll work of these substructures and make them flexible, promoting them to the dignity of decorative arabesques. But it was to Gabriel Fauré, who completely freed the accompanimental arpeggio, that it owed its elegance, fantasy and richness. He handled it like a rope which permitted him to lasso the unseen and the impossible.

The arpeggio, as he uses it, is as alive, as sensitive and as expressive as the melody along with which it moves and with which it amicably converses on the basis of perfect equality.

The Fauréan arpeggio treats the subject matter as carefully as the melody. It completes a phrase and it states precisely, at times, what the voice doesn't dare to, or what it would be incapable of expressing. Moreover, it has control over the movement of the modulations, taking the knowing turns, which adroitly bring about a change of direction. It no longer blindly follows the melody, it leads it.

At every stage in his development Fauré delighted in using this harmonic refinement whose charm is inimitable and which, in all types of composition, allowed him to bring to his works conclusions whose ingenuity were without equal. Jankélévitch, who took the trouble to extol a great number of them, discovered a ravishing way of defining that charm which consists in exasperating our desire by prominently visible refusals and in misleading our ear in order to better sharpen its need for a certain direction. "Fauré," he said, "will always be the wizard of modulation. He has measured the outer limits of desire of the auditory memory." As a matter of fact, such is the case with the rules of this perverse but charming game.

The uninterrupted series of Fauré's first vocal works concludes with two duos for sopranos. One is based on the poem of Victor Hugo, "Puisq'ici-bas, toute âme," whose Romanticism inspired Fauré to compose a piece which interprets the spirit and atmosphere of the text and capitalizes on the supple interweaving of the two female voices of the same timbre. The other, the "Tarentelle" by Marc Monnier, constitutes a novel flight toward an imaginary Italy (Fauré was not to visit that country until forty-six years later!) whose ambiance and mysterious intoxication he captured. The conjectural Italy of Fauré, at the same time Venetian and Neapolitan, was created without the help of any descriptive means. What the musician had the ability to evoke is the essence of a countryside, and not its external appearance. Also, he had no need to work from nature. All takes place in the domain of intangibility and imagination. Chabrier, Debussy and Ravel were soon going to reconstruct for themselves, without needing to cross the Pyrenees, a Spain by using traditional rhythms at all times. Fauré's Italy, which was entirely a product of his imagination, was also the creation of the poet.

Vocal polyphony also attracted him from an early date. As we know, he was still at the École Niedermeyer when he produced, as a student assignment, his *Cantique de Racine, Op. 11* for chorus, organ and strings or orchestra. Its elevated ideas, contemplative mood, the technical skill and sonorous balance are surprising for a pupil. From the first, this beginner had discovered what could be called his sacred style, that is to say, a noble and serene language which owed nothing to routine parish musical activities or to spectacular conventional religious ceremony.

At the same time, a second subject tempted him. He set to music for chorus and orchestra Victor Hugo's *Les Djinns*. We can understand the attraction that this difficult acrobatic poetry might present for a beginner with its change of meter for each stanza to bring into relief, typographically, the two "blasts" of a crescendo and diminuendo. In *Les Djinns, Op. 12,* the description of an attack of evil demons coming quietly out of the shadows, rushing onto an oriental village, laying siege to it with a terrifying fracas then going off and disappearing into the night, presented an amusing rhythmic problem to put across musically. The young student attacked the problem, but did not find a particularly brilliant solution. For the first and last time in his life, he applied himself to a task which did not agree with his temperament.

This poem was essentially descriptive and graphic. Ever since his youth, Fauré did not show any intuitive affinity for this style. Moreover, the juggling represented by this lozenge-shaped curiosity whose two vertical ends are verses of two feet and the two horizontal ends are Alexandrines narrowly subjugated the composer to the dictatorship of the words which had laboriously constructed this geometric figure. Whatever the cost, he welded their contours and slavishly respected the ebb and flow of the strophes which were, as we know, anti-Fauréan in the first place. It was an impossible task to rework these so solidly forged lines into fluidity and to a point of fusion which would have permitted him to "musicalise" them in the way he wanted. Therefore, the attempt could only succeed in giving us a conscientiously correct work which, composed by someone else, would have been much esteemed.

Until he was thirty years old, Schumann needed no other interpreter for his dreams and emotions than the piano. It was only then that he called upon the human voice to translate his more impassioned excitement. Fauré, to the contrary, began by writing songs, but did not dare, before reaching, like Schumann, his thirtieth birthday, attempt instrumental music. Seven important compositions appeared one by one: a sonata, a concerto, a quartet, a berceuse and the three *Romances sans paroles, Op. 17.*

The sonata is the famous *Sonata No. 1 for Violin and Piano in A Major, Op. 13* which was not understood when it first appeared but which has since taken its rightful place in the repertoire. One wonders today how music lovers of 1876 could have resisted so much freshness, happiness, communicative ardor, palpitating life, aural voluptuousness and misunderstood such a charming masterpiece. In a famous article, Saint-Saëns took his hat off with sincere enthusiasm to the marvelous debut of his student in the realm of chamber music. He declared that Fauré had defeated the German school, which had no rival in this area. And, he added, "One finds in this sonata all that which can charm the fastidious: formal novelty, the quest, refinement of the modulations, curious sonorities, use of the most unexpected rhythms. Over this hovers a charm which envelops the entire work and makes the crowd of ordinary listeners accept as very natural the most unexpected touches of boldness."

This first violin sonata has yet another merit, that of respecting the most traditional rules of the form while rejuvenating them and easily and elegantly enriching the form with new properties. Fauré knew how to create a sonata with a personality, new proportions and unsuspected balances, which make his work a great deal more solidly constructed than those of certified architects who base their plans on the substructure of a classic masterpiece and start over again and again with the same prefabricated houses. A quarter of a century before Debussy, in his first chamber music work, Fauré demonstrated that one could and should create his own form for every new work by attaching less importance, as Louis Laloy said so succinctly, "to classical symmetry than to the written rules for lovely lines and harmonious movement." Such is the revelation that is brought to us, without any noisy, clamorous declarations of faith, nor with dogmatic manifestoes, by the composer of this work whose opening *allegro* carries us away on wings toward the highest and most mysterious regions of impassioned lyricism; whose *scherzo* makes one think of a sunlit field; whose *andante* is rounded off with a meditative arabesque of a moving expressivity; and whose *finale* is galvanized by an irresistible rhythmic ebb.

The concerto was a work for violin and orchestra. Fauré wrote a first movement, had it performed at the Société Nationale, declared himself unsatisfied with it and with his usual professional conscientiousness abandoned this project. Forty-five years later, on the threshold of death, he took it up again and used the two themes of the first *allegro* in the first movement of his *String Quartet, Op. 121.* This once again shows the lack of watertight compartments that people wanted to set up for his works.

The *Piano Quartet in C Minor, Op. 15* is the first of the two works in this form in which Fauré intended to show that the combination of three stringed instruments and a keyboard instrument was not as deceptive as one was willing to believe. Certainly, the piano takes shorter breaths than the violin and the sound of a hammer striking a string is not easily blended with that of a string caressed by a bow. This mixture often produces mediocre results, but we would not be very well acquainted with our poet of the keyboard if we were to doubt the facility with which he could resolve this problem. His two *Piano Quartets, Ops. 15 and 45* and his two *Piano Quintets, Ops. 89 and 115* are shining examples of this style.

The flexibility of the pianistic writing is wonderful. Enveloped by the arpeggios, chords and scale passages of the piano, the strings freely weave their homogeneous pattern which the piano solidifies. Fauré creates, in this fashion, a fabric of rare richness and sumptuousness. He uses this to reveal to us, as early as his first essay in this form, a new side of his talent—his virile energy which hides under the gracefulness of his style and whose secret presence can be uncovered at every stage of his production.

The *Piano Quartet No. 1 in C Minor, Op. 15,* whose themes are robust and muscular, silence the underhanded insinuations of critics who habitually relegate Fauré to the ranks of the "weavers of charm."

Yet the vigor and powerful impulses which animate the first *allegro* and the exciting *finale* of this very vital and dynamic work do not prevent the composer from abandoning himself in the *andante* to a poignantly melancholy meditation and inventing a *scherzo* of infinite delicacy. And what a discovery the *trio* from this dazzling *scherzo* is, as it suddenly softens the mood and allows the three stringed instruments to mesh together in a silken blend of muted sonorities in order to state a caressing phrase while the piano continues to move around them!

Some critics attributed the unusual solemnity of the *andante* to the chagrin caused by the composer's broken engagement to Marianne Viardot. Nothing, in my opinion, warrants docile acceptance of such a sentimental and imprudent thesis. Fauré's reserve always prevented him from following the example of Romantic artists who allowed the whole world to witness their personal frustrations. Everything one knows about him contradicts this theory. Capable of enlarging his style to treat a pathetic theme possessing something universal, Fauré would never have consented to express himself in such a spectacular manner. Moreover, we have ascertained that the works dating from this period do not carry any trace of the wound which he concealed with so much delicacy and dignity.

This first piano quartet is very promising. From the beginning of its first movement, we admire Fauré's art in all of its grace and intelligence. Eluding none of the formal requirements of chamber music, he found a way to soften and sweeten its strictness. He complies with the classical rituals of the exposition, the development and the recapitulation, but he knows how to make one forget the tyranny of academicism. The thematic fragments, the cutting up and crushing of the germ cells by other composers in an architectural fashion are often nothing but inert, passive and interchangeable material with as much personality or expression as tile, bricks or rubble. With Fauré, the smallest rhythmic or melodic motive has a meaning, a musical interest, an individuality. Not a single note is extraneous, not a single note is banal. All came from the heart. While the change from major to minor generally constitutes a sort of formality, the changing of the mode here is knowingly calculated. When the virile theme appears, in the minor, at the beginning of the exposition, it hides its true face. It enters the lists, its visor lowered to prepare for a surprise effect when the visor is raised to receive the glorious light of E flat Major.

In order to escape from the melodic and rhythmic monotony of a disciplined development section based on amplification, Fauré exposes other secrets. First, he makes us hold our breath and sustain our interest by the audacious, ingenious and unexpected modulations. Elsewhere, he alludes to the two contrasting themes alternately, in order to vary the pattern and articulation of his discourse. Frequently in the course of his career we will find these linguistic elegances. This *Piano Quartet No. 1* contains the seed for Fauré's magnificent later works.

One of the most dazzling is assuredly his *Piano Quartet No. 2 in G Minor, Op. 45*, a masterful work which permits us to successively admire all of the characteristic aspects of Fauré's genius and the virility of his art. The first *allegro* begins vigorously over a piano accompaniment. The strings present, in unison, a warm and proud theme—a melody completely suitable to chamber music.

Fauré excelled in inventing motives which take us into a spiritual world where a pathos removed from our daily existence prevails. In the course of the development it will suddenly become Major and will shine forth with incomparable radiancy. A meditative second theme calms the agitated movement of the first. Along with the melodic and rhythmic elements of these two contrasted motives is a lighter section of surprising ingenuity whose details are worthy of attention.

The *scherzo* begins decisively. This time it is the strings which create the accompanimental rhythm and the persistent driving energy, while the piano scatters lively scales. There is no methodical development section. However, without slowing the movement down, several fleeting allusions are made to the two main motives of the first movement and this *moto perpetuo,* which lasts scarcely half a minute, dissipates rapidly and draws to a close on a peremptory chord. Like the first movement, the *scherzo* is in the Minor. Also like the *allegro,* the *scherzo* seems to want to prove that music in the Minor is not necessarily used to designate melancholia, and that effects of indisputable lightness can be drawn from it. The *finale* again demonstrates this.

With the *adagio ma non troppo* we reach one of the peaks that one could call Gabriel Fauré's metaphysical lyricism, that is to say, his miraculous gift for deep pathos. He makes us hear, first, over rocking fifths, those faraway bells of the village of Cadirac whose twilight ringing was forever engraved on the memory of the little Ariégeois child. Following this soothing passage, which returns to play a role in subsequent developments, comes a dreamy and tender phrase in the viola which impregnates the entire *adagio* with an inexpressible sweetness.

The keyboard and the strings begin an impassioned dialogue. They are superimposed. We can't use the term accompaniment, for the two conversants are developing their thoughts quite independently, although on a common harmonic basis. At this point, the bells introduce their soft chiming under the viola's theme which the piano has taken for its own. The whole section is brimming over with purity, nobility and grandeur. It leads us to one of those magical and decidedly Fauréan musical conclusions whose charm is supernatural.

The mechanism is of such simplicity that analysis does not reveal its mysterious power. Two parallel fifths, like those of the bells, connect two perfect chords which seem to have the intention of imposing two tonalities—B flat Major and G flat Major. But a lower appoggiatura and a passing note enrich this harmony with such poetic intensity that when the lovely viola theme sounds above it, it undergoes a moving transformation.

As for the last *allegro*, ardent and energetic, it burns its bridges behind it by firing themes with a strange rapidity. The composer carelessly throws in a half dozen of these musical ideas, abandoning some and bringing others back according to his fancy and mood. One is aristocratic, another roguish, a third sad, another commanding. A tumultuous coda where scales, arpeggios, and chords vie with each other to come in first, closes this magnificent score.

The *Berceuse, Op. 16* for violin and piano which forms part of this group needs no introduction. Its tenderness and caressing melodic charm have made it Fauré's most popular work. It is an exquisite piece and one cannot reproach it for its prodigious success at popular concerts.

The *Ballade for Piano and Orchestra, Op. 19* was originally written for solo piano. It was in that form that Saint-Saëns showed it to Franz Liszt in Weimar. And it was this version which prompted the famous remark of the emperor of the piano who read the first few pages of the score and said with discouragement, "It's too difficult."

This observation did honor to Gabriel Fauré's individualism. It is quite evident that in the virtuosic hands of the composer of the *Hungarian Rhapsodies* no part of the *Ballade* would present the least difficulty, especially the first pages. But for one who was so enthusiastic about German Romanticism, the disarming simplicity and disconcerting modulations had something disturbing and disquieting about them so that the old Wagnerite had not the inclination to investigate further. He would have had to study the calm and mysterious language more closely in order to discover its secrets. This was in itself a "too difficult" task and that particular day Liszt read no further.

From this first piano work, Fauré had already so completely embodied the specific qualities of "la sensibilité française" that his music could not easily gain an audience in other countries. Even today it is met with misunderstanding and opposition by non-French musicians who sincerely admire modern French composers. The admirable German pianist Walter Gieseking, who was the incomparable interpreter of Ravel and Debussy, one day expressed to me his sadness in not being able to understand this masterpiece of Fauré. He had wanted to make it and Fauré's other piano music part of his repertoire. He had practiced the *Ballade* assiduously and without experiencing the least aversion toward the music, but he could not discover its meaning. For him, as for Liszt—"too difficult."

The final version of the *Ballade* which this time had an indispensable orchestral accompaniment was performed in Paris in 1881 at the Société Nationale. Since then, it has made its way out into the world, but into a world of connoisseurs.

It has been suggested that it was inspired by Fauré's remembrance of Wagner's *Forest Murmurs* from *Siegfried*, which had charmed him when he heard the Ring cycle at Bayreuth. Certainly, there isn't the least trace of Wagner in the score either in its mood or in its compositional style. What Fauré seems to have wanted was to make a typically French forest sweetly sing for us. He contented himself with creating around a quietly meditative piano piece a stylized atmosphere evocative of the "warbling of birds and singing branches."

A light, quiet pizzicato in the basses is the signal for the beginning of this forest stroll whose tempo and rhythm are to be regulated by gentle chords. A meditative phrase of inexpressible well-being unfolds. Once the stroller's communion with the essence of things is complete, the forest carries on a friendly conversation. As a matter of fact, the flute will answer the piano by taking up its theme in canonic imitation.

Observe how something magical happens here. The canon, an intellectual exercise, a scholastically stylistic procedure par excellence, seems, by nature, improper for the expression of any kind of poetry. But Fauré is so much a master that he willfully makes a canonic imitation as poetic, as expressive, and as free in appearance as a melody. The whole of this contemplative exposition, a miracle of delightful clarity, balance and proportion, leads us to a peaceful conclusion.

A new, and more animated theme appears and takes charge of the walk. It is young, agile, and quicker in step. Its development is ingenious but one is never aware of any effort. Fauré had the innate ability of subtly giving his ideas a character of spontaneity which increases their persuasiveness. The initial theme recurs and the two become participants in a fantastic tournament during which they skillfully compete with one another.

A short *andante* introduces a languid and dreamy feeling which leads into a joyous, animated and impetuous *allegro*. Two sparkling piano cadenzas bring back calm and serenity to this scene, now illuminated by reflections, plays of colors, and the lustrous sparkle of the first two themes, reappearing in the accompaniment patterns.

When one thinks that, at the time when Fauré was composing this new and daring work, it predated by three years Debussy's tantalizing and charming harmonic vocabulary of *L'Enfant prodigue*, one then realizes the importance of the discoveries of this precursor, who created and used the neologisms that we admire among his juniors.

At the end of his life, forty years later, Fauré was to write a second work for piano and orchestra, the *Fantaisie, Op. 111*, whose performance he refused to authorize. After his death there was no delay in ignoring this wish and, in spite of the clearly expressed position of its composer, this *Fantaisie* has been heard in the concert hall. Reasons can be found for this resurrection. In principle, they are condemnable, but they can be found. Nothing that a musician of genius has created can leave us indifferent, and it is an act of piety to gather up all that has fallen from his pen. Besides, pianists were in a hurry to incorporate a new *Ballade* in their repertoire, since Fauré had not written a piano concerto for them. So be it! However, the veto of a composer whose critical sense was very astute, tempts us to look more closely. Certainly this *Fantaisie* is a very agreeable piece for piano which composed by someone else would be well received in concert. Why did Fauré retract it? Perhaps he was not pleased with the orchestration, which has its faults. But to correct them would have been easy. I believe, rather, that the remembrance of the *Ballade* must have dissuaded him from bringing forth a less charming sister.

There is a chasm between these two works and the *Fantaisie* suffers by comparison. The basic theme of the latter work is excellent and leads to typically Fauréan developments, but while in the *Ballade* these developments appear spontaneously one after the other like blossoms on the stalk of a gladiola, those in the *Fantaisie* are visibly the result of the intellect. It was the infallible professionalism of a master composer which dictated these harmonies, these cadences, and these modulations whose use is so familiar that they combine and separate quite automatically with an acquired fluency as soon as the composer's mind has given them the signal to start. Fauré certainly was aware of this and he didn't want his listeners to guess it.

Although he always had a happy disposition, Fauré never was attracted to the comic element in music. It is with difficulty that one pictures him involved with the composition of an opera buffa. Humor and even irony have found no place in his work. The austere Vincent d'Indy was not afraid to write an operetta while, in spite of his jovial nature, our tone poet never succumbed to that temptation. One day, however, under quite exceptional circumstances, he attempted a parody. He was returning from Bayreuth with André Messager, and the realizations brought about by having heard the Ring cycle had plunged both of them into a state of exaltation and indescribable enthusiasm. In Paris, they discovered some Wagner lovers and met with them in order to relive together their impressions and memories.

Aside from the powerful emotions stirred up by the four days of the Ring cycle, they amused themselves by keeping track of the leitmotives. It was the sort of distraction comparable to a child's when his parents give him a box of tinker-toys. The Walküre's motive, those of Siegfried, Loge and Wotan, and those of Hunding or of Erda became, among the initiated, familiar toys which proved diverting without being irreverent as soon as they were taken out of context.

So, one must not be shocked and cry out "blasphemy" and "sacrilege" in learning that, in order to entertain this circle of Wagnerites, Fauré and Messager had the happy idea of composing an extravagant potpourri on the leading motives of *Der Ring des Nibelungen*. There was no sarcasm, and no trace of impiety in this naive outburst of good humor which relieved the emotional pressures of these young artists. It was for them a way of having fun and throwing their hats into the air, in front of the statue of their god.

This hurried piece of writing was not, certainly, intended to leave the clique in which it had been born. However, it was found and under the title of *Souvenir de Bayreuth,* published and recorded as an historical document. And it was justifiable, for when one hears this fantasy played brilliantly by its two composers in a four-hand arrangement, to the great joy of an audience, one immediately recognizes the mark of two perfect musicians, two men of intelligence and taste. The imitation of Offenbach's style and the rhythmic and harmonic travesties that the themes undergo are plentiful. The *Pastourelle,* in particular, based on the *Song of Spring,* the love theme, the Rhine Maidens, the Rhine, and the Forge of the Dwarfs are surprisingly successful and deserve to be preserved by us.

From this time on, the songs and instrumental compositions were produced at the same rate on parallel paths. The most striking successes followed one another uninterruptedly. Let us open, to begin with, the second collection of songs. It is abundantly filled with pieces of astonishing diversity. There are works here which, because of their color and style, the choice of their poetry and their technical writing, reveal to us each time a new and unexpected aspect of their composer's personality. Not one is without interest. The simplest ones, in appearance the most familiar, which seem to be popular only because of their pleasant charm, like *La Fée aux chansons, Op. 27, No. 2; Barcarolle, Op. 7, No. 3; Aurore, Op. 39, No. 1; Notre amour, Op. 23, No. 2; Chanson d'amour, Op. 27, No. 1;* or *Fleur jetée, Op. 39, No. 2,* still contain, whether in harmonic invention or in modulation, melodic line or accompanimental figuration, small but happy discoveries which, bearing any other signature than Fauré's, would have made the best composers of his day proud, but which have paled next to his innumerable bursts of genius.

Examine *Nell, Op. 18, No. 1*, which is so supple, flexible, filled with flights of infinite grace and carried along by little caressing arpeggios which gradually propel it by imperceptible displacements of one of their notes and lead the theme off to enchanted horizons. What refined elegance beneath the apparent ease of the vocal arabesque! What ingenuity in the modulations which entwine and separate with such tender nonchalance in the central phrase, *"Que ta perle est douce au ciel enflammé . . ."* Among all of the impressive touches created by a Fauré arpeggio, the one from *Nell* with its outward simplicity, its youthful purity and freshness is one of the most charming.

Following this spontaneous cry of love are two serious and meditative pieces, *Le Voyageur, Op. 18, No. 2* and *Automne, Op. 18, No. 3*, based on two poems by Armand Silvestre. The first, somber and almost tragic, creates a vague and oppressing menace of some evil fate which follows implacably in the steps of a stranger on his way to his destiny. This muffled anguish is transformed into music by means of a harsh obsessive rhythm, quite unusual in any of Fauré's works. In the first and final sections, an obstinate C, the dominant of the key, lugubriously tolls the knell for some deathly ghost. The most compassionately tender harmonies glide by without weakening its pained sadness and when it is stilled in the central portion, *"Voyageur, presse donc le pas . . . . ,"* it can yet be heard under the most distant modulations which are preparing for its adroitly managed return. *Automne,* equally sad, finds in the "foggy skies and painful horizons" of autumn's end nostalgic and sentimental memories, as a syncopated bass stirs up and disperses the disillusioning images.

A small triptych, *Poème d'un jour, Op. 21*, summarizes the three stages of love—*Rencontre, Toujours* and *Adieu*—giving Fauré the opportunity to paint three canvases of genius that a singer can interpret in different ways. He can take Grandmougin's couplets very seriously and, in this case, he will fill the three songs with great sincerity of emotion by greatly slowing down the final song which then becomes an elegy. This is a relatively recent interpretation. He can, on the other hand, be slightly ironic, which could very well be part of Fauré's character, in the sense of the tragicomedy of the "eternal sacraments." The poetry probably calls for the second interpretation, for *Rencontre* and *Toujours* are somewhat verbally exalted with more than a hint of the dramatic stage. In any case, *Adieu* adopts a tone of mocking scepticism, *"les longs soupirs, les bien-aimées: fumées . . . A vous l'on se croyait fidèle, mais, dans ce monde léger, les plus longs amours sont courts et je dis, en quittant vos charmes, sans larmes, presque au moment de mon aveu: Adieu!,"* which are words that do not easily lend themselves to an interpretation colored by despair. Fauré's music leans toward this second conception despite the indications of the opening movement.

More than one critic intuitively pointed out the insincere emotion in *Rencontre* and the "lack of inspiration" of *Toujours* which "strives for passion." Under these circumstances, *Adieu*, with its little chords to which the dotted eighth notes give a mocking character and the disengaging manner in which the lover reclaims his liberty, *"presque au moment de son aveu,"* perfectly justifies a progressively more animated, lighter interpretation. Examine the accompaniment patterns of the final section of the last selection of this lovely triptych and you will notice how it is a lot more suitable to a carefree and "tearless" *scherzando* than to a melancholy *andante* bathed in tears.

Two poems were going to take Fauré's feelings in other directions. Armand Sully-Prudhomme, in discovering the synchronism of connecting massive vessels rocked by great swells with cradles that mothers tenderly rock, gave him the material to write one of his most justly popular songs, *Les Berceaux, Op. 23, No. 1* which was set into motion by gentle *arpeggios* which create a sentimental mood.

Armand Silvestre's enigmatic poem "Le Secret" is surpassed by Fauré's music (Op. 23, No. 3) which penetrates well beyond the words into that mysterious region forbidden to all the other arts and in which Fauré has always moved about with ease. A simple change on the fourth scale degree gives, from the beginning, a sensual character to the key of D Minor (reserved for the two sealed secrets) while, in the middle section, a fleeting enharmonic elegance endows with more brilliance the boldness of the text. Simple chords move calmly in a stepwise direction with each beat and succeed one another with a kind of religious solemnity. Then, gradually thinning out, they are extinguished for an instant in a chord which perfectly describes the mood of the poem. I consider *Le Secret* as one of the keys, a tiny key, which, in some ways, unlocks the greatest number of doors to the mysteries of Fauré's art.

Another song, *Notre amour, Op. 23, No. 2*, inspired by the same poet, is not as good as expected. It is criticized because of its facileness, its light grace, and its candid joy which is carried along on a single wave by a rapid and carefree theme.

On the other hand, the songlike *Clair de lune, Op. 46, No. 2*, whose success does not happen to dull the power of its magical charm, leaves us with the feeling of absolute perfection. Isn't it a miracle to have captured in the lunar surroundings of the key of B flat Minor all the fairy nostalgia of Verlaine's "Fêtes galantes" by transforming the musical version of its poetry into the shape of a phantom minuet? What attention to detail in the musical transformation of the poet's images! When Verlaine has his imaginary characters sing "in the minor mode," what an example of legerdemain, giving us by this means the feeling of being duped, by introducing a D-natural which destroys the Minor key of the minuet but ironically tricks our ear and produces the desired result.

Les Présents, Op. 46, No. 1, has only thirty-six measures, each bar being the signal for a change of key. Such a procedure could make us fear for an exaggerated fragmentation of the melody which is undergoing these unceasing breaks in flow. Such is not the case. These regular alternations of tonalities create, to the contrary, a mysterious and very favorable balance for the somewhat enigmatic mood of Villiers de l'Isle-Adam's poem. And the listener will sense that each of these tonal metamorphoses has been thought out with extraordinary skill by Fauré in order to give us some pleasant surprises. The evocation of the "ancient ballade," of "roses full of droplets of moisture," of the "flower of the dead," of "tombs," or of "doves" is realized with magical knowledge.

It is a very different technique to achieve the pacifying rocking of the cradle which makes the perfume of *Les Roses d'Ispahan, Op. 39, No. 4,* so sensual. Its success, like that of *Clair de lune,* has caused dissatisfaction among the Jansenists of music. Their protective smiles do not prevent the exoticism of these unique pages from being efficacious and enriching Leconte de Lisle's poetry with lively color. In *Les Présents,* the tonality changed with each measure. In *Les Roses d'Ispahan,* an oriental languor would not be suitable for this kind of movement. In order to dream of seducing his pure Leilah, her lover will have to remain lazily stretched out on the broad and massive couch of D Major. It will momentarily rise up a third to mourn the flighty character of his mistress and will again assume the comfortable beginning tonality to cherish the hope for the quick return of the unfaithful one.

This song, with its whiff of intoxicating and perfumed sensuality, is immediately followed by the angelic *En prière* (no opus number) of the infant Jesus asking his celestial Father to grant him the strength and mildness necessary to accomplish his earthly mission. No entreaty could be more striking. Fauré's genius always identifies faithfully with inspirational subjects since he treats them all so convincingly with music.

Listen to Fauré's song *En prière* and the famous *Panis angelicus* by Franck. No one could doubt the religious sincerity of the *Pater seraphicus,* and the mystical composer of *Rédemption* is evidently more qualified than the composer of *Les Roses d'Ispahan* to kneel down before the Eucharist. And besides, the *Panis angelicus* is really only a very agreeable and carefully

73

written piece of music with a weak canonic imitation that one might find in any collection accessible to the humblest of the faith, but you will not find in it the touching confidence, the fervent glow of faith or the tender humility which makes the Fauré prayer more moving than the one which is most representative of the "pious laity."

Between the second and third collections of songs appears Fauré's masterpiece, the *Requiem, Op. 48.* This requiem is an absolutely unique work. It has no musical or religious connection with the most famous compositions which bear this name. Mozart's *Requiem,* Verdi's, Brahms', Berlioz', to name only the most famous, all have features in common, in spite of the diversity of their composers' temperaments. This one is the only one of its kind.

We have just said that Fauré was not a religious man. He was incapable of intolerance or sectarianism, but his agnosticism was complete. It was that of an indulgent philosopher, but one without illusions. He never hid anything from himself. It was he who, after having read a manifesto of faith in an important Catholic journal, was not afraid to write, "How nice is this self-assurance! How nice is the naivete, or the vanity, or the stupidity or the bad faith of the people for whom this was written, printed and distributed!" Only his natural courtesy and his professional conscience allowed him to carry out his duties as an organist with absolute correctness and with the least amount of hypocrisy to write a certain number of religious works, a Low Mass of angelic purity for three women's voices, his *Cantique de Jean Racine,* of which we have already spoken, several elegantly ingenious motets and his extraordinary *Requiem.*

This *Requiem* is, if I dare say so, the work of a disbeliever who respects the belief of others. One need not have faith to accompany with contemplation and emotion one of his own to a final resting place. A requiem's purpose is to assuage the grief of a family or a crowd in prayer, while reminding them of the vistas their religious beliefs can open to them when they enjoy eternal rest. A Verdi or a Berlioz constructed their scores like gigantic sonorous cathedrals. These composers spared us no painful detail. They stress all of the threats contained in the sacred texts. They created the atmosphere of fear. Their main purpose was to solemnly remind the faithful of the eternal torture which awaits them if they die in a state of sin.

This view of divine justice evidently did not suit Fauré. His music played a more compassionate role. Fauré thus begins by abandoning the nightmarish representation of the *Dies irae*, a dramatic interpolation conceived in the century of the "Danses macabres" which disturbs the serenity of the funeral service. He makes only a fleeting allusion to the reassuring promises God made to Abraham and his descendants in his *Offertory*. Of the liturgical texts, he only retains those which have the character of a prayer, of supplication, of a look toward heaven and not toward hell.

The work is composed for soloists, chorus, organ and orchestra. The *Introit* is grave and majestic. It immediately brings to mind the pathetic grandeur of the subject about to be treated. The brass instruments of the orchestra and the organ unite in a powerful chord which the hushed voices of the choir timidly echo. The composer does not indulge in any realistic description inspired by the theatrical *Tuba mirum*, whose spectacular possibilities have so often been exploited. He scorns these easy effects as unworthy of him. He interprets in the logic of pure music, the suggestive force of his thoughts and feelings. This grandiose and mournful chord sounds three times, each time lowered one step.

What the chorus murmurs is the fervent supplication which rises to the lips of any sensitive human being when he finds himself in front of a tomb. *Requiem aeternam donna eis, Domine!* The broad expanse of the *Lux perpetua* charitably illuminates this prayer and injects an element of peace and hope in death. An ascending and descending motive in the cellos sustains the broadly stated melody of the *Kyrie* against which the transparent and luminous voices of the women are heard, with the *Te decet hymnus* finishing softly.

The *Offertory* is treated in quite a different style from the *Introit* and *Kyrie*. Apparent here is the very personal harmonic vocabulary of a virtuoso of shock modulations, of clear evasions which flower into a distant tonality but then only abandon it in a single movement as soon as he has extricated from it a reflection which enchants the ear. The tender feminine appeal *O Domine Jesu Christe* precedes and prepares the entrance of the baritone solo which will develop the thread of the *Hostias et preces tibi*.

It is here that one can observe one of the most elegant characteristics of Fauré. This melodic phrase is in reality only a long hold on the dominant which, with a few passing undulations, dominates the prayer. And under this serene line, extended from one end of the verse to the other, is a gentle rocking of beautiful chords which closely and by degrees follow one another with inimitable ease and charm. It is there that one hears, for the first time, in augmentation, the theme that is going to be shortly transformed into a winding pattern in the *Sanctus*. Finally, this episode ends on an angelic *Amen* which climbs toward heaven with the spiritual purity of children's voices.

The *Sanctus* is a small masterpiece of conciseness and simplicity. It begins with female unison voices over a continual embroidery of harp arpeggios. The male voices softly echo them and mirror their image. A muted violin arabesque weaves between these two choirs and closely entwines, interlacing them. This moving prayer has the tenderness of a berceuse and possesses an extraordinary power to pacify. It soothes and quiets human suffering, but becomes vigorous suddenly in the *Hosanna* in order to exalt divine glory. Massive chords and trumpet blasts explode and weld the choruses together in an enthusiastic but brief section.

The architecture of the *Pie Jesu* is also very simple. The immaculate melody is entrusted to a solo soprano. The orchestra is still, attentively listening, and only dares intervene very discreetly between the stanzas of this simple melody. And yet tenderness, compassion, and affecting confidence reign from one end of the *Agnus Dei* to the other before the return of the opening *Requiem* section.

With its "background" which underlies the regular and lightly syncopated *pizzicati* of the strings, the organ supports the voice of the baritone solo in the *Libera me*. The curve of this melody is broad and noble. When it meets with the menacing words evoking the destruction of the earth and heaven, it treats them without weakening and without terror. Only the choruses give a short shudder at *Tremens factus sum ego*, but the recurring vision of tranquility on the horizon restores faith and hope.

And it is now that the theme of the *In paradisum* rises up. Its serenity is the peaceful and comforting conclusion for the Office of the Dead.

The great philosophical merit of this admirable farewell to life is in its sensitivity and its modesty. Fauré could look death in the face without flinching and make the necessary adjustments to accept the modest place he had to occupy in life. The music of Fauré's *Requiem* supplies, with its customary ease, the harmonies for the inevitable modulation of a being. There is no crying out, no common fright, no romantic outbursts.

Fauré's third group of songs is neither less rich nor less varied than the preceding ones. Only a more marked complacency toward texts dealing with suffering can be detected, like *Larmes, Op. 51, No. 1; Spleen, Op. 51, No. 3; Prison, Op. 83, No. 1;* and *Au cimetière, Op. 51, No. 2.* He treats these with particular conviction. There is in the sobbing rhythm of *Larmes* a desolate harshness quite unusual for the highly compassionate composer of the *Requiem*. His *Spleen* is so nostalgic and disheartening that we can no longer listen to Verlaine's poem in any other musical setting than this one.

The same thing must be said for *Prison* which also spoils for us all other versions of this poignant picture, made so sad by the almost cruel portrayal of the "simple and peaceful" life, whose distant reflections the prisoner catches sight of from the window of his cell. Fauré understood the eloquence of this silent message coming to the captive from over the rooftops. To convey this, he used two intervals of a third which, held closely together with small chords, interrupt at regular intervals the gentle ringing of two octaves striking a B Minor chord, sounding much like a bell. And it is by obstinately maintaining this peaceful succession of equal values that Fauré wrests from the guilty repentant the tortured cry, "What have you done with your youth?"

There is a great consoling serenity in the admirable *Au cimetière,* where rustic tombs surround a village church. Again there are small consonant chords of equal value which synthesize for the musician the rhythm of happiness. Fauré then replaced the first chordal reprise by an arpeggiated triplet to change the mood and scene. The sea is before us in all its ferocity as a devourer of men. Each measure creates the sound of a wave beating against the sides of a boat snapping under the impetus of two dissonant chords which sweep it to the depths. And isn't the decrescendo, which in four measures quiets the waves and leads back to the initial rhythm, strengthened by the return in the bass of the dominant of C Minor which prepares us for the conclusion, a model of expressive conciseness?

After these melancholy pages, a good humored springtime bursts forth in the sensuality that *Arpège, Op. 76, No. 2,* offers to Sylva, Sylvie, and Sylvanire, the "beauties with the devious blue eyes." *"Allez vite, l'heure est si brève,"* the tender intrigue which makes *Le plus doux chemin, Op. 87, No. 1,* poetical, *Le Ramier, Op. 87, No. 2* and *Madrigal, Op. 35,* and the overflowing sensuality of the *Chanson de Shylock* (in Op. 57) are evidences of an enthusiasm toward life made more precious and desirable by the proximity of visions of death. Fauré's hedonism bursts forth here in rhythm and accents which are his alone and which endow his musical speech with a gentleness which does not prevent him from treating with the same success the subtly melancholy texts of *La Fleur qui va sur l'eau, Op. 85, No. 2, Accompagnement, Op. 85, No. 3,* and *Dans le forêt de septembre, Op. 85, No. 1.*

It is also in this collection that the five "Venice" songs are found, *Mandoline, En sourdine, Green, A Clymène* and *C'est l'extase, Op. 58, Nos. 1–5,* of which I will speak later. And it is here that we also find several of the high points of Fauré's art with *Le Parfum impérissable, Op. 76, No. 1,* whose title alone represents the best definition ever found for his art, with his *La Rose, Op. 51, No. 4,* a lyric apotheosis of Aphrodite's charms, and, above all, with *Soir, Op. 83, No. 2,* which defies comment by its genial concentrated writing and extraordinary harmonic construction.

Fauré has never consciously pushed the boundaries of tonality so far as in these continuing series of unusual resolutions, interrupted broken cadences, anticipations, suspensions, everything which can give the ear the feeling of instability and vagueness which the agony of the fading light at the end of a day can bring to our senses. Never did he unite more closely and more subtly visual suggestions with the most delicate emotional nuances or the touch of compassion. *Soir* brings together in a strikingly abridged version all that is most profound, deepest and personal in Fauré's harmonic palette and the infinite delicacy of his imagination.

Fauré composed about a hundred songs. Sixty of them are divided chronologically in three collections which are not related psychologically or esthetically. But there are exceptions—the five so-called *"Venice Songs," Op. 58,* the nine songs of *La Bonne Chanson, Op. 61,* the ten couplets of *La Chanson d'Ève, Op. 95,* the eight settings of *Le Jardin clos, Op. 106,* the four *Mirages, Op. 113,* and the four songs of *L'Horizon chimérique, Op. 118,* forming balanced and homogeneous collections whose pages obey a common law and whose construction has been minutely studied.

The "Venetian" collection (*Cinq Mélodies, Op. 58*), which is the first of this series, does not fulfill these architectural conditions. The popular title only indicates the place where the author conceived of the musical settings for five Verlaine poems. Fauré had profited from his first contact with Venice by composing *Mandoline* which is as much "Versaillesque" as his *Clair de lune* and did not finish the rest of the collection until his return to Paris. There is nothing "Italian" about these songs.

It is known that this preoccupation with locale is frequent among the creative who find in their imagination richer sources of inspiration than in copying reality. It was in a Burgundian village that Debussy patiently studied the play of waves for *La Mer* and in his lodging in the Batignolles that he condensed, without having crossed the Pyrenees, the intoxicating perfumes for *Ibéria*. Two well-known anecdotes of Fauré and Ravel confirm this observation. To an admirer who begged him to reveal the divine countryside which had dictated the sublime harmonies of the *Nocturne No. 6 in D flat Major, Op. 63* to him, Fauré answered with a secret satisfaction, "the Simplon Tunnel." And Ravel, during a trip to Morocco, confessed, "If I were involved in composing Arab music, it would be much more Arabic than the real thing."

We should not then be surprised to see the composer of *Mandoline* imaginatively boating on the Grand Canal while he is looking at the Tuileries Pond, and resurrecting Watteau on the day when he takes his first authentic gondola trip. This *Mandoline* is a ravishing piece which has fixed for all time the conjectural mood of the *Fêtes Galantes* which take place in an imaginary Versailles park, designed as much by Verlaine as by Le Nôtre. Its accompanimental arpeggios create an easy and graceful rhythm which is a real find which other works will echo. Three years earlier, the fairy-like *Clair de lune* had extracted from the same dreamy landscape all of its deep emotion. *Mandoline* completes this picture by putting the emphasis on its purely literary aspects. The spectral minuet from *Clair de lune* suffused moonlight over an unreal scene. The smiling arpeggios of *Mandoline* invite us not to take too seriously the elegant puppets with which the painter and the poet have populated it. Fauré has displayed in this perfect setting so much grace that none of the composers who set this short poem have ever succeeded in conveying it with such perfection.

This homage to Watteau, which is evidently non-Venetian, appears as the frontispiece to a Verlainesque anthology that takes quite another direction. *En sourdine, Green, A Clymène* and *C'est l'extase* foreshadow the amatory effusions of *La Bonne Chanson, Op. 61.* Nightfall in the first, the tender cajolery of the second, the great bursts of love in *C'est l'extase* are found again in the later song collection, but they are wiser, purified and candid. The subtle thoughts of *A Clymène* are the common thread which allows the poet and the musician to modulate the acknowledged sensuality which impregnates this first collection with the chaste reserve which reigns in the second. And this astonishing transformation of a courageous lover overcome with love is one of the important psychological features of *La Bonne Chanson.*

The nine songs which constitute *La Bonne Chanson, Op. 61,* represent a unique moment of intoxicating excitement, due to a perfect meeting of Fauré's sensitivity and what is most secret and pure in Verlaine's feelings. The poet, who ordinarily cannot hide his troubles and torments from us, became involved with singularly saddening candidness and fervor. And the contagiousness of confidence in life and of optimism in love is such a strong force among men that Fauré, usually so prudish and reserved in expressing his feelings, has not hesitated to follow Verlaine through the poet's outbursts of happiness.

Une Sainte en son auréole is touching because it is the slightly childlike language of the poet's recaptured innocence but, by itself, it is tame and rather conventional. Fauré transformed it and spiritualized it. It has become unrecognizable. The music endowed it with a grandeur that the poem itself lacked. Its most banal imagery takes on color and shape. The Saint, the Lady, the horn, even the swan, can no longer escape from it. A calm little theme progressed unhurriedly from beginning to end, harmonized in four parts like a student work at the Conservatoire. The text makes it tremble in its course and a brief modulatory reaction, an alteration or a tonal equivalent, permits it to revitalize an image in flight. The tower of the medieval château rises up suddenly out of this modulation in C flat. Listen to the F flat which intones the note from a distant horn. The economy of means employed to move our subconscious could not be further extended and one finishes by concluding that the miracle of *La Bonne Chanson* owes more to Fauré than to Verlaine.

Let's not examine too closely the verses of the following poem, "Puisque l'aube grandit," by isolating it from the music. It still expresses the candidness of a young swooning lover who wishes only to put his hand in that of his beloved and to walk beside her. Still, the music makes the words divine. Svelte arpeggios, arranged in flowered arches, impose a supple rhythm on the musical description of this tender couple. Fauré feels their chaste happiness so deeply that at the moment when the word "aurore" appears, he composes a short vocalise on his melody, a stylistic procedure representing for him an effusive abandon which is really exceptional.

The graceful four-foot versicles which evoke the enchantment of a lunar landscape led the composer to make the third piece, *La lune blanche luit dans les bois,* the most poetic of all.

In the fourth poem, "J'allais par des chemins perfides," we fleetingly catch a glimpse of the uncertain Verlaine whom we well know. For an instant he is haunted by the image of his stormy past and "his devious ways" when he would lose his way and someone's "dear hands" would come to snatch him away from the perils which threatened him. But he soon turns away from these untimely memories and finds other language to thank this benefactress. Step by step, the music follows the expression of his remorse and of his hopes, describing with a few light touches the bitterness of his dark memories, the encounter of his guardian angel, his affectionate encouragement and, upon the reappearance of the initial theme which is accompanied by little ascending scales, the leap of energy, energy which has brought him back to the right path.

Regaining his serenity, the poet has so well recovered his adolescent purity that in the following song, "J'ai presque peur," he tries to analyze and to define his scruples in a kind of delicate but slightly precious madrigal where he excuses himself for the fright which seized him when he thought that his beloved had taken his soul last summer and reduced him to a state of slavery. He trembles to think that all his destiny will henceforth be suspended by one word, a smile, a gesture, or a wink of the eye by the sovereign queen who reigns over his heart . . . He only wants to see the future "beyond a great hope" resumed in the supreme declaration of love.

Fauré, who possessed the subtlest feeling for nuance, did not let anything escape from this text. A very quiet, rapid tempo and syncopated accents which are half-threatening, half-smiling, accurately convey the gallant homage contained in this fearful feigning, permitting him to avoid anything insignificant in this gracefully precious language which will conclude in a great burst of sincerity with the final declaration.

The sixth poem, "Avant que tu ne t'en ailles," again returns the lovers to Nature. The nocturnal reverie is over, the morning star pales, dawn is breaking. The poet, watching over his sleeping beloved waits for her awakening as well as that of the surrounding countryside. With the same suppleness and ease, the musical commentary describes the sky, sings along with the birds, warms up progressively with the approach of the sun, prepares for its entrance and sees it ecstatically unhook arrows from its first bursting rays.

Continually associating his love with the great rhythms of the universe, Verlaine makes the return of the sun a "party to his joy" in his seventh poem, "Donc, ce sera par un clair jour d'été." He asks it to make his beloved even more beautiful.

When night falls, it is to the stars that he addresses himself so that they may "benevolently shine" upon the couple. This presents a new opportunity for Fauré to display enchanting melodic touches, to surround a theme in thirds of an irresistible grace and charm with arpeggios and to fully capture the mood of the poem.

We again find this rather sad thirst for purity and modesty in Verlaine in the next to last piece in the album, "N'est-ce pas?" The lovers want to ignore the world and isolate themselves in their love, to walk hand in hand with one another. And it is they themselves who are proud of having rediscovered the childlike soul of those who love each other without concern or anxiety. The composer experienced the same proud feeling at this return to an original state of innocence, which makes him utilize unceasingly in this collection the most subtle arpeggios in his most refined accompaniments.

The song which concludes this cycle, "L'hiver a cessé," takes on the task of summarizing the entire work simultaneously by ingenious references to the themes taken from different episodes of this intimate poetry and by evoking various stages of its psychological development. It salutes the return of spring, which makes the saddest heart rejoice. Suddenly, the poet shows his ingratitude. Hasn't he henceforth an eternal spring in his soul? What matter the unpleasant seasons? Each one will charm him. And in a verse now famous, because it works for Fauré's genius for astonishing balance, he thanks the sister soul sense for the incomparable gift of revealing "this fantasy and reason" to him.

For critics for whom a rigid system of classification is so very useful, the year 1910 when the *La Chanson d'Ève, Op. 95* appeared, marks the official entrance of Fauré's genius in the arid and desert-like realm of old age. From this time on, they did not cease to uncover a drying out, an impoverishing, a progressive withering in his music. Those who loved him ascribed to this old man the guise of an ascetic disavowing his youthful sins. Others, who only admired him because it was the thing to do, easily resigned themselves to noticing in him the effects of an inevitable senility. Finally, others refused to follow until the end the evolution of a composer unfortunately gone astray into complicated and abstract styles, who also made of his esthetics something too obscure, making them flounder in a monotonous and discouraging black and white. All contributed in turning the public from Fauré's last works, a public traditionally the enemy of any creative effort and whom the scarecrow of boredom still frightens away. On the other hand, one cannot expect from performers the heroism and sacrifice which navigating against the current would have required. Under these circumstances, it is not possible to predict when and how this sad misunderstanding might have been dissipated.

There is among all this pity, sincere or obligatory, which discredits in one breath some thirty important scores by an artist who preserved up to his last breath an extraordinary youthfulness of spirit and heart, a considerable share of injustice. Certainly, no one would think of denying the existence of the three indisputable ages that every living being passes through and Fauré, who worked until he was seventy-nine, could not escape the dawn, midday, and twilight. But one must not commit the error of hearing senility in his music, for his mind did not age at the same rate as his body. At the most, one can attribute to his deafness a certain change in melodic and harmonic style. His chord schemes expanded less broadly than before. They were confined, their notes crowded together often in the middle range of the piano which corresponded to the least sclerotic portion of his ear drums. His vocal configurations unfolded more prudently and deviated only with reluctance from the tonic and dominant. An old man takes smaller steps than an adolescent, but the path upon which Fauré set out was less adventurous than the one he followed until now.

The irreparable damage of time and sclerosis affected him only in terms of pure creation. During the last part of his life, Fauré did not create many new themes, melodic contours, or novel rhythms. He was less occupied with being an explorer or a conqueror. But from this period on, far from repudiating his past, as has been suggested, he took pleasure in depending on it and drawing from it.

He had only the difficulty of choosing from among his former methods of thinking and writing, his ingenious harmonic system, his subtle modulatory mechanism, his favorite cadences, his conception of tonal and modal style and his preferred melodic inflections. In short, all of the elements which would allow him to rest on his laurels and continue to compose songs and instrumental works up to the end. Fauré's mastery of his profession never aged and could have guided his hand for many more years.

Those who heard his new works recognized numerous reminders and details belonging to earlier works. Consciously or not, these borrowings came only from his youth or the fertile period of his maturity and consequently meant neither denial nor repentance. Even if one were to contest their originality, it would be absurd to deny their charm.

His chamber music works, by their very nature, hid these expropriations more easily than his songs. The development of themes held a more important position, and since it required much inventiveness and fecundity to cover up the rigidity of formal structure, Fauré's way of composing at times betrayed his age. We will see that his last quartet is at times a sad but quite moving testimonial to this fact.

One must, moreover, take into consideration a very particular circumstance which has misled superficial observers. What one has labeled the privation of a repentant and ascetic is only in reality an intuitive search for formal purity and an economy of means whose presence is quite frequently felt in Fauré's final works. This hypersensitive musician could not have remained in this climate without being impregnated with an inner Hellenism whose traces are present in all of his succeeding works. *Pénélope*, in particular, exercised a tyrannical influence on his style. One does not have to look far for the origins of the *Le*

Jardin clos, Op. 106, La Chanson d'Ève, Op. 95, or the *Violin Sonata No. 2 in E Minor, Op. 108,* for you will find them in this obsession with Greece which this Latin did not abandon for forty-five productive years and which by no means constitutes a late discovery of his old age. Florent Schmitt spoke the truth. Fauré had no successive styles, but parallel ones which progressed side by side at the same pace along the long road of his masterpieces.

The incidental music Fauré wrote in 1898 for the performance of *Pelléas et Mélisande, Op. 80,* at the Prince of Wales Theater in London included, in the third act, a song based on an English poem which has not, like the four sections of the orchestral suite, survived. The music for this song had first been used in *Crépuscule,* a work by the Belgian poet, Charles van Lerberghe. This poem was part of a collection whose study enchanted the composer and inspired in him the desire to make a new song cycle in the manner of Schubert and Schumann. This happy formula which was to produce masterpieces such as the *Le Jardin clos, Mirages,* and *L'Horizon chimérique* was particularly dear to him. This resulted in that pure marvel which is *La Chanson d'Ève,* a cycle of ten songs based on a quite developed description.

Not forgetting that the sweet face of Mélisande had been associated with the first version of *Crépuscule, Op. 95, No. 9,* Fauré introduced in *La Chanson d'Ève* the five mysterious notes which, in the incidental music to *Pelléas* summarize the melancholy destiny of the remote and enigmatic princess.

Van Lerberghe's poem could appear a bit exotic at first glance, but Fauré knew how to penetrate to the subtle nuances and reproduce them with extraordinary fidelity. The general theme of the work was for his own pleasure. Far from an orthodox confession, the poet puts us in the presence of God, entrusting Eve with the mission of gathering life's emanations, guessing at and soaking up its secrets, and listening to the voices of nature and the elements. In a symbolic Paradise, where Eve has just "awakened to God," the Creator converses with his creature, whose receptiveness he wants to develop. He sends her to earth to study the essence of things and to discover the deep sense of all which surround it. "Give," he says, "to all things I have created, a word from your lips." The word will be able to clarify the great laws of universal harmony out of the chaos. Eve, who represents the human senses, must thus complete the Creator's work.

Fauré, who had immediately realized that it was here a matter of honoring a superior pantheism by searching everything for a reflection of divine presence, easily found the musical style suitable for this meditative text. He adopted in it, with the most perfect logic, that technique of "abstracting," of simplifying and making the writing transparent. Yet another proof of the error committed by well-intentioned critics, who reserved for Fauré's final stylistic period that expiatory vocabulary invented by a repentant esthete. At the time when he began to compose this masterwork in 1906, Fauré's genius was fully mature and very far removed from this supposed road to Damascus and his imagined conversion.

The first song in this cycle, *Paradis,* is striking. "It is the first dawn of the world . . . An amazingly wonderful garden begins to glow . . . everything is still in a state of confusion and everything is mixed together, the shivering of leaves, the singing of birds, the brushing sound of wings . . ." The music evokes this budding Paradise with moving poetry obtained by means of conscious simplicity. The melody floats between heaven and earth. It is only accompanied by light touches on the piano, especially when Eve becomes sleepy and "disrobes in the silence of a wonderful dream."

He only uses simple chords, almost always consonant ones, but he strings them together with a sense of magic which is uniquely his. Each phrase opens a mysterious window onto an infinite variety of landscapes. The vocal line unfolds serenely, pausing for lengthy pedals over the dominant which broadens the vista until the horizon can no longer be seen. This extraordinary score defies all descriptive analysis, and seems to have been inspired by one of the phrases of its text which in the presence of this awakening of the world silently tells us of "its endless murmuring."

The birth of the world, the blooming of life finds a faithful musical rendering in the slow efflorescent harmonies, emerging one by one from the initial fifth, hollow and transparent, giving the impression of an infinite emptiness. Its fundamental E resists all tonality, suggested by diatonic or chromatic displacements of the bass and of fleeting cadences built on full harmonies. In the course of these peaceful atmospheric metamorphoses appear the first manifestations of rhythmic activity when the Creator speaks to his creature.

Eve carries out her mission in *Prima verba* (second song). She has sprayed the dew of sound over all things from her flower lips and the earth has heard her song. Now, on static chords, rhythmless, the *prima verba* make their way out into the universe.

The *Roses ardentes* (third song) which perfume "the immobile night" create a gradual sense of elation in the composer, and over a syncopated accompaniment he is obliged to salute the source of energy and vitality represented by the triumphant return of the sun, for it is from this that Eve "reaches her God" on a magnificent progression in *Comme Dieu rayonne* (the fourth song).

L'Aube blanche (the fifth tableau) draws her gently from her dreams. The music describes the progress of daylight, while Eve, tenderly answering its call, looks ecstatically on the world. Strings of harmonies of exquisite grace make this daybreak poetic.

The sixth song, *Eau vivante*, reveals her charms. Little murmuring scales gush from all sides mixing their babblings and their reflections.

Eve communes so profoundly with the forces of nature that in the depth of night she tries to find, in the world of fragrances, the scented path that day left behind. "Veilles-tu, ma senteur de soleil?" she says in the seventh song, searching to capture, floating in the air "its bee-like aroma," its sweet honey smell as she questions the "warm lilacs and roses." The purity of Eve and her song, without losing any of its serenity and nobleness, is filled here with a disquieting passion and the musical accompaniment shivers with voluptuousness. In *Dans un parfum de roses blanches* (the eighth song), this thrill of sensuality is appeased. The singing becomes murmuring and only the quiet crackling of a falling petal can be heard.

Crépuscule (the ninth song), which was the generating germ for the whole collection and whose first notes are dedicated to Mélisande, brings a breath of sadness. A dull and secret dread which is allied to the feelings of the small abandoned girl who cried at the water's edge, is translated into these disturbing questions: "Who is sighing? Who is crying? Who comes to flutter on my heart like a wounded bird?" Eve wonders if these threatening thoughts which trouble her come out of the past or the future. She gives a cry of fright but soon recovers her calm and her confidence in the benevolence of things.

For this benevolence is of her death. *O Mort, poussière d'étoiles* (the last song of the cycle) brings the voluptuousness of the highest abandon to her. In a pathetic outburst, whose deep sincerity galvanizes the melody, the pantheistic fervor reaches its culmination. And it brings to this masterwork of poetry, of music, of metaphysics and philosophy, a conclusion of incomparable grandeur.

La Chanson d'Ève should be among the highest products of universal thought. Condemned by its very quality to acceptance by a small but discerning circle, it will doubtless never know the glory it deserves, but it will hold a privileged place in the mind of the initiated. This is so well expressed by the line from the poem, "Her voice is quiet, but it can still be heard."

Le Jardin clos! This title for the second collection of poems that the composer of *La Chanson d'Ève* asked of Van Lerberghe has always seemed to me to have been badly chosen. First, because this closed door intimidates the apprehensive and secondly because there is no work more magnificently brilliant and "open" than this one. The text for *Le Jardin clos, Op. 106*, did not, however, furnish the composer with as rich an invitation to dream as the meditations of *La Chanson d'Ève*. These amorous effusions are tender and moving, but without great depth and mysterious connections with the subconscious. These are impersonal confessions, some being born on the lips of women others on those of a lover. They are not the confidences of any particular couple, but timeless expressions of love. The poet's vocabulary here is less subtle, less nuanced, less filled with thought. He utilizes basic words, more familiar shapes and asks the composer to aim for simplicity.

From the first page of this collection, we observe that Fauré uses the calmest, the most limpid and ingenuous of his accompanimental arpeggios, the one which helped him in *Soir, Op. 83, No. 2*, to create an atmosphere of peaceful reverie. From beginning to end of this first page, this elementary figure escorts a melodic line of perfect serenity, seldom avoiding the dominant and moving often by step-wise motion, faithful to that "supple, easy and proud bearing" which characterizes *Nell, Op. 18, No. 1*, as well as *Lydia, Op. 4, No. 2, Le Secret, Op. 23, No. 3* and the most charming of his youthful works. This virginal thread which floats with such lightness is enveloped with changing harmonies, obeying the cinematic technique which makes an image slowly disappear while a new one appears simultaneously, a procedure for which Fauré discovered the exact musical equivalent well before the invention of motion pictures and that he continually used in all of his style periods.

What can one say of the explosive and ardent sensuality which shapes the second song? "When you look deeply into my eyes, I fill yours completely. When your mouth unloosens mine, my love is my mouth alone. If you lightly brush my hair, I only exist as my hair. If your hand brushes my breast, I rise up like a sudden blaze . . ." Over gently pulsating chords, these confessions escape the lover's lips with tantalizing immodesty. The harmony and the melody have the enthusiasm of the intoxicated adolescent.

The joyful arpeggios of *La Messagère,* the third song of *Le Jardin clos,* sound a spring-like note. They peal the Angelus for the renewal of spring in the air. They sing April's resurrection with an easy-going joie-de-vivre which are not the sentiments of an old man denying his youth. Hope and renewed budding light are here. And the music, still more than the poem, climbs skyward with irresistible happiness.

What tender and loving confidence in life emanates from the fourth piece, *Je me poserai sur ton coeur.* There is no bitterness, no discouragement in this evocation of a sea gull letting itself be rocked by the waves and gathering its strength anew by obeying the laws of Nature and the summons of the sea and wind.

Are they less sensitive and less stirring than those of *Le Parfum impérissable, Op. 76, No. 1,* these slow and peace-inducing chords which maintain in an unreal atmosphere the thoughts which visit the dreamer and show her a radiant feminine apparition in a mysterious Eden, with its fairy illuminations? The magic vision generates a growing excitement and produces a crescendo of astonishing amplitude which little by little rises to the heights, then calms itself and falls back when it makes contact with the reality of life. One knows that, in his pleasing conclusions, Fauré avoids as much as he can the classic ending of having the chord of the dominant seventh resolve on the tonic. His style of writing which is so adroitly modal, and the artistry with which he utilizes all the resources of the plagal cadence render him precious service here. One therefore expects to see a final cadence of this kind concluding the description of this beautiful dream, but one is surprised to hear suddenly a humble dominant seventh with a retardation of the leading tone which then goes into the tonic with all of the matter-of-factness suitable to a deceptive return to reality after a dream.

What is there to say about the conclusion of this cycle, *Inscription sur le sable,* so completely impregnated with love's mystique, of this complaint whose text and imagery are weak and poor but whose composer has created such a fetching reverie against such a gloomy background? We find ourselves here in the presence of a purely musical miracle. The supple and strong genius of the composer of *La Bonne Chanson* was alone capable of carrying out this transformation, for he has literally transfigured the poem. And, if one thinks that it was a septuagenarian who could weld to this communicative adolescent enthusiasm the rather precious octo-syllables of the eight strophes of this hymn to Aphrodite, one is amazed and full of admiration. Do you find the least trace of austerity or renouncement in this music which is so clear, tender and pulsating with life? The entire score uses only a familiar and congenial vocabulary. The melodic style is not obscure and the accompanimental figures are all borrowed from the composer's earliest and freshest works! Isn't it disconcerting, considering this, to witness such a protracted misunderstanding, stupidly favoring the separation of Fauré's last masterworks from the public and professional singers to whom their difficulty of comprehension has been denounced?

Mirages, Op. 113, is a small collection. In many scores of three hundred pages, the most patient person would have difficulty in finding such a great quantity of beautiful music.

One should closely examine the progression of these modest chords, written for the most part in three or four parts without doubling in order to understand this paradoxical charm. This conscious style is essentially an intelligent style. It progresses by allusion, reconciliation, function, union, comparison, by artifice, pretense, daring touches, fake exits and entrances, by various and devious means. The note that one expects reveals itself, a subtle retard maliciously indicates its hiding place. At the moment when one thinks one has it, an unresolved appoggiatura already is carrying it off in another direction. The chords are transformed with disconcerting facility. Full of unusual dissonances, none of which is arbitrary, they change color like chameleons. And one sees above all in these knowing games an ease and logic which are absolutely inimitable with a touch of nobility because the thought is never sacrificed to the wealth of stylistic devices.

Take the first song of the collection, *Cygne sur l'eau*. Observe the imperceptible impulse which delays by gently holding back the melody. It is a slow and almost silent progression. Velvet harmonies melt together in the wake of a melody which progresses, almost constantly by stepwise motion, with a proud indolence.

Without ever condescending to slavish descriptive means, this music never loses sight of the most devious innuendoes in Baronne de Brimont's text. With light touches, without insisting, the music clarifies and underlines the imagery. Notice with what mastery the gliding of the swan is portrayed. A charming harmonic progression cleaves through the tranquil waters of the beautiful lake of music and as it progresses, makes the chords which open and shine like flowers disappear one by one.

And what extraordinary effects this great virtuoso of the seventh chord draws from the sudden juxtaposition of these daringly misplaced chords without causing confusion, disorder or musical inversion which brusquely transforms the shading of the melody. "Beautiful and vain Swan, renounce this slow journey toward a dark destiny. . . ." Then Fauré suddenly leads you back to the initial key by one of those miracles of ingenuity whose secret only he possesses!

The fluidity and transparency of water have never found a better artist to describe them than Gabriel Fauré. The second song in *Mirages* is *Reflets dans l'eau*—all freshness, reflection and clear crystal. The shock of a C sharp makes the liquid sheet of water ripple for an instant. Large circles form on its surface, broadened by triplets and push the ripples toward the river where they die out in a lull of binary rhythm. Never has such a striking evocation been obtained until now by means as supple and at the same time as refined without leaving the domain of pure music. And never has a musician-magician succeeded in producing anything as colorful as what is carved on the swan's mottled wings.

There is still greater simplicity in the *Jardin nocturne*. There, the style of writing is thinned out to the limits of the intangible. When the water trickles "drop by drop down the side of gently rounded basins of fountains" it is really with the sole discharge of two little harmonious droplets that the composer succeeds in expressing the poet's thoughts without renouncing the logic of his musical discourse.

I don't know whether this tour de force is not eclipsed by the one in *Danseuse*, where a delicately balanced sixteenth note gives birth to the image of a tireless gyration.

Let us add that *Mirages* will give useful lessons to more than one composer. Few musicians possess as much as Fauré this mysterious sense of the rhythm of French words which is so fleeting, so light, and so deceptive. French, as we know, doesn't have the elastic and singing inflections of Italian, nor the sharp profile and energetic accentuation of German. Its melodiousness is to be found on a more limited scale, but its harmony is fine, precise. Gabriel Fauré makes us aware of his singularly skillful procedures. He imbues it with a kind of continual artificial flexibility by employing syncopations which communicate with his audience. This recipe is not without its drawbacks. It can only be applied by a master who knows the limits of resistance of a vowel and the possibilities of melodic extension of a syllable between two accentuations borrowed from current speech. Anyone other than he would fail in this endeavor. The composer of *Le Don silencieux, Op. 92*, draws effects unfailingly from the best and most adroit means in order to match the poem with musical colors.

Unfortunately, the esthetic of this music is based on an aristocratic intelligence and a heart which unpityingly selects its followers. We shouldn't be surprised, then, to see this music not only so often compromised, but so often betrayed. Haven't the

95

interpreters capable of defending this transcendental music whose brilliance is veiled with a sort of jealous prudishness become all too rare? Works more assertive in appearance are accepted without resistance by musicians for whom Fauré's style remains an impenetrable mystery. This purity, this profundity, imbued with nonchalance, this power with sweetness, these modest sounds, all appear paradoxical to many listeners who cannot perceive such discrete genius.

Louis Aguettant, the most authentic and orthodox Fauréan whom I have ever met, succinctly stated the case for Fauré in these excellent terms: "Fauré's music is the place for reconciling opposing forces: the normal and the unusual, refinement and simplicity, charm and power, sensual detail and organic unity. In this collection of balances we recognize the concept of classicism. If it is the proper function of real classicism to subordinate everything to the expression of what is essential, few composers have been worthy of being called classicists as much as Fauré."

L'Horizon chimérique, Op. 118! This abused title is inscribed on the frontispiece of a collection which is enveloped with nostalgia. As a matter of fact, when one thinks that the author of these four poems, Jean de la Ville de Mirmont, was a young poet of great talent who was taken away by World War I and whose verses, four years later, would furnish Gabriel Fauré with the opportunity of composing his last vocal masterpiece at the age of seventy-seven, it is with a tug at the heart strings. The two collaborators, without having met one another, seemed to have sensed their approaching deaths, for a heavy anguish reveals itself in this cycle.

The first song, *La Mer est infinie,* is addressed to the limitless sea, upon which troubled souls would like to watch their dreams sailing along like sea gulls. The poet would like to follow their movements in the wake of "ships that his heart has followed in pursuit." Freed from earthly cares, they would recognize the extent of his considerable bitterness and would become drunk from the caresses "of the sea which consoles and washes away tears." What a thirst for escape in this passionate desire. What a need to be relieved of the burdens of daily living and to give flight to thoughts in this invitation to voyage! With what haste the composer rushes after the poet and at times gets ahead of him! And the astonishing sweetness which results from the modulation on the word "tears" proves to us to what extent Fauré has faith in the rocking of waves to maternally lull our disappointments to sleep.

It is yet another invitation to a voyage that the second song, *Je me suis embarqué*, brings. The poet and the composer have embarked on a ship "which dances and rolls broadside, and pitches and rights itself." The obstinate pulsation of a stressed grace note, analogous to the one which sustains the gyration of *Danseuse, Op. 113, No. 4*, creates the sensation of the regular rhythmic motion and balance of the boat as it sails along. The flight comes to pass. "My brother, I have suffered on all of your continents," cries out the liberated prisoner. He feels himself delivered from all of his bonds, "the tears at departing no longer burn on his eyes," and he no longer even remembers the distant port where he left his suffering behind.

The third meditation, *Diane, Séléné*, comes about by the appearance of the night stars whose impassiveness annoys us. "O moon, I am angry at your limpidity, an offense to the vain troubles of wretched mankind." The anguish reappears and reveals before this scene the indifference of nature in the presence of perpetually tired and agitated hearts which despairingly aspire to the peace of this "nocturnal lustre."

Finally, the last song—*Vaisseaux, nous vous aurons aimés*— is the heart-rending adieu that the voyager left on the shore addresses to the boats that he "loved in vain," for the Western horizon "took away so many open sails, that this port and his heart are forever abandoned." And he confesses his weakness and his misery: "I belong," he says, "with those whose desires remain on earth." He lacks the courage to follow the adventurous ships, but he suffers from hearing their calls for he feels a great unsatisfied desire to depart.

There is, in this noble poetry, a singularly moving expression of the piercing nostalgia from which those corrupted by nature with ideals do not escape. Fauré was really the most qualified composer to set this poetry faithfully to music and the fact that these are the last words he put to music attests to his eternal, youthful spirit. Also, with the young poet as with the old composer, a singularly penetrating and oppressive melancholy impregnates the poetry and harmonies. These four songs reveal to us one of the most moving aspects of Fauré's sensitivity, in a discrete and serene form which is his aristocratic birthright, but whose powerful spell is boundless. This album betrays, once again, the infinite torment which troubles superior beings. None of Fauré's works formulate with more frankness than this one the straightforward confession of this obsession.

Parallel to the composition of so many vocal masterpieces, Fauré enriched the piano repertoire with a series of pieces of great importance—six impromptus, four valses-caprices, nine préludes, eight *Pièces brèves*, the *Dolly Suite, Op. 56, Thème et variations in C sharp Minor, Op. 73*, thirteen barcarolles, and thirteen nocturnes—a crowning achievement which spanned almost forty years of his career.

Before looking at these collections and discussing selected pieces, it would perhaps be useful to draw attention to the unfortunate attitude of the French middle class to an instrument which is not always regarded with the admiration and respect that it merits.

You will object and say that for several years the number of piano virtuosos has grown. Statistics of recitals and symphonic concerts indicate the progress of this mounting tide. But, if the wave of professionals is on the increase, the number of amateurs clearly is on the wane. The reasons for this are not mysterious. In past times, young girls of good middle-class upbringing were capable of accompanying an operatic aria or a popular song on the piano. Today the sudden eruption in our homes of recordings, radio and television has cooled the zeal of our youth who are overjoyed to be relieved of the sometimes thankless practicing needed to attain a particular musical skill. The sight-reading sessions, the four-hand playing and the little intimate concerts have become anachronistic diversions in the suburbs as well as in Paris.

At the same time, abandoned in private homes, the piano has no immense prestige among the musically ignorant. Perhaps the repetitive scales and arpeggios which pupils inflict on their neighbors have something to do with this collective hostility. Saint-Saëns, himself a brilliant pianist, is associated with this popular malice by putting virtuoso and student pianists in cages in the zoo (*Carnaval des Animaux*) and by classifying them among the undesirable mammals. And one knows that the touching performances of *Prière d'une Vierge* in middle-class living rooms have ridiculed the young woman of marriageable age of the last century.

The piano is reproached for its mechanical nature. You press your finger down on a key in the same way you would a door-bell, and immediately a sound comes out of nowhere, pure, precise, and on pitch. Anyone can do this. Quite another thing occurs with a violin or horn, a trombone or a clarinet, if you were to place this instrument in the hands of a musical ignoramus. They are respected because their complexity protects them.

Is it necessary to point out the absurdity of such a misconception? The piano does not automatically distribute sounds. Why, for example, did Walter Gieseking enchant us with his sonorities, velvet timbres and an infinite variety of rainbow-like nuances when he played the works of Ravel and Debussy? If the action of the hammers on the strings were automatic, any pianist using the same piano as Gieseking did, could produce the identical sonorities, and all the credit for his magical touch would go to the manufacturer of the instrument.

Just imagine that the manufacture of a single piano requires the assembling of thousands of precise parts. This collection of levers, pivots, springs, hooks, wire shanks, hammers, movable works, cloth, metal and felt possesses a suppleness, a nervous system, and a prompt reflex action which are amazingly human. Technology has produced a miracle of clarity and precision in the communicating machinery of 88 points of contact which connect the pianist's fingers to the steel wires that he has to activate. The hammer has really become as sensitive as the pianist's hand.

That is why one hundred virtuosos will produce one hundred different sounds on the same concert grand for, thanks to the suppleness and the tractability of its mechanism, there are a hundred different ways of depressing a key and putting in motion the numerous and sensitive machinery which allows a performer to control his hammers. It is in this way that the hammer striking a hidden string can produce a dry or mellow, drab or brilliant, radiant or fluted sonority. Add to all of this the decisive intervention of personality and temperament and the infinitely subtle play of the two pedals and you can gauge the extent of stupidity which has so marred the reputation of this instrument.

The piano has, besides, the advantage of developing the harmonic curiosity of the composer who consults it. It can be observed that in each generation and in every country it is to the composer who loved the piano—think of Liszt, Chopin, Debussy, Ravel and Gabriel Fauré—that we owe that heritage of sonorous discoveries. When one considers the pianistic works of Fauré at a moment when his pupils are rejoining the man in the street in this absurd disdain for the piano and when certain present-day schools of thought relegate it to the percussion family, it is perhaps not altogether useless to have reminded the reader of some basic truths.

How did Fauré play the piano? There are many answers to this question. Virtuosos have not shown themselves to be very indulgent toward his performances, which were limited to accompanying his songs or to playing in those chamber music works which call for a piano. I could never align myself with this critical severity. He played not like a stage prima donna, but as a composer. This, certainly, is a point in his favor, for the musical interest of his work benefitted from his interpretations.

It is convenient to distinguish very clearly the Fauré of the concert stage from the one of intimate performances and especially the Fauré one heard before 1907. His hearing troubles were to separate him little by little from the public. On stage, he sometimes gave the impression of a man in a hurry to finish an unpleasant job and he would accelerate the tempos. It is possible that this was because the feeling of his growing infirmity had made public appearances quite painful for him. But, like a true dilettante, when he was asked for the exact tempo required for such and such a song, he would elude the question by a retort like this: "That depends. If the singer hasn't much talent, I rush the tempo, but if she is good, I take my time." Apparently his metronome indications were not binding.

Having had the privilege of hearing him privately from 1900 to 1907, at the time when his hearing was intact, I remember his playing very well. His technique was suited to his personal charm and style. In the same way that the rich and epicurean playing of Debussy made me feel the sensations he was searching out in the magical sonority of certain progressions, Fauré's fingers, in the same way, built arpeggios and chords totally his own.

Familiar with organs, he often altered the fingerings so that the felt hammers would produce a true legato. He knew how to turn the most delicate phrase. But his agile fingers were equally adept at ornamentation, virtuoso figurations and the rapid scales which abound in his *scherzos*. Technically, his playing was not up to academic standards, but was perfectly suited to the basic requirements of his writing style. He was evidently superior to any other in making us understand his most secret intentions primarily by the correctness of his melodic line, his rhythmic accent and the personality of his style.

One can observe the exceptional importance he attached to the attack and volume of his bass notes. "A nous les basses," he often said with a humorously official air. As a matter of fact, the bass was for him the generating cell for a harmonic creation, the trunk of a tree which unfurled its consecutive thirds, arpeggios, appoggiaturas and passing notes. If all this ornamentation were not solidly attached to the roots, his compositions would have lost their meaning.

One incident permitted me to understand the importance given to his basses. I was listening to a recording of a Fauré song, interpreted by an excellent singer, with a composer-pianist as accompanist whose dislike for Fauré is legendary. This attitude had always shocked me. Listening to his accompaniment, I suddenly understood this phenomenon. He did not realize the importance of Fauré's basses and did not give them any more prominence than the various notes of an arpeggio or a chord, which weakened the brilliancy of the accompaniment. Under these conditions, one can well understand the impossible task the accompanist had in penetrating the secrets of this style which was so different from that of Roussel's which, for example, so often does without harmonic "roots."

To hear Fauré play his works alone was a precious initiation into his style. Those who have had this privilege will always feel a certain irritation at the patronizing tone certain virtuosos take when speaking of his pianistic abilities. Even making allowances for the respect and admiration that Fauré inspired in me, I scarcely can believe that my remembrance of his pianistic style was mistaken to this point.

In Fauré's piano works, the six impromptus have a curious place. In the two years before reaching his fortieth birthday, Fauré had written the first three. He lost interest in this type of composition for twenty-three years and it was only after having passed his sixtieth year that he composed the last three, the sixth being, in reality, only a transcription for piano of the harp *Impromptu, Op. 86.*

It was with an impromptu that Fauré inaugurated his rich collection of piano works. This choice has a symbolic meaning.

The word "impromptu" designates a musical style which theoretically only refers to its spontaneity and free fantasy. It modestly accepts being considered as a kind of improvisation, a sketch. In reality, for a Gabriel Fauré, an impromptu is written with the minutest care and often becomes a piece in a collection. But it is satisfying to the spirit to see the composer of *Nell* try his hand at a purely pianistic style by choosing the form of composition to affirm the affectionate intimacy that he wants to uphold with the piano. Thus, a concert artist awakens his keyboard with a caress by trying out some rapid passage work and some capricious chords to introduce the performance of an important work.

This *Impromptu No. 1 in E flat Major, Op. 25* does not present us with a characteristic model. Written in 6/8, its first theme sounds like a whirling kind of a waltz. Less rapid, freer and elastic, the second motive gives us a more exact notion of the compound rhythm. Nevertheless, an equivocal meter subsists and the elegant passage work which surrounds the melody accents rather than dissipates it. This is one of the principal charms of this lovely piece.

The *Impromptu No. 2 in F Minor, Op. 31,* in contrast to the first, fully justifies its title. It begins decisively in a 6/8 rhythm whose accentuation and division are immediately recognizable. This time, woven in a wreath three by three, the eighth notes take joyous leaps, revealing a melodic sail that the wind blows. As soon as it seems to die down, a quick breeze inflates it. Thus, bit by bit it rises in the air until, tired by the play of the wind, it descends to earth by means of a series of light and bouncy chords. A sweet arpeggio greets it, a peaceful theme takes its place for an instant and is developed with accents of tenderness and caressing harmonies. The frolicsome eighth notes return to assure an inimitably graceful conclusion.

The *Impromptu No. 3 in A flat Major, Op. 34* is still fresher, younger, and more carefree than the second. It seems to have been composed in a state of intoxicated enthusiasm. It pulsates with youthful exaltation. It reaches heights of irresistible vigor and concludes with a triumphal gesture. And then, quickly, a serious theme causes this inebriated adolescent to calm down and become thoughtful. The pensive mood is soon cast aside by the return of this veritable hymn to spring. The serious theme returns for two more unsuccessful attempts and it is the youthful theme which in the end evicts it and remains master of the territory.

The three other *Impromptus*, which are separated from the first three by more than a quarter of a century, follow quite different paths. Fauré was not the man to quietly take up an already exploited formula for the sole pleasure of terminating a collection in the same style. The initial theme of the *Impromptu No. 4 in D flat-C sharp Major, Op. 91*, begins with a sort of hesitancy and later catches its breath during ascending passages. It is followed by a slow and expressive motive whose step is more sure and whose mood is more serious and profound. This motive will be used in a thoughtout development section before the return of the first theme. This reflective *andante* seems to have really forgotten the rules governing an impromptu, but this piece is very lovely and filled with happy touches.

The *Impromptu No. 5 in F sharp Minor, Op. 102* brings a surprise. Fauré amused himself in writing it by using the whole-tone scale which was to become one of Debussy's favorite devices. With his customary ease and skill, Fauré fluently used this new language and drew scintillating and mirror-like effects of astonishing luminosity.

As far as the *Impromptu No. 6 in D flat Major, Op. 86b* is concerned, its origin cannot be hidden from us. From the very first notes, Fauré admits that it was not conceived for the piano, but for the harp. The fact that he transcribed it for piano does not deceive us. The chord progressions and the arpeggio patterns have that special characteristic which distinguished the direct attack of a plucked string from the strike of the piano hammer. Without seeing, we guess at the position of the fingers of the performer caressing the strings of the harp. This *Impromptu No. 6* which unknowingly owes its presence here to the foresight of a publisher, is one of the bravura pieces of great harpists. It loses none of its charm if one substitutes for the plucking of the human finger, the felt shank of a hammer on the great horizontal harp which is a concert grand.

Although he had been welcomed in the most aristocratic drawing rooms of Paris, Fauré was never the slave of society matrons who annoyed him and for whom he never made concessions. If he wrote four valses-caprices it was not in order to evoke the atmosphere of the brilliant evening parties at which he was often a guest. It was to contribute to the classic pianistic genre held in esteem by the most illustrious of his elders. The valse-caprice which at the beginning used the charm of the "dizziness of triple meter" very quickly liberated itself in order to stylize itself by adding ornamentation and embroidery, brilliant passage work and modulations. Fauré was to excel in this.

The *Valse-Caprice No. 1 in A Major, Op. 30* outlines an exquisite melodic line that graceful arpeggios and crystalline figures seem so intent on covering with jewels. This beginning is followed by a second motive attacked vigorously and in quite an opposing rhythm. By broadening the tempo, in a very Viennese tradition, a new theme, a great deal more robust, ennobles and strengthens this conquest by developing it continually with elegant melodies. A fourth theme, soft and expressive, introduces a note of sadness before the brilliant conclusion.

A lullaby charms the *Valse-Caprice No. 2 in D flat Major, Op. 38*, less capricious than its companions and more faithful to dance rhythm. This caress is immediately followed by a lightly elastic jumping motive, then by a long, flexible arabesque which undulates with grace and *brio* before the return of the balanced opening rhythm. A theme in C sharp Minor taints these amiable *divertissements* with melancholy, but in enharmonically exchanging the four sharps for the five flats of D flat Major, it suddenly shines resplendent with brilliant light and brings back the optimism in the development section. There is a final return to the cradle rhythm, then the scintillating theme draws the piece to a happy conclusion.

Cleaving a path between syncopated basses and flowing arabesques which slide about it, the theme of the *Valse-Caprice No. 3 in G flat Major, Op. 59* is quite melodious and dance-like without the slightest rhythmic uncertainty. It is developed with complacency and its broad *grupetto* furnishes more charming details for this admirably conducted discourse. Slower and more sensitive, the melodic phrase is not afraid to expose itself to view with assurance. And a fragment that was just heard before becomes a final *presto* full of happiness.

The *Valse-Caprice No. 4 in A flat Major, Op. 62* has less abandon than the preceding ones. This work is filled with surprise modulations; from the exposition of an affirmative second theme and a passage of floating tenderness, it unceasingly evokes with exceptional refinement a mood of very studied tonal instability which leaves nothing to chance. It concludes the album by enriching the formula for the valse-caprice with a refined bit of writing.

Between the publication of *La Chanson d'Ève* (1910) and *Le Jardin clos* (1918), eight years had elapsed during which Fauré ceased to confide in the human voice and again took up his affectionate relationship with the piano. It was during this period that five new barcarolles, three new nocturnes, the fifth impromptu, the *Sérénade, Op. 98* for piano and cello, the collection of nine préludes and nineteen instrumental works of the highest order were created. This means that, theoretically, the collection of préludes is part of the list of works from the autumn period.

The prélude, like the impromptu, is a form of composition which was to particularly suit Fauré's temperament, for it constitutes a genre whose structure allows composers great freedom. Learnedness does not play a very important role here. Imagination, however, is vital. This type of composition has some illustrious precedents in the past which define its attitude and its bearing in a quite definite manner.

Bach, by assigning the prelude the task of prefacing his fugues, imposed a certain style on it similar to introductory remarks. Elsewhere, organists have given it another flavor. In the church service, the prelude plays the role of a meditation of variable duration according to the requirements of the liturgy. The performer must always be ready to abandon it at the first signal. In order to create a prelude he puts his foot on the pedals and produces a tonic full of gravity and peaceful contemplation. Upon this solid foundation, he will erect, stone by stone, his sonorous edifice by making use of the innumerable resources of counterpoint.

Fauré, who was an organist and a great admirer of Bach, could have adapted himself quite naturally to these noble disciplines. Such was not the case. First of all, one must not forget that not only didn't he give his works descriptive titles, but by employing abstract labels, like "impromptu," "barcarolle," "nocturne," or "prélude," he did not restrict himself. For a realistic description is not suited to him. These *Neuf Préludes, Op. 103* are of an extremely free and varied construction.

The first begins calmly, serenely and a bit dreamily. The right hand sings out alone, like monody, slowly note by note spinning out a melody which opens behind, in its wake, harmonies whose changing reflections are mirrored in the left hand. The ear is surprised and charmed each time by the ingenious way in which this simple melody produces unforeseen harmonic vistas at each turn. An ordinary C, presented as the tonic, can quickly be called upon to change to a mediant, subdominant, dominant or leading tone in a variety of different keys, and the composer exploits the diatonic or chromatic ambiguities with a skill, artistry and originality which are inimitable. Nobody has defended better than Fauré the sense of tonality by paradoxically feigning to betray it in order to increase our need to find it again, intact, after these unending evasion tactics.

The second *Prélude* forms a striking contrast to the first. Here the theme is rapid, light and impassioned. Then it quiets down and finishes sweetly. The third is a conscious or unconscious homage to the melodic Romanticism of a Chopin, but the harmonic personality is so much that of Fauré that we are never left in doubt as to whose signature appears on this page.

These three first *Préludes* were written, one after the other, during the year 1910. The following year, the other six were completed. The fourth possesses a characteristic seldom utilized in the entire collection, that of a pastoral naivete, of a popular, idyllic song, happy and carefree, full of freshness but naturally garbed by an excellent tailor.

A dark agitation pervades the beginning of the fifth. Then, a cantilena in the minor that seems to have some vague archaicism from the distant past, creates round itself an atmosphere of penetrating sadness. And in defiance, with a suppleness and ease which are paradoxical, the sixth *Prélude* has imposed upon it the inflexible deceptiveness of canonic construction. An alteration of the leading tone gives it an agreeably modal flavor, while the second theme vacillates between the delightful ambiguities of Major and Minor. This tour de force of writing is carried off with miraculous aplomb and gives no hint of the difficulties overcome by this smiling musician.

The seventh *Prélude* is filled with a suppressed secretiveness. It possesses great expressive power, but has nothing of a personal story in it.

In order to atone for this moment of seriousness, Fauré gives us an eighth *Prélude* which is nothing but a graceful play of repeated notes, whose light leaping speaks to the eye as well as to the ear. Puck never danced with more grace and speed. The conclusion of the collection comes to us in the form of a beautiful melodic theme in the Minor punctuated by chords and given to the right hand, while the left hand, reversing the arrangement of the first *Prélude*, outlines an independent and single bass theme which by its anticipations and its suspension carves out of the movement of ephemeral harmonies a bare line of astonishing daring.

In the whole of this collection, if you carefully scrutinize it, you will not find a single sign of weakness. To the contrary, you will admire a freedom of construction, a generous melodic and harmonic vocabulary and, let me repeat, a disconcerting youthfulness. Why do pianists, those whose authority and public fame should allow them to try this without danger, pretend to be ignorant of this collection and never program one or two of these *Préludes* together with those of Chopin or Debussy? Not one sincere and faithful music lover could resist their charm. And by absorbing in small doses their richly concentrated music, the listener would in the end become initiated into their enchantments and move with more ease within the confines of this *jardin clos,* so to speak.

The barcarolle indicates powerful suggestive elements by its title. The word immediately brings to mind the sights of Venice. But the title is also an invitation to amorous reveries which are cradled on a mirror of water.

As with his nocturnes, Fauré decided not to make his thirteen barcarolles submit to rules too imperious for such an evocative title.

The *Barcarolle No. 1 in A Minor, Op. 26* respects the traditions of this type of piece. It gracefully rocks and has a nonchalant and charming theme which softly cleaves the water of one of those lakes beside which Fauré had so often dreamed. In several of his barcarolles, Fauré often, after his first theme, introduced a second, entirely new idea, changed the tonality or the mode to introduce a third motive equally original and independent which played the role of the trio in the minuet. The *Barcarolle No. 1* is constructed in this manner. Three charming themes follow one another.

In the *Barcarolle No. 2 in G Major, Op. 41, L'embarquement pour Cythère* is invoked. The first part is hesitant and seems uncertain of what route to follow. It is only with the second motive that one perceives the undulations of waves. The composer's imagination until then had been oriented toward quite different rhythms. But now, a certain excitement is generated and arpeggios and scales maintain it. The craft moves on. The end of the second motive will be utilized in a subsequent development. Carefully guided, prepared and prefaced by a delicate transition section, a third motive, more sensitive, more moving and sadder, sings charmingly. But the docile initial theme returns, this time to the rhythm of the oars, and the crossing is achieved poetically and with a feeling of euphoria.

Definitely melodic and with aristocratic elegance, *Barcarolle No. 3 in G flat Major, Op. 42* navigates without incident, and the regularity of the motions of its oarsman assures us an uneventful crossing. The general plan adopted in effect is already known: three different motives of which the last functions as a trio. The second carries out alluring and graceful play which, until the final chord, enchants us by its ingenuity. One knows that Fauré was without rival in the art of modulating effortlessly to the most distant keys. But he does not practice with less virtuosity what one could call the science of "modal modulation." In the same way, he creates ambiguities between major and minor by borrowing scales and cadences from Greek and ecclesiastical modes whose archaism he transforms into audacious harmonic novelties.

The *Barcarolle No. 3* is almost entirely devoted to this subtly oscillating modality which continually modifies the face of the melody. It benefits from a double rocking motion which creates waves of clever arpeggios which leave and return unceasingly to their point of departure and produce a regular alternation of modes. It also gives importance to two motives of rolling and pitching. It is the complete barcarolle.

Two arpeggiated waves glide along the length of the peaceful gondola which is the *Barcarolle No. 4 in A flat Major, Op. 44*. Very simple and melodic, it doesn't present any architectural subtleties and unfolds with ease. But it decides upon a rhythmic refinement to spice the melody. The duple pulsating measures lend themselves quite naturally to the depiction of an undulating movement. The 6/8 meter is the typical notation for a barcarolle theme. The uneven structure of each beat endows it with an inimitable interior flexibility. "I prefer unevenness," Verlaine judiciously said.

When a measure is comprised of six eighth notes, it is divisible either by twos or threes. You can extract from it at will two groups of three eights or three groups of two eighths. The total value will remain constant but by displacing the weak and strong beats one can completely transform the spirit of the phrase. Composers have quickly understood the choice between alternating or superimposing these two separate and unrelated formulas of uneven pairs, which create a sensation of slight imbalance.

Fauré did not deprive himself of this exciting stylistic resource. In the *Barcarolle No. 4* he challenged the complacency of our ears. We only know that Fauré's art consciously practiced this mischievousness as a means of whetting our appetites for tonal stability by concealing tonality through crafty modulations, by wandering to the extremities of our orthodox harmonic system, by multiplying the audacities which seem to make it go beyond the boards. In allowing the supple accompaniments of his barcarolles to follow their inclinations to balance their binary rhythm, he tops them upon occasion with themes in clearly ternary rhythm which create a delicately syncopated melody. And the eventual return to strongly accented beats is all the more delectable for it.

Until now the barcarolle had only sailed on lakes or lagoons. The *Barcarolle No. 5 in F sharp Minor, Op. 66* seems to carry us off to the open sea. The accompanimental rhythms have hardened. Some are jerky, uneven, as if waves were crashing against the hull of a ship and one senses that the navigator is obliged to struggle against the storm. There is lyricism and excitement in his full-voiced song. If this is not Fauré's precise intent, very probably it is a metaphonic equivalent and one that we can use to describe the purely musical evolution of this stormy page which, bursting with sound and dynamic accents, differs so radically from those which preceded it. However, the work returns, at its conclusion, to the serenity which is its only concession to its title.

We find in the *Barcarolle No. 6 in E flat Major, Op. 70* an atmosphere, a smooth expanse of water. The melodic configurations and the pianistic passage work of its flexible initial theme unite in a smiling happiness. A second motive which seems to be about to be ruled by the more rigid ternary rhythm returns quickly to the soft binary arpeggios and scales which make this short scene so amiable and charming.

Briefer yet is the *Barcarolle No. 7 in D Minor, Op. 90*. It is a bit disconcerting at first due to the somewhat disquieting and hesitating accent of its melody which advances by little spurts and stops repeatedly to catch its breath. One senses, however, that this voyage is deeply meditative and that it is accompanied by darkly disturbing thoughts. Whether this is philosophical or emotional, the music guards its secret well.

The *Barcarolle No. 8 in D flat Major, Op. 96* is graceful, light and greatly unconstrained. But soon, thrusts of passion from within animate the discourse and sparks fly from heated accents. And abandoning the technique of drawing alongside without colliding with all the other barcarolles, this short voyage concludes on a crescendo and a vigorous final chord whose violence can rightfully be disconcerting.

There are many breathless hesitations in the *Barcarolle No. 9 in A Minor, Op. 101*, which is strangely constructed. Around a very nostalgic minor theme whose shape is curiously reminiscent of the melody "Voyageur, ou vas-tu, là-bas? . . ." are erected systematic repetitions, echoes between the extreme parts, sad passages which the luminous scales do not dispel and between which the navigating theme slowly ploughs a passage.

The melancholy of the Minor also disturbs the *Barcarolle No. 10 in A Minor, Op. 104* which surprises us by the conscious monotony of its melodic design repeated indefinitely in the course of strict progressions which form a single thread through this introspective composition.

With the *Barcarolle No. 11 in G Minor, Op. 105, No. 1,* the horizon lightens, but Fauré abandoned the melodic themes developed from one impetus so common in the preceding works and more and more adapted the developmental technique of short repetitive rhythms and ascending or descending progressions. We meet a fresh example of this here.

The *Barcarolle No. 12 in E flat Major, Op. 105, No. 2* stresses calmness even more. It easily attenuates the serenity which could result from this process by introducing here and there tiny ornamental details.

And it is also under this mark that the *Barcarolle No. 13 in C Major, Op. 116* closes the series. Thoroughly melodious, it breathes gaily and with carefreeness. It has at times a springlike naivete which astonishes us for an artist of seventy-six, ending a collection begun before his fortieth year and which scorns the difficulties of classification that will be imposed on it by "experts" who set up the official catalogue of works reserved for the third period.

The small album of eight *Pièces brèves, Op. 84,* victim of the modesty of its title, has scarcely held the attention of pianists who make a great error by neglecting these charming pieces. In place of performing them all, several could furnish encore pieces of the highest quality.

The most diversified styles are represented here. These pieces bear such titles as *Capriccio, Fantaisie, Fugue, Adagietto, Improvisation, Allégresse* and *Nocturne.* Certain ones resemble sketches. The *Capriccio in E flat Major*—so graceful, so lively with its witty embellishments—contains the promise of a charming impromptu. The *Nocturne in D flat Major* might have easily become a barcarolle or a fifth valse-caprice. The *Adagietto in E Minor*'s pulsating eighth-note rhythm which gives it the tempo of a noble and meditative march could easily be transformed into a moving funeral march. The two miniature figures, reduced to the essential elements of their ritualistic architecture, are models of clarity and design. The counterpoint of the second possesses an ease and an incomparable elegance. The sensitive, calm and dreamy character of the *Fantaisie in A flat Major,* the suppleness and the expressive melodies of the *Improvisation in C sharp Minor* and the spring-like enthusiasm of the *Allégresse in C Major* make this collection a precious and charming one.

Before perusing the last of Fauré's piano masterworks, the nocturnes, let us examine the two isolated scores written while the large collections were being penned. These two compositions, *Dolly, Op. 56* and *Thème et variations in C sharp Minor, Op. 73* are strongly contrasting. One is a graceful childlike fantasy, the other of a more noble construction with an imposing façade.

Dolly is the happy homage that all modern composers have wanted to offer to children since Schumann's *Kinderscenen.* The inspiring subject, whose unusual character should have endeared itself to composers of all times, is of relatively recent vintage. This tenderness before a cradle dates from the days of Romantic sentimentality. The classicists, and for sterner reasons, the primitives, ignored it. From the seventh to the nineteenth centuries when a child was born, no family circle thought of applauding it with great cries and no composer felt the need of celebrating this event in music. The reign of the infant king, in the arts as well as in society, doesn't pre-date 1830. But since then, what a return of the young sovereign. One can no longer count the small masterworks in this category. In general, scores which make use of this subject matter have a curious tendency to be too complicated. These homages interest children less than their parents. It is among adults that one exchanges amusing and tender observations and knowing winks. Remember Debussy's touching scruples in feeling the need to dedicate to his dear little Chou-chou his delicious *Children's Corner* and to present to his little girl his tender excuses for what was going to follow.

It was also a charming little girl who inspired Fauré to compose the six ravishing little *tableaux* which comprise the *Dolly Suite*. Fauré found his graceful model in the household of a friend, where "Dolly," later Madame de Tinan, was the daughter of Mme. Emma Bardac who was some years later to marry Claude Debussy. The child's games are described to us with exquisite delicacy. The *Berceuse* can be applied as well to Dolly as to the doll she cradles maternally. On the soft regular rocking of an accompanimental arpeggio in E Major, a simple and familiar melody, like a popular folk song, is heard. A second phrase which employs the same rhythmic motives follows in C Major and leads into a small development section. Then there is a return to the first theme, this time in the form of a canon at the octave. This is not the least of this piece's charms, this unexpected utilization of the austere canon to obtain such graceful effects. Several of the pieces in *Dolly* draw upon these strict canonic imitations which result in a surprising distinctiveness. This scene concludes in peace and calm for Dolly has been tenderly rocked and has fallen asleep.

Miaou is not an imitation of the sound of a cat in music. It is the name of a kitten who brought pleasure to this family. You will notice its capricious leaps, its abrupt turnabouts, its zigzag movements and its sudden cajolery when, tired of running about wildly, it falls asleep on the lap of its little mistress.

The *Jardin de Dolly* depicts the fresh and prosaic impressions that an infant has upon discovering the fairyland of flowers as she slowly walks along the paths of her garden which she later regretfully leaves. *Kitty-Valse* represents the light grace usually displayed by a dancing young girl who is already developing the seductive ways of the woman she will grow up to be. *Tendresse* is the touching picture of an infant cradled in the arms of his mother. His small heartbeats are in the same rhythm as hers and this is indicated in the delicate canonic imitation appearing with the second theme before the return of the affecting opening melody. Finally, this suite of perfect miniatures concludes with a joyful evening dance of mid-Lent where Dolly is disguised as Carmencita and skips about beating a little Basque drum.

We have already had the opportunity to admire Fauré's dexterity with the most abstract and severe musical forms. Under his hand canon, fugato, imitation and other contrapuntal designs lost their scholarly dryness and became exquisite and novel means of expression. Nothing proves this better than Fauré's pianistic masterpiece, *Thème et variations in C sharp Minor, Op. 73,* a work of nobility and grandeur which might seem foreboding were it not for the fact that it is an uninterrupted musical enchantment.

The "variation" was originally, among Classical composers, a quite childish exercise in composition. It was at first necessary to choose a simple and short theme which had been already engraved on our minds. A popular song or a children's melody was admirably suited to this purpose. The theme was first exposed with the greatest simplicity, then it was taken up with different ornamentations. Stylistic practice had even created in this area a certain number of traditions that were usually respected. The theme was to be alternately Major, Minor, fast, slow, joyful, sad, sentimental, or martial. But the important thing was to always make clearly perceptible to the least sensitive ears the basic melody, despite its succession of disguises. The satisfaction of recognizing it during the course of the piece sufficed to reward the listeners.

In the Romantic period, this style became more complex. Composers took a certain teasing pleasure in complicating the masking of the theme. It was obscured behind tricky rhythms, hide-and-seek was the game played, a game which became more and more ardent and impassioned.

Not only did this type of composition have a faithful following but, curiously, it triumphs today among fanatical specialists, those who furiously applaud the most famous virtuosi of *le jazz-hot,* New Orleans style. The technique of these "aces" consists, in effect, of suggesting a theme instead of stating it, in ornamenting only the high points of the melody in place of a continual line, inviting the connoisseur's ear to fill in the spaces created between their elusive accentuation and elliptical syncopations.

The instrumental, percussive or melodic sections calmly accompany the invisible and ubiquitous ghost theme, while the intoxicated soloist titillates it with daring passage work, encircles it with cunning caresses and affection which lightly touch it without stripping it of its indiscernible silhouette. His motion is like that of a painter or sculptor who takes pleasure in outlining in the air with a sensitive thumb the fleeting contour of forms which will bring his paint brush or his sculpting tool to life. Without realizing it, the faithful followers of the great jazz improvisors render a singular honor to the modern variation which, in the hands of Brahms and Fauré, became an incredibly refined means of expression.

Fauré takes his departure from an irreproachable Classicism. His theme possesses the anatomy of extreme simplicity. It moves rhythmically by successive thrusts along an ascending Minor diatonic scale which doubles back upon itself four times in order to return by conjunct motion to its point of departure. A brief answer, still utilizing these same conjunct degrees, is no less elementary and, like the first motive, does not hint at the hidden riches it conceals. Laid out in equal values, this phrase should be absolutely neutral. Scanned by noble chords, it is presented here as a march, characterized by a certain solemnity, but it does not betray any of its secrets.

The first variation is a completely new presentation of the theme in the bass. It seems to be a question of imposing itself upon the mind of the listener and certainly the precaution is useful, for the theme soon undergoes some rough treatment. Above it, arabesques of rare elegance float and undulate. It allows us to glimpse all that a melody with a severe aspect can

117

contain in terms of poetry. For it is really the theme, heavily articulated in the left hand, which note for note gives rise to exquisite counterpoint played by the right hand.

The fun begins with the second variation. In a lively tempo, the bouncing rhythm of a *scherzo* replaces the solemn march. It begins to break up the theme, to soften it, to give only a suggestion of it, slightly altered yet still identifiable. Progressively, the rhythmic inventions, the sparkling colors of the modulations, the harmonic discoveries disperse the constructive notes of the theme.

The third variation transports us to a metrical terrain. The ternary division of the beat destroys the binary balance which had been in effect until now. The triplets introduce, in the unraveling of the melodic line, an agile and smoothly-moving passage. The vital breadth of the theme grows in the fourth variation. The right hand makes broad and brilliant responses which cover a vast stretch of the keyboard. Small broken scales animate and adroitly propel the fifth variation whereas in the sixth, now meditative, the bass, emerging slowly from the depths, marches calmly to meet the melodic descending line which inclines in its direction.

It is with a discretely syncopated elocution that the seventh variation indicates some personal trouble or other, some growing inquietude while ingeniously partitioning the melodic line, presented thus in an unexpected guise but, in spite of all, faithful to its origin. The eighth is a model of simplicity and discretion. Short and balanced, it outwardly appears to be a transition in order to have us effortlessly pass from the seventh to the ninth, whose entrance is secretly prepared by its conscious humility.

The ninth is a masterwork of delicacy and poetry. It develops in an atmosphere of serenity, in the "vast and tender peacefulness." Divided at the center of the keyboard, the two hands move away from each other by small and somewhat hesitant steps in order to gradually reach the two extemities of the keyboard. The hand which reaches the treble register seems to cautiously open a curtain which allows a crystalling G sharp to filter in. Answers in thirds of an angelic suavity descend from the upper register to the middle range of the piano, before ascending again.

The two final variations are very contrasting. The tenth surrounds light and winged chords with capricious staccato passage work which leap about in a charming frolic. The conclusion of this admirable work is worthy of the infallible taste and tact of its composer.

A series of variations usually ends with a brilliant vigorous finale, a piece of bravura calling imperiously for applause by the public. We would misunderstand Fauré if we believed him capable of using such a recipe for success. To take leave of us, he has found something quite different.

The first variations are so adroitly diversified, so full of constant discoveries, that they all have kept their Minor tonality without for one moment giving rise to a feeling of monotony. One is not even aware of the fact that the composer had neglected to fall back upon the traditional change of mode in order to facilitate his task. He hid his own personal ideas on this subject. To pass from a Minor variation to a Major variation is only often a kind of social formality, a bit of savoir faire, a rite consecrated by usage. Fauré endowed his music with more elevated functions.

After having maintained his theme in the feeble illumination of the four sharps of its Minor tonality, six times in succession, he thought that the unexpected appearance of the Major in the final variation would form a poetic and radiant conclusion. He had, until then, deferred this surprise effect and it is a ravishing effect to suddenly penetrate, thanks to three additional sharps, that zone of well-being and peacefulness that one finds in the initial theme in the bass surrounded by strangely translucent modulations and chord progressions. Once again, Fauré enriched a simple scholastic procedure with a sensitivity and an emotional power which place it in this enchanted domain of pure creation.

This magistral score, because of the abundance, the richness and the variety of its rhythms, offered a marvelous musical basis for a ballet for some intelligent and sensitive choreographer. Orchestrated by D. E. Inghelbrecht, it permitted Carina Ari to extract from it a very noble realization in dance entitled "Moonbeam," which she created for the Paris Opéra in 1926 and which was performed with great success.

The nocturne is not a definite musical form. It is a psychological mood, a state of mind. The nocturne is the most complete realization of man at peace with the magic of the elements.

Fauré wrote thirteen nocturnes which are intensely poetic masterpieces. However, one must guard against giving this title an anecdotal or figurative meaning. This collection is not a collection of thirteen moonlit evenings. At the most, one can consider Fauré's nocturnes as a symbolic homage to night's serenity which prepares dreamers for meditation.

As usual, Fauré refused to be grouped with the landscape painters. It is not the scenery which interested him, it is the mysterious force which inhabits it. Moreover, certain of the nocturnes which are not given to description plunge us into the magical atmosphere of the night while others, which one might call "metaphysical," contain violent outbursts and are strangers to their title if one preserves the definition as applied to the nocturnes of Field and Chopin.

The composition of Fauré's thirteen nocturnes extends over a long period. The first three date from 1883 and the two following from 1884. But ten years separate the fifth from the sixth and there are ten more years between the seventh and the eighth. The series was finally completed in 1922, that is to say, close to forty years after the birth of the *Nocturne No. 1 in E flat Minor, Op. 33, No. 1*, which inaugurated the set. Therefore, one must not be surprised to discover many different techniques between the first and last pieces in this magnificent collection.

It is considered proper to speak with a tone of light condescension about the first three nocturnes, *E flat Minor, Op. 33,*

No. 1, B Major, Op. 33, No. 2 and *A flat Major; Op. 33, No. 3,* written by Fauré at thirty-eight. Their affability, clarity and grace have prevented some serious judges of esthetics from taking them seriously. These men have deprived themselves of a delicate pleasure, for the works are charming. At thirty-eight, Fauré had already composed his first *Piano Quartet, Op. 15,* his *Ballade for Piano and Orchestra, Op. 19* and various songs attesting to his very high qualities of invention and style. He possessed a mastery which should have opened many more doors to his credit.

His *Nocturne No. 1 in E flat Minor* proves that he deserved this credit. It is impregnated with great melancholy. Its first theme, slow and expressive, is stated over a regular throbbing of small close-knit chords of three notes which cling to it and produce a harmonization in four parts of rare sobriety. A melodious reply in the same vein follows, becomes animated for an instant, lightly fills out the pianistic figuration and then leads back to a peaceful conclusion in E flat Minor. Without changing key or mode, a new episode is introduced. In the same grave tone, two groups of six notes, of which the second curiously does away with its penultimate sixteenth note, outlines a very characteristic scallop pattern which will serve as an accompaniment formula for a broad and quite somber phrase. This, then, progressively consoles itself, and begins a graceful dialogue in echo fashion between the melody and the bass. A brilliant burst of arpeggios which fall back into scales leads us to think that this great sorrow is gone, but we are returned to the sadness of the initial theme, which this time is surrounded by a rhythmic reminder of the peaceful episode. The little scallops in sextuplets twice reappear fugitively in the bass, and a sincere coda realistically recalls the plaintive inflections of the *Chanson du pêcheur, Op. 4, No. 1,* composed almost twenty years before.

Although one can observe certain similarities between the first two nocturnes, the *Nocturne No. 2 in B Major, Op. 33, No. 2* evolves in a different atmosphere. It is pleasant, carefree, a bit capricious, and permits itself at times the graceful freedom of an impromptu. From the exposition of the first theme, it brings to the fore two stylistic pleasantries. One consists of establishing continual echo effects between the melody and its accompaniment. The other delights in creating a clever friction with the interval of a second which gives rise to suspensions, anticipations, ornaments and extended appoggiaturas which occur simultaneously with the actual note. In the work of composers who are clumsy, these dissonances introduced without discernment sound like "wrong" notes and offend our ears. With Fauré, to the contrary, they are so adroitly prepared, so logically executed, so intelligently justified by what precedes them as by what follows, that they take on a refined elegance. The whole first theme unwinds in an expressive *andantino* and this dual virtuosity asserts itself without losing anything in the way of grace or spontaneity.

It is followed by a quite unexpected *allegro*. Rapid sextuplets distributed in both hands surprise us because of their fervent agitation. As early as the second piece in his collection, Fauré shakes off the connotation of his title. This stirring piece which finishes forcefully really has nothing in it which evokes the serenity of night. We can admire here one of the melodic and rhythmic touches so dear to our magician. In order to give proof of the plasticity of his music, Fauré often takes pleasure in introducing in his instrumental works a single theme which he makes in turn virile or lyrical, brutal or caressing, agitated or dreamy. Here, the nervous and irritable sextuplets that we have just heard in the left hand reappear in an entirely transformed guise.

Of the entire collection, the *Nocturne No. 3 in A flat Major, Op. 33, No. 3* is certainly the most indulgent for timid ears. In the reassuring key of A flat Major, it immediately introduces an elegant melody to which a constant alternation of binary and ternary rhythm promises a particularly graceful movement, sustained by very simple chords which escort it in syncopation. The two hands sing in turn, and at every third repetition the composer introduces a new theme quite as charming as its two brothers and accompanied with as much discretion. The construction is here quite simple and is reduced to its essential elements, but the variety, ingenuity and charm of the harmonies of these three melodies prove to us that Fauré's eloquence has no need of any rhetorical complicity to produce irresistible touches.

The *Nocturne No. 4 in E flat Major, Op. 36* is clear, logical, and without mystery. Its first theme is broad, simple and cordial. Beginning as if from a great distance, on regular chords, it is then repeated in octaves and gives way to a swinging pattern of double eighth notes on which are posed calm half-notes which peal sweetly like distant bells. A second motive introduced by a pianistic cadence introduces to this reverie more lyrical elements and abandons itself to a certain exaltation. New pealing of bells reestablishes the calm. We find the first theme with a more enveloping accompaniment. The conclusion employs for the last time the mysterious angelus surrounded by its vibrant halo, then four large perfect chords close the door to this enchanted garden.

The regular accompaniment of syncopated chords will again be used to present the theme of the *Nocturne No. 5 in B flat Major, Op. 37.* It is at the same time dreamy, nonchalant, affecting and unfolds gracefully. Its pace is different from the preceding nocturnes. Until now, all the nocturnes have adopted breathing spaces of four measures. Here the phrase prolongs itself until the sixth measure and takes a double breath, while a passage of double eighth-notes evaporates softly into the air. To increase the feelings of freedom and flexibility that this unexpected division produces, it next uses breathing points of five measures before submitting to the classical phrase divisions. However, don't trust this apparent abandon. Fauré's languor is always of short duration and is quickly followed by energetic movement. The first part does not keep its deceptive calm to the end. Its melodic line, its accents and chords establish themselves progressively in a second theme, and it only concludes peacefully in order to lead us to the threshold of an *allegro* in ⁶/₈ meter which is going to establish the color and the feeling of the piece. The melody passes in the bass where it sounds dark and a bit threatening. There it is surrounded by agile arpeggios. It is broadly developed and borrows a fragment from the second theme. After much exuberance, it surprises us by bringing back with feigned candor the charming initial *andante*, which again radiates optimism and serenity.

By universal assent of music lovers the *Nocturne No. 6 in D flat Major, Op. 63* is the most brilliant piece of the entire collection. Its penetrating poetry, its pianistic interest, its clarity and grandness strike all listeners alike. No easy solution is to be found for the unanimity of such an opinion. Fauré always remains himself, naturally distinctive and aristocratic without describing the enchantments of the night.

Its principal theme unfolds with a calm majesty. It moves unhurriedly and its answer echoes its calm. A whole mood is established about us. A second motive, more animated and familiar, appears in C sharp Minor. Soon there is a series of modulations which fugitively open and then quickly shut doors through which one glimpses other horizons. But then it dies out with a return of a fragment of the first melody. A shivering measure of thirds rises out of the silence. The last note of the preceding theme whose eyelids have been closed by a D flat awakens a C sharp and, in this new light, a third theme is created. In a supernatural peace, the lovely initial phrase then reappears, claiming for an instant possession of its magic empire and takes leave of us in four berceuse-like measures whose charm is unforgettable.

For some time the *Nocturne No. 7 in C sharp Minor, Op. 74* has been dangerous competition for the *Nocturne No. 6.* Assuredly not with the public at large, for this music is serious and does not reveal its troubled secrets at the first hearing. But the almost popular success of the *Nocturne No. 6* has caused the initiated who have closely studied Fauré's style to group themselves instinctively around the slightly enigmatic message with the egotistical satisfaction of not having to share its qualities with too many listeners. The two nocturnes are so dissimilar that it is not fair to compare them. For musicians who are not ashamed of being charmed and seduced by Fauré's melodic invention, the *Nocturne No. 6* retains all of its prestige in the face of the severe beauties of the seventh, which is also an authentic masterpiece.

We find in it one of those heavy, obstinate rhythms Fauré consciously uses like a spring to propel one idea after the other with the regular but light firing of short appoggiaturas. This procedure takes place in a variety of ways. We can observe it in the *Danseuse* from *Mirages,* as well as in the sea-bound boat in *L'Horizon chimérique.* Here it expresses a profound oppressiveness and by the use of appoggiaturas from above and below, the theme seems to have more weight at each step of the way. It is quite evident that for an average listener the spontaneous flow of a flexible and free melodic arabesque is more attractive than the precise mechanism which produces the cells of a theme one by one where the role played by intellectual calculation is greater. It is in this area that the sixth and the seventh nocturnes have no common ground and could not be favorably compared to one another.

The first theme is heard twice with two accompanimental formulas and two different cadential terminations. It also returns several times to establish its mood of sadness when the discourse seems to be avoiding its serious duties. This is the case for a second idea, made more animated by the little broken rhythm which slides in between the melody and the bass. However, life wants to reclaim its rights. Four sharps in the treble, like silver bells, intone some unknown call to leisure. A small sunny phrase in two parts, enough to brighten the most worried brow, intones in C sharp Major and dominates the development. In spite of the heaviness of the activity held around it, it ends by cleaning the atmosphere. In any case, it gives this depressed nocturne a taste for the Major, and when the *molto lento* slowly mounts the twenty steps of a chromatic stairway in order to bring about the conclusion, the clouds have disappeared. Delicate scales flower from exquisite "escapist" modulations ending this euphoria, this reflective concentrated work whose musical substance is of such an exceptional richness that its concentrated harmonies seem to have been crystalized by evaporation.

After this capital piece, a calm relaxation establishes itself in the *Nocturne No. 8 in D flat Major, Op. 84, No. 8.* It had been inserted at first in the collection of the eight *Pièces brèves, Op. 84,* then it came to assume its position in the group of nocturnes. Entirely melodic, it seems written from a single impetus, since both of its themes have amiability and ease. Liquidly mobile wreaths of sixteenth notes running the length and breadth of the keyboard surround it with their light arabesques. There are few subtle harmonic nuances, but the left hand plays a delicate chain of fourths and fifths twice, a real treat for the ear.

A little motive, very simple and of naive charm, announces the beginning of the *Nocturne No. 9 in B Minor-Major, Op. 97.* A grumbling response in the bass which rises up by conjunct motion from the depths contrasts violently with the graceful childlike quality of the beginning and leads to a very methodical development of the initial theme. Then, one becomes aware of a curious incompatibility of mood, between the bass and the melody. The bass remains consistently sullen while the second melody is always pleasant. In the course of their interaction, some ingeniously stressed ascending and descending harmonic progressions whose formula Fauré never tired of reviving, reappear. The bass steals away for an instant from the candid little motive of the beginning, but its impatiently hoped for return is maliciously refused us.

The *Nocturne No. 10 in E Minor, Op. 99* does not choose to be melodic. From the beginning, it is engaged in a play of tightly constructed progressions and echoes between the extreme parts. A distant emanation from *La Bonne Chanson, Op. 61* appears before its conclusion to make this reverie, which has already left the Minor key and whose obstinate syncopations fall like tears, a bit less somber. Engaged until then in the activity of the development which has broken it up, the melody finally and imperceptibly disengages itself, but is only left with a few measures to gasp its swan song.

Without representing anything of a descriptive nature, the *Nocturne No. 11 in F sharp Minor, Op. 104, No. 1* has a subject. Here are more tears from which a doleful syncopation falls drop by drop. Fauré planned to do an affectionate homage to the memory of Noëmie Lalo in this nocturne. He carried out his plan with his usual delicacy and tact, not allowing his sorrow to show too blatantly. For an instant, however, the tone seems to rise up in a motion of revolt against the cruelty and injustice of blind fate, but the tender imploring, whose reserve is so sweet and suitable to the evocation of a feminine mystique, soon regains its elegiac serenity.

A long struggle between the Major and Minor is established in the *Nocturne No. 12 in E Minor, Op. 107.* Its first chord is Major, but it is immediately overshadowed by a Minor scale whose sadness is overwhelming. One doesn't know what the composer's state of mind was when he composed this poignant hand-to-hand combat, but it is striking to observe the perpetual thrusts toward the light which hurl themselves against the bars of this gloomy prison. A second theme, whose chords are also wounded by the bites of the seconds which tear at its flesh, perpetuates the combat. When it reaches its end, one thinks that the Major will be victorious but a Minor chord returns alone to the field of battle and, curiously, has the last word.

It is always arbitrary and somewhat conformist to want to romanticize Fauré's *Nocturne No. 13 in B Minor, Op. 119,* which has stirred up so many contradictory opinions. One can, without being irreverent, accept a suggestion of Charles Koechlin, one of Fauré's best students and most fervent admirers. The date when this melancholy piece was written, 1922, caused musicologists to assign it automatically to the category of

Fauré's declining works, with all of the misunderstandings that this entails. Koechlin logically claims that it is not a question of a work of old age, but of a work dedicated to old age by a man whose brain and heart have not aged and who has kept all of his mental faculties intact. The fact that at seventy-seven years of age Fauré became involved in the tactical difficulties of chess and often sought this diversion proves to us that age had weakened none of his abilities. But his body was becoming more and more sclerotic. His illnesses became more aggravated and he clearly and very lucidly observed that the hour of supreme renouncement was approaching. Koechlin perceived in this nocturne the menacing evocation of this twilight crossed with the luminous memories of past years and resigned to the sadness of the approaching reality.

Examination of this score confirms this hypothesis. There is an infinite sadness in this first theme which, at the first opportunity, becomes animated and tries to find the energy and the hopes of the past. But it must renounce them and fall back for an instant into sad reverie. However, the old man does not admit defeat. He leans on his past for support and revives the exalted images of his youth. Over a brilliantly pianistic accompaniment, which is fluent and busy, his adolescent dreams, ambitions and enthusiasm sing a flowing hymn to life written by an untrembling hand and attest to the paradoxical freshness of an imagination and a sensitivity which the years did not take away. Such a piece is the best answer to those who dare speak of the autumnal aridity of Fauré's imagination.

Two strangely subterranean rumblings harshly interrupt this trip, reversing the time machine. The first theme reappears implacably in its sad guise of disenchantment. It moves slowly and inflexibly toward a tonic chord at the extremity of a scale and heavily falls back. And it is, as a matter of fact, a tomb which is being shut, for this chord of B Minor closes the series of Fauré's piano works.

Fauré left us two sonatas for piano and violin, Ops. 13 and 108. The author was thirty years old when he composed the first. He was in his seventies when he wrote the second. The close relationship between these two works, separated by forty years, reveals once again Fauré's incredible vigor and strength. Everything we have said about the *Sonata No. 1 in A Major, Op. 13* can be applied to the *Sonata No. 2 in E Minor, Op. 108.* The same strength of thematic invention, the same youthful ardor in the stride of the conquering allegros, the same variety of melodic mood permitted the composer to borrow themes from certain earlier works without breaking contact between the ideals of the old man and those of the adolescent.

Such is the case with the *andante* from the second sonata, which is moving because of its serenity, the breadth of its inspiration, the elevation of its thought, and the sovereign mastery which characterizes all of the works of this period. This movement comes from the *Symphony in D Minor, Op. 40* that he wrote a few years after the first sonata and which he had not wanted to be published because certain details did not satisfy him. The quality of this piece, now in the form of an instrumental duo, makes us think that the severe self-criticism which the composer imposed upon himself was perhaps excessive. Observe that at this period, the less than forty-year-old composer delighted in making a theme sing by constructing it out of conjunct steps. It is an effective method, a heritage from his organ technique.

What a perfect model of composition is this first allegro, whose initial feverish and agitated theme is heard on the piano then quickly joined on the violin and whose second theme is calm, severe, sweet, tender, and peaceful and possesses at the same time that *affetuoso* character which is a Fauréan trademark. Under a shower of arpeggios, both make their way with a sure step.

Fauré created themes which suggest the notions of strength or weakness, of masculine virility, or feminine passivity, of tenderness or anger as absolutes. These themes are love, joy, sorrow, melancholy, charm, or violence in themselves and are beyond the human. To reach as high as possible above that which is, is the constant ambition of this composer who transforms and spiritualizes all human passions by means of ethereal language.

One must never forget his declaration of principles after the analysis of the first sonata by his son Philippe, an analysis which he recognized as "so applicable that one might really believe that this *finale* describes all there was to see in it." Having thus rendered homage to the ingenuity of this work, Fauré very honestly added, "I must admit that I did not think of anything like that. Actually, I thought of nothing at all in this circumstance . . ." But he did take the trouble to explain the effect of the ringing of bells which appears at the beginning of the *adagio* of his *Piano Quartet No. 2, Op. 45.* He wrote, "Almost unconsciously, the very old memory of a ringing of bells came to me when, in evening during my childhood, this sound wafted across from the west, from a village called Cadirac. Musing on this, I began to dream. But it would be difficult to describe this vagueness into words. Isn't it often that an exterior event fills us with these kinds of thoughts, so imprecise that in reality they are not thoughts but something in which we take pleasure. Perhaps the desire for things which don't exist. And that is really the domain of music." These basic statements make it clear why Fauré's chamber music works, without ever being descriptive or anecdotal, create a whole universe of dreams and, if one can say so, a galaxy of unreality.

Like the first *allegro*, the *finale* of the *Sonata No. 2 in E Minor* is rich, ardent, and animated with an intense inner life. However, the mood is gathered into a sort of smiling euphoria. One notices in many of Fauré's works written after *Pénélope*, the frequent use of an octave leap but with a recognizable hint at the Ulysses motive which unconsciously haunted him and inspired him until his dying day with so many happy melodic inventions.

The fate of Fauré's *Piano Quintet No. 1 in D Minor, Op. 89* is really unusual. Written in 1906 and published in New York the following year, it has completely disappeared from circulation. When the *Piano Quintet No. 2 in C Minor, Op. 115,* composed fifteen years later, became famous, the first was henceforth lost in oblivion. Once the stock was exhausted in America (and there were always difficulties in importation to France), it was practically abandoned. Fauré enthusiasts knew of its existence, but for many years there were no clues to the whereabouts of this masterpiece and it appeared to have been definitely lost.

Since I couldn't bear to have the readers of this study remain ignorant of the beauties of this work, I moved mountains to have it revived for one brief hour, thanks to the devotion of the efforts and the talents of the great pianist Joseph Benvenuti, the celebrated quartettist Joseph Calvet and the valiant Parrenin String Quartet who, by generously lending themselves for this project, this attempt at momentary resurrection, have well merited membership in the Fauréan cult!

This *Piano Quintet in D Minor* presents particularities common to several scores dating from the same period. It is more serious than meditative, sterner than the second, which dates from 1921, and is infinitely younger and more carefree than its older relative.

Its general architecture surprises us by its apparent indifference to the classic stylistic tradition. Its three movements without a *scherzo* tend toward having a certain unification of tempo. The first *allegro* is "molto moderato," that is to say, "it moves," but less decidedly and with less energy than customary. On the other hand, the *adagio* with its metronome indication of 54 to a dotted quarter note does not allow for any possibility of slowing down when one wishes and is thus related to the preceding movement. As for the third part, it is an *allegretto,* an even-keeled *moderato* which is closer in speed to an amiable *scherzo* rather than to a racy *finale.* The unity of the work is inherent in its general atmosphere of calm balance rather than in the rhythmic or thematic work.

The first Minor motive, sustained *pianissimo* by crystalline piano arpeggios, is presented by the second violin which severely announces its first four measures. When this is repeated it is doubled at the lower octave by the cello which imbues it with more body and solidity. The viola soon reinforces this unison and the first violin crowns the edifice by adding the octave above. All this time the piano has not stopped stringing its arpeggios while this unison becomes richer every four measures with the collaboration of each new stringed instrument. Thus, one sees this beginning as a resolute evasion of the traditional formula of the first movement of a quartet.

A second theme, still in D Minor, more cheerful and disengaging, follows the first strongly modifying the mood, and one can observe in the entire work a concern to conserve an internal "melodiousness." This quintet is essentially melodic. It sings unceasingly and inexhaustibly with lyricism and passion. There are no spectacular oppositions of themes or rhythms, and no exterior conflicts. The melodic current never leaves the four stringed instruments and the frequent return of the unison on three levels which gives much expressive intensity to the singing lines only accentuates this characteristic. One must make an especially concerted effort to realize that the play of echoes, imitations, answers, displacements, and modulating structures, hidden under this melodic exaltedness, ingeniously assures the architectural equilibrium of the development. A clever employment of the triplet in the piano part and in the melody softens the angularity and sustains interest in the movement.

Here is another significant observation. One knows what scruples hindered the composition of Fauré's only string quartet for such a long time. The piano had always been indispensable to him in the construction of his chamber music works. In his *Piano Quintet No. 1*, he seems to have wanted to give more independence to the strings and trains them to manage by themselves. The piano was long confined to the role of accompaniment, a delectable role, certainly, but not as an active participant essential to the structuring of the discourse. It was only required to support an unobstrusive web of arpeggios. In this regard, the first piano quintet constitutes a sort of preparatory exercise for the liberation of the strings which will be a fait accompli in his last work.

The second movement is inspired by the same lyric and songful spirit. It is rich in pure music, it has the same long breadth of the same impetus, the same ardent movement toward the heights. Its two themes are interrelated in the same ways. This time, the piano is permitted to participate in the developmental activity and to announce the *dolce cantabile,* the first four measures of the second theme, after which the strings take over and exploit all of its expressive possibilities. The important unisons return to increase the inner tension of the melody and we meet the most authentic Fauréan touches in the modulations and cadences.

As for the *finale,* it puts the piano first in importance by giving it the initial theme, an amiable melody moving by conjunct degrees and etched in unison by both hands two octaves apart. One knows that this disposition gives the piano the charming sonority of a glockenspiel or celeste, whose aerial lightness is helped by the syncopated pizzicato accompaniment in the four strings. Fauré draws a continuous variety of effects from this motive.

His theme passes quickly to the bass to allow the first violin to gravely sing the second motive which is modeled after the first with that heavenly ease which is one of Fauré's secrets. With these two basic elements, the composer enchants us with his unceasing attention to detail, leading us effortlessly and excitedly to a very classic conclusion. This masterpiece, which is so balanced, so overflowing with music, gives us the impression of having heard sonorous effects of such exceptional richness that we are astonished to see Fauré waiting eighteen years before giving us his *String Quartet in E Minor.*

The *Piano Quintet No. 2 in C Minor, Op. 115* has the paradoxical merit of bringing together the two generally incompatible virtues of youth and serenity. It has that juvenile freshness, ardor, generosity and persuasive tenderness, and also possesses the refined gifts of wisdom, of sublimated passion, of sensual and lovely balance and reasoned tranquility.

The form of this Quintet does not, however, seen at first glance, offer to a musician the opportunity to display such varied emotions. The traditionally severe character of chamber music, its voluntary disdain of dramatic expression and its intellectual sentiments, have often paralyzed the sincerest out-pourings of composers. But Fauré's art contains precisely the essential ingredient of the "pathétique" which has no need to be exteriorized by many words or large vocal forces. It is concise, discrete, subtle and eloquent because it has the Verlainian cour-age of "straining" toward eloquence. The ardent or light dia-logue of the strings permits him to say everything with an extraordinary clarity and a moving profundity. For him the most strictly regulated musical style and the most carefully woven phrasing are never in the domain of intellectual diver-sion or decorative art. Whether they want to or not, Fauré's melodies, like certain landscapes, always remain a mood.

The first movement of the *Piano Quintet No. 2* is an *allegro moderato*, very alert, very lively but beginning softly. Its strength and its agitation are controlled. The first movement of a composition of this kind complies ordinarily to almost theat-rical convention. The silence is decisively broken. Thrown to the winds is a solidly constructed phrase, presenting a charac-teristic profile and typical ornamental trimmings, a generally energetic phrase of proud bearing which plays at being noble. Without it being possible to define why these arched melodies are so easily recognizable, they carry within them their devel-opmental destinies. The composer who meets one by chance might immediately say to himself, "That would really make an excellent theme for the first *allegro* of a sonata, quartet or symphony."

Gabriel Fauré scorns this little traditional gallantry, this salute to the public. He has chosen a sober theme, announced by the viola in the second measure with a sort of affectionate simplicity where the piano makes discrete use of the first three notes to develop surrounding accompanimental arpeggios. After just eight measures, the whole work has an unmistakable signature.

The composition has all of the imperceptible and mysterious touches immediately reminiscent of the inimitable magician of *Soir*. The melody is made up of simple note values, with some rhythmic oddity making it supple and flexible like a vine; pure phrases whose every segment suggests rich harmonic possibilities and which, in concluding, alights softly on the tonic. One again finds the characteristic elasticity of the accompaniment which, scarcely changing its position, reveals at every turn delectable views of neighboring or distant tonalities, the implied harmonies indicated by adroit voice-leading progressing by conjunct degrees and unceasingly transforming the shading of the theme. This imperceptibly intoxicating color, this nonchalant richness, this winged grace and lucidity is Gabriel Fauré's whole style solidified and liquefied at the same time.

One of the most astonishing aspects of Fauré's style is the ease with which he can pass without a jolt from a firmly established rhythm to a new phrase division. Many composers become prisoners of a beautiful rhythmic pattern. In the first *allegro*, the soft initial sixteenth-note arpeggios balance so well that it could be indefinite with the composer suspending it when he wants to, reinserting it, or replacing it by syncopation or triplets with an infallible timing. And its return is on a well chosen chord, achieved with an elegance and deftness that is ravishing to the ear.

The themes happily follow one another. In the first tempo with unexpected seriousness, a short phrase is announced of almost scholarly austerity, fashioned like a chorale. Immediately in opposition to its male pride is a seductive melody which archs and stretches with a feline languor. It is marvelous to see these always novel and unexpected musical effects that the composer knew how to draw from the eternal conflict between sensuality and reason. And you can guess what verbalizations accompany these surprises with their irresistible intoxication of sevenths, and tender repose on the sixth, technical subtleties whose mechanics are not a secret but seldom used with more artistry.

The *Scherzo* rocks us at first in an agreeable state of indecision between tonality and modality, thanks to a little serpentine scale bristling with alterations which ascends, falls back, and babbles like a tiny fountain. The violin holds back, marking time, fusing certain passages with pizzicatos. Suddenly, the first violin imposes a magnificently long and flexible phrase, a rich melody covering twenty-four measures in one breath without repeating itself, a symmetrical, noble lyric, outlining a fine delineated curve which furnishes the elements for an ingenious development.

Let us invite, in passing, the adversaries of contemporary music to consider phrases of this kind in order to realize the absurdity of their favorite complaints. They incessantly reproach today's musical language for not giving any importance to melody and breaking everything up into little fragments. Gabriel Fauré, and after him Debussy, then Ravel, perfectly applied the contemporary vocabulary generously and to an absolutely exceptional extent to melody. Do we not find in Bach, and in the loftiest and so geometrically compartmentalized masterpieces of the Classic period, a melodic effusion of liberty, spontaneity and splendor?

The powerful sap which is in Fauré's melody makes it expand for a second time above a murmur of pianistic droplets before the conclusion of the work. If one feels in this grave and impassioned *andante* that all of the voices come close and lightly touch in the intoxication of a fervent ecstasy, how can one remain untouched by the ardent life of the *finale* which races along with a light step on such simple rhythms and avoids showy ornamentation.

After an interval of forty years had elapsed between the birth of this *Sonata No. 1 for Violin and Piano in A Major, Op. 13* and the composition of the *Sonata No. 2 for Violin and Piano in E Minor, Op. 108,* Fauré wrote his two cello sonatas, almost one after the other. The first, in D Minor, is Op. 109 and the second, in G Minor, is Op. 117. After the second, there were only three more scores, *L'Horizon chimérique, Op. 118,* the *Nocturne No. 13, Op. 119* and the *Trio, Op. 120,* before the final *String Quartet, Op. 121.*

The first sonata for cello and piano is serious and meditative. It does not willingly part with its Minor mode and openly exploits its natural melancholy. From the appearance of his popular *Elégie, Op. 24,* we know that Fauré greatly appreciated the deep sonorities of the cello rather than its high register to which the acrobatics of the instrument give a forced quality.

Is it to react against this frivolity that Fauré wanted to remind one of the instrument's true mission? In this first sonata, an inhabitual seriousness is preserved. The initial movement is somber with harsh rhythms in the piano. It progresses breathlessly by fits and starts. The entire work is permeated by obstinate rhythmic accents. The first thrusting theme is restrained by a sort of severity which makes the second theme, by contrast, appear more supple, graceful and charming. A technique of echo and answer is employed in its development which is very characteristic. We will find it again in the other two movements.

In the *andante,* the lion's share is saved for the cello. In the two sonatas, the piano is content to support it with deference and modesty. Here it sometimes ventures to escort the triumphant melody by following in its footsteps, by echoing it in the higher register, but without any attempt to compete with it as a solo partner. It produces discrete counterpoint and the movement of its bass is as interesting to observe as the melody's. The *finale* gives the keyboard back its liberty and allows it to take charge of animating a development where the famous altered theme of Ulysses from *Pénélope* will play an important role, as it did in all of the works of this period. The shadowy threats are dissipated, optimism claims its rights, and the sonata ends with a sense of well being.

The *Sonata No. 2 for Cello and Piano in G Minor, Op. 117*

has a lot in common with the first, including the same ternary meter and the same movement indications. Even the same care is taken to make the stringed instrument the most important factor and to impose a certain modesty on the piano which keeps the same rhythm going for a long while and multiplies the responses and the soft echoes as the melody unravels. Beginning with the first *allegro*, we find ourselves in a much gayer atmosphere. The main theme is amiable and almost joyful. It is young and active. The piano, then the cello, presents with good humor the secondary theme which takes the lead. Each instrument shows its interest in the progress of its associate by imitations which are at times strict or very free. And the parallelism of these two twin activities gives this first section such an engaging movement that its conclusion is reached with surprising rapidity.

An unexpected contrast is furnished by the *andante* which has a funereal tempo. You will not be surprised to learn that Fauré used a theme originally destined to commemorate the centenary of Napoleon's death. The piano resigns itself to playing repeated chords while the cello meditatively gives free rein to its emotions. The accompanimental chords lead to an episode of calm serenity in A flat Major which dissipates our anguish. The initial phrase tries in vain to sadden us again. The two themes borrow the light of the Major mode to chase these chords away and bring about a happy conclusion.

As for the *finale*, the piano is again given the liberty so long denied it. It profits from this freedom to throw itself impetuously into a maelstrom of scales and arpeggios. Proud of its regained independence, it initiates more daring things. Three times it alone dictates new thematic material to the cello. The sonata ends in a mood of adolescent joyfulness.

At the École Niedermeyer, the stage evidently did not smell too clean. Any other viewpoint would have been abnormal and illogical in a milieu where the theater had always been considered one of the most dangerous dens of the devil. The Conservatoire itself was suspected by the Niedermeyer choir directors because its composition classes were methodically and solely oriented toward the opera and the lyric stage. Certainly, one can't blame them for considering Bach as a more respectable director of musical conscience than Ambroise Thomas. And, we have already stated that Gabriel Fauré, when he held the destiny of the Faculté Nationale de Musique in his hands, rightfully denounced the absurdity of the Concours de Rome which refused to recognize any talented composer other than those who produced theatrical cantatas. Don't be surprised to learn that he accepted with pleasure the offer to compose incidental music for the five acts and prologue of the Alexander Dumas tragedy, *Caligula,* that was to be produced at the Théâtre de l'Odéon in 1888. He was to distinguish himself in this place of perdition.

This score, Fauré's Op. 52, is content to be introduced by a prelude replete with fanfares and to furnish the *entr'actes* with musical interludes. It takes part in the action by means of a choreographic episode of oriental languor and a delectable female chorus which sings about the inebriating effects of springtime, the hours spent in battle, and happy times while voluptuously lulling the Emperor to sleep. These pages reveal a sensual and pagan Fauré who so well understood the carnal intoxication of ancient Rome and the decadence with which Charles Koechlin was able to lure us. This allowed the composer to impregnate his music with a color and perfume so subtly evocative that it accurately recreates the epoch and the circumstances of the action. To be able to establish by way of pure music so precise a distinction between the Hellenic atmosphere and that of the Roman Empire is a tour de force which reveals the sensitivity of Fauré and the astonishing richness of his creative imagination.

The following year, L'Odéon asked him for another theater score. This time, it had to do with quite a different subject, since they were going from the Rome of Caesar to the Shakespearean Venice of Shylock. Edmond Haraucourt had made an adaptation in very careful verse. Once again Fauré—who became acquainted with Venice two years later—found no difficulty in creating the atmosphere needed for his new score (Op. 57). He designed a tender and dreamy Venetian soul, and wrote under the direction of an inner vision a *prélude*, a gallant *chanson*, an *entr'acte*, a *madrigal*, an *épithalame*, a *nocturne*, and a *finale* which are of a truly delicate nature.

Nine years passed, and a new commission obliged the composer to immerse himself again in a very different atmosphere, that of the very old and darkly mysterious Nordic château in which Maeterlinck housed the melancholy story of *Pelléas et Mélisande*. The production took place at the Prince of Wales Theater in London. Fauré himself was invited to conduct his score (Op. 80) which was made up of a number of quite brief orchestral interludes, a theme and four important pieces which furnished material for a suite which has often been performed at symphonic concerts.

The tender and nostalgic *Prélude* immediately created the legendary color of the drama. It was then used in turn to evoke the forest where the enigmatic princess wanders, and the feelings of anguish which afflict her at the threshold of some unknown destiny. The distant horn calls from Golaud heard at the end of her painful meditation makes the tragic sense of this meeting vivid for the audience. A *Fileuse* betrays Mélisande's youthful, carefree spirit and symbolizes the calm life of the fugitive recluse in her new dwelling place. A *Sicilienne* introduces an intermezzo, quite inexplicably sunny considering the misty and medieval atmosphere of the old castle. This interlude was probably added at the last moment and is borrowed from a previous work, for it is completely foreign not only to the action, but to the style of the rest of the score.

The noble *adagio* of the interlude which precedes Mélisande's final moments brings us back to the heart of the subject. The language of suffering takes on a nobility and profundity which are extraordinarily moving. A noble and profound interpretation can curiously transform the psychological atmosphere. Certain orchestral conductors, by stressing the grace note of the melody, make it a funeral march, accentuated like Chopin's. In this case, one sees the vision of the solemn funeral ceremony for Prince Golaud's wife, which is, by itself, a very lovely picture. But other conductors, by making it more flexible, extend the elasticity of the phrase and make a tender and dolorous meditation at the bedside of Mélisande. This piece is played while Mélisande is still alive. This fact, plus the orchestral color of the piece, makes the second conception more plausible.

The effect of the theater on Fauré's sensitivity grew. After the success of these three essays in incidental music, he became bolder and planned larger projects. His friend Saint-Saëns introduced him to Castelbon de Beauxhostes who, each year, organized impressive outdoor theatrical performances and decided to commission Fauré to write music for a tragedy of Jean Lorrain and F. A. Hérold, inspired by Aeschylus' *Prometheus*. Their very free adaptation was opportunely conceived in the form of a series of contrasting scenes, capable of sustaining the interest of a public which was not too knowledgeable about Greek drama.

If this libretto attracted Fauré, the conditions under which this flattering commission was offered were quite disconcerting, and the composer realized the pitfalls too late. First of all, the time given to the composer to complete the score was clearly insufficient. The score itself was subjected to questionable uses. It was to be inserted in a play in which certain roles were spoken and others sung. It was supposed to have a sonorous volume of sound as titanic as its hero and utilize imposing forces: a chorus, two wind orchestras in addition to a symphony orchestra, and an enormous complement of harps to fill the immense open air stage. Besides, Fauré had to be satisfied with instrumentalists who were not very dependable. This was due to the fact that, in order to staff two wind orchestras, one had to depend on amateur musicians from a local music society and the military musicians from a Montpellier regiment. All this also meant such a great deal of work in furnishing orchestral materials, parts, plus rehearsals in Paris and in the province, that Fauré was hard pressed to meet the deadline and had to give the conductor of the Montpellier unit the job of orchestrating his score.

Fervent admirers of Fauré suffered greatly seeing him involved in such an unfortunate venture. Our consternation was even more pronounced when we saw him the victim of innumerable catastrophic defections and deceptions, the usual by-products of any large-scaled open-air spectacular since they involve too many collaborators. But, in spite of all these trials, Fauré kept calm and in good humor. I can still see him, perched on a high platform, a straw hat on his head to protect himself against a burning sun, standing with his two arms lifted toward the sky to conduct his three orchestras, choruses, and imposing his will on the eight hundred performers under his direction, a slender silhouette on which all attention was riveted, an emanating post from which silent messages radiated to a crowd of singers, a minuscule vital center of a universe peopled with heroes and gods . . .

He was spared nothing. At the final rehearsal, a violent storm raged over Béziers. A torrential rain transformed the arena into a lake and the thunder, too occupied in conforming to the stage action, struck the scenery at the precise moment when Prometheus was to carry off the celestial fire. But the next day, under a radiant sky, the performance took place without difficulty and was marvelously successful. The crowd, less sophisticated than the refined Fauréans, following their scruples, theories and preconceived ideas toward a certain defeatist attitude in the presence of such a paradoxical work; the crowd which knew neither *La Bonne Chanson* nor the *Nocturne No. 6* nor *Le Parfum impérissable* and, consequently, was not encumbered by any complexes, was immediately won over by the nobility of this spectacular drama and the healthy simplicity of its music which was so well suited to the requirements of an outdoor performance.

Once more, the quintessential magician had shown the most virile side of his talents and had effortlessly treated this, the most gigantic subject of all of Greek dramaturgy. In this respect, Prometheus represented in Gabriel Fauré's output a proof of strength and an athletic prowess which confounded all of the superficial observers who thought they saw in him only a kind of Paul Delmet, an expert in harmony.

Unfortunately, circumstances did not permit this ravisher of fire to efficaciously repeat this useful demonstration. Two unfortunate attempts to transplant *Prométhée* to the old Hippodrome and the Opéra brought discredit to this magnificent work which was conceived for the out-of-doors. It is deplorable that this composition has not been heard more frequently. Even if Fauré's sensitivity is more naturally in tune with Verlaine than with Aeschylus, it is still exciting to observe how, in the majestic prelude to *Prométhée* in the first crowd scene, in Gaïa's prophecy, in Titan's invocation in chains, the serious Fauré as opposed to the spontaneous and intuitive Fauré who outlines with such a purity of line Pandora's touching face, finds the right touches to describe the chaste funeral. One cannot rationally allow this work, which was such a precious witness of the astonishing multiplicity of Fauré's genius, to be forgotten.

The year following the creation of *Prométhée*, Fauré had the chance to write a new theater score of infinitely more modest dimensions. It was to be used to accompany, at the Théâtre de la Porte-Saint-Martin, a play by Georges Clemenceau entitled *Le Voile du bonheur* (Op. 88), a little Chinese morality piece which was about a blind mandarin pampered by a loving wife and by the care and esteem of respectful children and faithful friends. The patient blesses the gods each day for having granted him perfect happiness. Heaven, touched by his piety, sends him a marvelous physician who restores his sight. He begs his saviour not to mention having cured him in order to allow him the personal joy of surprising his entourage. He savors this pleasure in advance by excitedly observing what takes place around him.

He notices that his wife is cuckolding him with his best friend, his children secretly making fun of him, and his faithful friends are betraying his confidences. Crushed by these cruel revelations, the unfortunate man realizes that his infirmity was a blessing in disguise and in order to avoid being a victim of the calamities that sight brings, he asks the doctor to take away the fatal gift so that he might regain the illusions which assured him happiness. Thirty years earlier, Fauré had already treated this theme in an abridged manner in his song *Après un rêve*. "Hélàs! triste reveil des songes, ô Nuit, rends-moi tes mensonges . . ."

Such a subject did not require a lengthy score. Fauré contented himself with writing seven pages of far Eastern atmosphere for a little offstage orchestra, rich in delicate percussion instruments. The effect was most charming. Unfortunately, the original score and the orchestral material were mislaid by the personnel of the theater at the end of the play and have never been found. Because Fauré did not keep a copy, these little Chinese postage stamps have been lost. But the time was approaching when the composer's attention was going to be taken up with something quite different in importance.

It was, as a matter of fact, in 1907 that Gabriel Fauré, who had just passed his sixtieth birthday, suddenly decided to compose a large and entirely lyric work. The memory of the excellent performance of his *Prométhée* was to haunt him and it is known that in spite of all the ordeals, fatigue, deception, and bitterness, the theater exercises a lasting spell on those who once tasted its grandeur and its demands. René Fauchois, with a kind of miraculous foresight, proposed a subject to Fauré which corresponded exactly to his aspirations and his temperament.

144

We have spoken many times of Fauré's Hellenism. Although he had harmonized a *Hymne à Apollo* discovered at Delphi and transcribed by Theodore Reinach, Fauré never became a professional Hellinist. But he possessed what one could call a natural Atticism which impregnated his esthetic sense in many ways. Having made this distinction, it is quite evident that the purity, the nobility and the eurhythmics of a legendary drama from Greek antiquity should particularly interest him.

In this case, it was a striking episode from the *Odyssey*, the one where we witness the clandestine return of Ulysses to his palace in Ithaca. Disguised as an old beggar, this hero used this ruse in order to enter his own house where arrogant pretenders intended to steal his wife and crown. The heroic Penelope courageously opposed them for she didn't want to believe that her husband was dead. At the same time, ambitious princes who were harassing her in an increasingly threatening manner, were already dividing her estate. With the aid of his old porter, Eumee, and his faithful shepherds, Ulysses drew his enemy into a trap, massacred them and, casting off his rags, opened his arms to his sublimely happy wife.

I don't know if Fauchois gave his collaborator an entirely complete libretto or if he only wrote it after having received suggestions, but Fauré could not have asked for a text more suited to his wishes. These three clear and well balanced acts, divided into single scenes, offered the composer attractive and varied musical possibilities. The beautiful servant girls, boldly flattered by the pretenders, a graceful choreographic episode, the insulting ultimatum of the princes summoning Penelope to marry one of them, the arrival of Ulysses in disguise, the compassionate greeting by the queen, the pious pilgrimage she makes every night when she climbs a hill from where she can see the vast ocean which one day will return her husband to her, the subterfuge which indefinitely slows down the weaving of Laërtes' shroud, the strategy permitting the fake beggar to seize Ulysses' long bow, the massacre of the pretenders and the apotheosis of the conqueror, as well as tableaux of very diversified color, permitted the composer to run the gamut of emotional expression.

But what Fauré was to value above all else was the simplicity of speech adopted by Fauchois. This unaffected language gave him the opportunity to treat the action with great human sincerity. An academic and solemn grandiloquence would have certainly not been suitable while Fauchois' conception gave it added enchantment. Let us note in passing that forty years later, Cocteau, in the same spirit, was to cover himself with glory by "taking off the makeup" from other Greek texts. But the librettist of *Pénélope*, like all of his precursors, did not reap these benefits.

Fauré settled in Lausanne and began work immediately with a joyful ardor. His letters revealed that this exciting work was a veritable obsession. He lived continually with his hero. He quickly began the *prélude* which, without being Wagnerian, announced the two characteristic themes representing Pénélope and Ulysses. He soon abandoned the *Prélude* to begin the initial scene of the first *tableau*, the one where Pénélope's servants lazily dreaming at their spinning wheels, comment on the events which are taking place at that moment. For twenty days he labored on the threads which envelop this frivolous conversation with light murmurings. Each of his daily letters shows him fretting about the difficulty of making these damsels sing while stretching, yawning, and exchanging candid observations on their boredom.

Honest as always in studying this problem in depth, he came to this conclusion: "It is not what they say that is important, it is the atmosphere of their nonchalance, of their activity, mixed with reverie. Consequently, it is the orchestra which should begin all this and their words should be sung over an uninterrupted movement of music." He jokingly added, "It is astonishing how hard one must work at depicting people who don't work!"

If one wants to be aware of the detail of this work and the methods he employed, read this very interesting passage from another letter: "I finished the three strophes of the spinners . . . that should get a prize. It began to develop at the moment when instead of finishing the movement is suspended over a harmony in which the reverie of the maidens is lost, one hears in the distance a burst of laughter revealing the presence of the pretenders. Here I am on a new phrase. The servant girls are going to tell us who these pretenders are and what they are going to do, Pénélope's resistance to them, etc. I found a theme for the pretenders that I am trying out, something which will give the impression of brutality and complete egotism. And when I say I am 'trying out' the theme, this is what I mean. I try to discover all the combinations I can according to circumstances. For example, a servant girl says, talking about one of the pretenders, 'Antinous is handsome!' It is necessary at this point that my theme spreads out its tail like a peacock! . . . . It is also necessary that it can combine with Pénélope's theme. I attempt to draw varied effects from it, whether in its totality or by fragmenting it. In a word, I make memos to myself which will serve me in the course of the work. I made sketches as an artist does for a picture. This indispensable job takes me a great deal of time, but it enormously facilitates my work in the long run."

That was the spirit in which this admirable score was fashioned from beginning to end. It remains to be discovered by the majority of musicians the world over.

Begun in Lausanne on July 28, 1907, continued in Lugano and in Hyères with frequent interruptions, the score of *Pénélope* was completed in Lugano on August 31, 1912. Two important theaters were impatiently awaiting it: the Monte Carlo opera which presented it on March 4th of the following year and the Théâtre des Champs-Elysées (under Astruc's direction) which presented it to the Parisian public two months later. The work enjoyed a triumphant success in both places. Unfortunately, these exceptional performances did not assure it a lasting career. There have been attempts to revive this moving work, but its preparation poses such difficulties that it is not easy to win over everyone and the work has suffered because of this handicap.

All of its roles, from the smallest to the most important, have to be filled with superb artists because of the quality of style and musicality required. If the pretenders, who only have a few measures to sing, are to be brought to life by weak choristers, the overall balance of the score will be compromised. Is it possible, even by drowning them in money, to recruit a stellar aggregation of great singers willing to perform these minor roles? The spinners, who are in the same position, would be no less problematical. The role of Eumée is a major one. Euryclée is no less so, and I am not mentioning the superhuman characters of Pénélope and Ulysses. These could only be brought to life by stars of the first order, possessing physical and vocal endowments rarely united in opera singers.

Finally, in this world, how many orchestral conductors exist who possess the gifts that constitute the "essence of Fauré," that is to say, the subtle instinct which will allow them to guess the inflections of such delicate phrases, the curve of those supple melodic configurations, the exact shading, the right accent, the precise color which suits this patrician music? It takes very little to make the first act of *Pénélope* dull when performed without sufficient attention to detail. Not having found favorable conditions in Monte Carlo, Fauré himself said, "I have the feeling of having created a wearisome and lifeless work."

We have just seen with what psychological and musical scruples Fauré wove the thread of each scene of his score. Apparent is a delicacy of touch and the hand of a virtuoso composer of chamber music. One should not hesitate to scrutinize certain pages of the orchestration where the strings play an important role with such nuance and care, as if they were playing a *scherzo* or an *andante* of a string quartet. It is only by doing

148

this that this music can reveal the interior life which pulsates within it.

For the professional as well as the public of today, such occupations are terribly anachronistic. Just as the capriciousness of snobbism is bent by the wind like ears of corn in an open field, the curiosity of our contemporaries will not have changed direction. One must give credit to Risler's clear observation in saying to Fauré, "Your work will last but it will take a long time to become implanted."

I believe that a perfect and truly Fauréan performance of *Pénélope* would be, for music lovers of every taste, a real revelation and would dissipate the misconceptions that have until now impeded the career of this opera. What musician worthy of the name could resist the charm of the first act's conclusion, "Take this mantle, old man, the breezes of the night are cool . . ." when the orchestra mysteriously concludes after Pénélope's aria so that the theme of Ulysses cleverly hidden, can reveal for us its dark warnings and its radiant promises?

Notice with what subtlety Fauré's refined musicianship knows how to utilize and transform the most abstract forms of composition. A canonic imitation escorts the queen who is going away. Why did the composer choose this form? Because, at that instant, hunching his tall figure, Ulysses takes in turn the road she is following, humbly following in her footsteps. All this fits the very definition of the musical discipline known as "canon." In the *Ballade for Piano and Orchestra*, Fauré had already made this mathematical exercise into something poetic.

What sensitive person would remain unmoved by the very simple and touching picture of *Pénélope* surrounded in her palace and holding her enemy at bay with all the firmness of her faith, her hope, and her love? Is it possible not to be struck by the nocturnal rustic atmosphere that the composer knew how to create at the beginning of the second act for the shepherd's watch, the calm resolve of the faithful Eumée, the prudent and circumspect conversation of the beggar and the queen, the joy of the shepherds upon recognizing their master and, in the following act, the scene of the bow, so cleverly developed, the punishment of the pretenders, and the serene happiness of the reunited couple?

All these episodes are treated musically with so much intelligence and penetrating sensitivity that they reveal such novel and captivating aspects of Fauré's genius and, in particular, his hidden qualities of strength and grandeur, that the three acts, apart from their uninterrupted musical enchantment represent a theatrical victory won, paradoxically, by abandoning all the sacrosanct traditions of the theater!

Thirteen years later, René Fauchois approached Fauré, who was already very weak, and submitted a project for a small spoken, sung, and danced divertimento for the Opéra-Comique entitled *Masques et Bergamasques*. It was the dramatic realization of a *fête galante* taking place in the eighteenth century in the purest Verlainian tradition, beneath the foliage of Versailles.

Loving couples stroll dreamily along the paths while the classic characters of Italian comedy, hidden behind trees, look at them with an affectionate malice and take them into their confidence. This likeable scenario, as much Fauréan as Verlainian, pleased the composer who, four years before dying, was able thus to make his adieu to the theater. He composed a ravishing overture, of a freshness, distinctiveness and happiness which, without borrowing a note from the melodic and harmonic vocabulary of Mozart, miraculously recreated his spirit.

We have now touched upon the outer limits of Fauré's production. Deciding later to try a string quartet, Fauré seems to have wanted to complete the cycle of chamber music works which comprised two violin sonatas, two cello sonatas, two piano quartets and two piano quintets by adding to his *String Quartet in E Minor, Op. 121* a *String Trio in D Minor, Op. 120*. He began and carried out the composition of these two works at the same time. The trio was completed a bit before the quartet. However, both scores tell us his last secrets!

These works carry no trace of sadness or anguish. Fauré, while quite weak, did not believe the end was so near. Until the last moment, he was making plans for the future. When his Op. 121 was finished, he wrote to his son, "The quartet is quite finished, such as it is. It will do; it would have been like my trio, in three movements, but as I am in no hurry to give it to the world, I will interpolate a fourth movement which could be played between the first and second. As it is not at all necessary, I will not tire myself composing one, at least not at this time . . ." One sees that these two works, composed in the euphoria of his annual stay at Annecy-la-Vieux, where the Maillot family surrounded him with affectionate care and kind attention, did not connote in his mind the character of funeral music that has been attributed to them.

This *Trio, Op. 120* is alert and lively. All of its themes are, at times, charming or full of ardor and optimism. The only thing which is indicative of the composer's physical fatigue is the overly methodical nature of his development sections which no longer have the same imaginative liberty as before, but are still organized distinctively and elegantly. One is equally struck by the richness and variety of sonorous effects Fauré draws from the three movements. In the first movement, the three instruments are interlaced with so much ingenuity that one thinks he is hearing a much larger ensemble. The *andantino* is a dreamy meditation which detaches us from reality and progressively reaches mysterious and spiritual spheres. And the *finale*, in taking us back to earth, abandons itself to gregarious good humor. From the beginning three calls are sounded, which curiously are a reproduction, note for note, of the famous *Ridi Pagliacci* by Leoncavallo! No evidence leads us to believe that this imitation was conscious and was meant to introduce an element of philosophical bitterness in the *finale*, which, by plunging us back into the cares of everyday living, tells us to hurry up and laugh, before we have to cry. It is probable that all of this was perfectly unconscious, but, from Fauré's pen, it is still strange and unexpected, to say the least.

Concerning the *String Quartet in E Minor, Op. 121* there has been much commentary, more literary and sentimental than musical. One must not be astonished. The circumstances which surround its composition so late in Fauré's career explain and justify the particular character of its exegesis very well. It is known that its composer was prey to self-doubts when he was about to approach the severe formal requirements of classical string quartet writing, admitting no other procedure of "weaving" than that of the gliding of the weaver's shuttle of four bows over the sixteen wires stretched across the wood. His two piano quartets, his two piano quintets, and his string trio had added to the sonority of the bowed string that of the struck string. The hammers of the keyboard permitted it to chisel certain details more clearly in its delicate language, to variate its timbres and articulate and enrich our auditory perception with a feeling of change, created by the conscious alteration of the subtle shock and the caress.

The fact that this excursion into a new genre was going to become for him, without his knowing, his swan song and musical testament, should rightfully place his admirers in a state of receptivity were sadness and respect more important than critical appraisal. And the very touching gesture of a master entrusting to a small group of students and friends the responsibility of deciding, independently and after his death, if this work was worthy or not of being published and performed had the effect of disturbing critics.

They wracked their brains to discover in the *String Quartet in E Minor* a new manifestation of asceticism, of contribution, of renouncement. These *ultima verba* were the confessions of a dying man casting a melancholy and undeceived look at his past. The more one loved this elite being, the more one found these words of farewell, and these avowals formulated at the threshold of the tomb saddening and painful.

Thirty-five years have elapsed since that first contact. Unfortunately, I was not wrong to doubt the coolness of the public at large as regards the *String Quartet in E Minor* which rarely appears on programs of French quartets. But this reception has singularly modified my own reaction as a listener of good faith. Reprieved from the funereal atmosphere which surrounded it, this score today appears to me in quite a different light.

I find it neither enigmatic, nebulous, nor disenchanting. It is serene and peaceful like most of the works composed at the twilight of Fauré's career, but it is, like the second violin sonata also in E Minor, and like his trio, full of life and persistent youthfulness. The best proof is that its first movement is based on two themes borrowed from a work composed forty-five years earlier, *Concerto for Violin, Op. 14*, which remains unfinished and unpublished. Nothing negative results from this audacious soldering process. We have noted the same significant phenomenon in the *andante* of the *Sonata No. 2 for Violin and Piano, Op. 108* which came from the *Symphony in D Minor, Op. 40* that Fauré had abandoned for thirty-three years, and these two "wild oats" were inserted in the heart of the two works of his late maturity without creating the least stylistic imbalance.

In reality, the string quartet contains all of the constructional elements of Fauré's vocabulary and his fundamental style. The brief first *allegro* which plays so gracefully with the Minor and Major theme sets them in opposition, entwines them, and superimposes them. The *andante* is impregnated with the harmonic atmosphere of *Pénélope* and is generously melodic. The *finale* is held together by nervous pizzicati. Fauré formally stated that it is a sort of *scherzo* of a light and pleasing character completely euphoric and even smiling.

It is startling to read certain biographers who say that this music is poignant, anguished, full of despair and that the composer abandoned the vertical conception of his first period and adopted now a "magnificently contrapuntal style!" The *String Quartet in E Minor, Op. 121* is neither more nor less "vertical" than his other works and there are none of the scholastic rules of counterpoint other than categorical imperatives of the most refined harmonies which rule his writing style and govern his polyphony.

Observe the profile of this theme. The handwriting experts attach the greatest importance to its evenness. The repeated horizontal strokes, the instinctive sloping, or the ascending movement of the lines we trace on paper constitute for them precise indications of our temperament. Graphic representations which glide involuntarily toward the bottom of the page betray laziness and intellectual weakness, while those which rise upwards are indicative of energy, ardent youth, and a taste for fighting.

What is true in the domain of writing is no less so in composing, since it also deals with an unconscious reflex. Fauré's predilection for ascending melodic lines, themes which thrust upward toward the heights, the regular progression which is endowed with an ascending force, is very characteristic. It even strikes the eyes if one examines at random any page in his scores. The string quartet constantly makes use of themes which climb the steps of an invisible staircase, one by one, slowly, but with assurance toward the light and seem to pull away from the mysterious chains which hold them back.

And shouldn't we salute the heroic fidelity that he kept to the last in the areas of his thinking, feeling and writing, to his developmental procedures by cell division, by melodic transposition, by echoes, by his employment of old modes not adopted as rigid scales but utilized in brief touches for color and in order to free himself from the tyranny of Major and Minor?

His string quartet tells us all of this, and the listener—without deciding—will understand it. But still there will have to be quartet players of talent worthy of performing it for us. Let us take it out of the shrine where the Fauréans of my generation have too piously locked it up. Let us allow it to breathe fresh air like a quartet of Haydn, Mozart, or Beethoven, and it will become a classic in its turn. Then it will lose its sad aura and echo from beyond the grave. And what sincere friend of Gabriel Fauré would not rejoice in seeing this artist of genius take leave of us with a bountiful smile on his lips?

Having come to the end of the homage I proposed to offer to Gabriel Fauré, I feel again overcome by the same melancholy I experienced writing the first sentence of this book. By pleasurably plunging my hands into the treasure chest where the gems chiseled by this incomparable jeweler are found, marveling at their splendor, handling them one after the other, watching them sparkle, and constantly discovering new riches, I had managed to forget the heartfelt shock I had experienced at the beginning of my task. I felt it again at the moment when it was finished. The more one realizes the magnificence of Fauré's genius, the more one suffers in seeing the profundity of the abyss which separated, until now, this exceptional being from the rest of humanity and still today banishes him in the history of our art to a position of "splendid isolation."

Furthermore, a feeling of remorse assails me. Considering the wall of incomprehensibility which his purest masterpieces have come up against, have I efficaciously served his glory by egotistically giving free rein to my enthusiasm? An Athenian, one day, demanded that Aristides be exiled simply because he was "tired of hearing him called, 'the Just One'!" Has not the spectacle of my fervor irritated readers who, having no explanation for it will be turned away from Fauré for the simple reason that they are "tired of hearing him called 'the Great One'?" Imagine, that with the best intentions in the world, I didn't seriously criticize a single one of his works. The most modest among them always contained enough charm, grace, ingenuity or learning to warrant my sympathy and support. People in general have always found this difficult to forgive.

Moreover, for all those who spontaneously or after following a methodical initiation have felt and understood Fauré's genius, his work has become a touchstone allowing them to reveal with certainty the degree of "musicality" that music lovers possess in their circle. For the person, amateur or professional, who admits to being insensitive or hostile to Fauré's artistry is afflicted with some pronounced deficiency in his perceptive powers. This person's sensitivity suffers from a localized paralysis. Instead of saying, "Tell me whom you love and I will tell you who you are," and as a matter of fact, certain tastes are revealed this way, Fauré's admirers flatter themselves in reaching a better result, psychologically, by saying, "Tell me whom you don't like."

Fauré's music belongs to the esthetic order of things, to a universe comparable to that of the position held by supersonic sounds in the science of acoustics. Fauréans pride themselves in having an extremely fine internal ear which can draw in what this or that friend does not perceive. And this is a pretention whose audacity is perfectly designed to exasperate their adversaries.

Because of this, Fauré's religious cult—for there is one—must now take refuge in small chapels instead of in temples worthy of it, since the taste which is now more and more widespread for "cerebral systems" in all of the arts directs the curiosity of new generations of scientists and explorers in a diametrically opposed direction.

A short time before his death, the creator of one of these systems, Arnold Schönberg, left us something to be retained and thought about. To someone who congratulated him on the success that his revolutionary technique had won for him, he answered with anxiety in his voice, "Yes, but will they be making *music?* . . ." The whole philosophy of the "case" for Fauré is contained in that reply. It shows us that Schönberg had, until the end, the wisdom of remaining faithful to that Verlainian saying that is too much scorned today, "Music above all things."

This saying was always Gabriel Fauré's. His music is nothing but music. It never borrowed anything from the sister arts. It owes nothing to literature and less to painting. In his association with the poets, he jealously protected all of music's rights. I am not afraid to confirm that the quality of a Fauré score, as measured in terms of pure music, is easily of a better grade than the most illustrious masterworks of our

156

time. It is perhaps this heavy concentration which constitutes an obstacle to its popularization for his music frightens audiences with lazy ears.

And it is precisely this peculiarity which makes Gabriel Fauré such a precious asset in the history of twentieth century French music. We have arrived at the crossroads in the history of universal art where the traditional dogmas of musical, pictorial, sculptural, and architectural techniques have been shaken loose from their foundations and when many words in our vocabulary have lost their original meaning. The word "music" is one of these. Today it is applied at random to all sorts of things which have no right to be called "music."

The most modest inventor of a new process of arranging notes on paper who substitutes the purely cerebral discipline of his calculated system for the collaboration and the control of his senses is convinced that he is making "music." And certain "laboratory technicians" who collect and mix vibrations to obtain "conglomerations" which furnish music with its raw construction materials, are too quickly taken for composers.

It would be absurd to prematurely discredit experiments and investigations which could result in great discoveries and bring to our art a wealth of unsuspected means of expression. The greatest architects in the world cannot do without the help of excavators, cement mixers, and stone cutters. But building corporations do not imprudently change structural appearances. A man of genius will always rise up with the knowledge to spark life from these inert materials. While waiting for this, it would be wise not to compound misconceptions by incorrectly using the term "music" indiscriminately.

At the beginning of the century, the brilliant mastery of a Fauré, of a Debussy and of a Ravel, the prodigious refinement of their technique, the unheard of subtlety of their language made their disciples uneasy because they sensed in this new style a dictatorial danger analogous to the threatening one which Wagner had represented. A few years before, in the

157

theater, the young composers impatient to turn over that page of French musical history hastened to make a declaration that this brilliant experiment was definitely at an end and outdated. One of their spokesmen penned this rallying cry: "And now we need some barbarians!"

Only an Attila, they thought, could unburden us from those quintessential affectations, those demoded elegances, those anachronistic "suavities." Openly, they wanted works of "shock" appeal, "cruel" music, "evil" music in order to cure the public of its sentimentality and its perverse taste for charm, grace, and the exquisite.

This was evidently an easy solution. The call for violence was quickly heard and gathered adherents. Some were fanatics, happy to rid themselves of the insupportable technical disciplines and anxious to kick up a row with impunity. But this revolutionary movement rapidly ran its course in the most unforeseen way. Instead of the wished-for Huns, one saw coming to the fore young men in glasses, studious, meticulous, and passionately devoted to mathematical theories, systems, abstract problems and procedures capable of imbuing music with a "cerebralism," and making the intervention of "talent" unnecessary in the creative act. In a word, it was a matter of creating music as if it were a science, not an art, by imposing on it conventions a lot more arbitrary than the original ones. This new postulate was, theoretically, a defendable one, but it was also the proclaimed intention of these reformers to take leave of their elders and to convince us to break all contact with the past without further ado.

It was to ask a very great sacrifice of us without any counter offer, only vague promises. There exists an enormous number of composers who never wanted to be cured of barbarisms, and barbarians who were to generate a rich musical style. The latter wanted, logically, to preserve the right of applying the expression "pure music" to the "A" of an inaudible tuning fork, which, from one century to the next, masters of all times and styles have used for tuning. It is its intangible sense, what harmonists call the "common sound," which closely binds creators as different as Bach, Mozart, Schumann, Chopin, Wagner, Moussorgsky, Stravinsky, Debussy, Ravel, Schönberg and Alban Berg to each other.

This "A", this common note, can be heard vibrating on every page of Fauré's scores but with an exceptional intensity and purity. Until now, no conqueror has gone as far as he along the labyrinth of discovery without ever losing contact with Ariadne's thread. Musical language has undergone, from the beginning of the century, a syntactical revolution and structural upheaval which have been more profound than the one which is taking place now. In showing us as he has done that "music" can suffer earthquakes without going against the laws of evolution, *natura non facit saltus,* Fauré has left us a tremendous example and an important lesson.

Until the day when the Messiah or a new Evangelism will have come to show us by deeds that what he brings us merits the abandoning of everything we had until now called "music," let us not commit the imprudent error of letting such a beautiful prize slip furtively from our hands.

❧ The Compositions of Gabriel Fauré

() denotes type of music and name of poet or librettist where applicable

c. 1865

Le Papillon et la fleur, Op. 1, No. 1 (song; Victor Hugo)
Mai, Op. 1, No. 2 (song; Victor Hugo)
Dans les ruines d'une abbaye, Op. 2, No. 1 (song; Victor Hugo)
Les Matelots, Op. 2, No. 2 (song; Théophile Gautier)
Seule!, Op. 3, No. 1 (song; Théophile Gautier)
Sérénade toscane, Op. 3, No. 2 (song; Romain Bussine)
Chanson du pêcheur, Op. 4, No. 1 (song; Théophile Gautier)
Lydia, Op. 4, No. 2 (song; Leconte de Lisle)
Chant d'automne, Op. 5, No. 1 (song; Charles Baudelaire)
Rêve d'amour, Op. 5, No. 2 (song; Victor Hugo)
L'Absent, Op. 5, No. 3 (song; Victor Hugo)
Aubade, Op. 6, No. 1 (song; Louis Pommey)
Tristesse, Op. 6, No. 2 (song; Théophile Gautier)
Sylvie, Op. 6, No. 3 (song; Paul de Choudens)
Après un rêve, Op. 7, No. 1 (song; Romain Bussine)
Hymne, Op. 7, No. 2 (song; Charles Baudelaire)
Barcarolle, Op. 7, No. 3 (song; Marc Monnier)
Au bord de l'eau, Op. 8, No. 1 (song; Armand Sully-Prudhomme)

La Rançon, Op. 8, No. 2 (song; Charles Baudelaire)
Ici-bas, Op. 8, No. 3 (song; Armand Sully-Prudhomme)

1863 (?)

Trois Romances sans paroles, Op. 17 (piano)

c. 1870

Puisqu'ici-bas, Op. 10, No. 1 (duet for two sopranos; Victor Hugo)
Tarentelle, Op. 10, No. 2 (duet for two sopranos; Marc Monnier)

c. 1871

Ave Maria, no opus number (three male voices)

c. 1873

Cantique de Jean Racine, Op. 11 (chorus, harmonium and string quartet or orchestra)

c. 1875

Les Djinns, Op. 12 (chorus and orchestra; Victor Hugo)

1875

Suite, Op. 20 (orchestra)
Allegro symphonique, Op. 68 (orchestra; first movement of the Suite, Op. 20)

1876

Sonata No. 1 for Violin and Piano in A Major, Op. 13

Concerto for Violin and Orchestra, Op. 14 (incomplete)

Piano Quartet No. 1 in C Minor, Op. 15

Souvenirs de Bayreuth, no opus number (piano four hands; composed with André Messager)

Berceuse, Op. 16 (violin and piano)
Nell, Op. 18, No. 1 (song; Leconte de Lisle)
Le Voyageur, Op. 18, No. 2 (song; Armand Silvestre)
Automne, Op. 18, No. 3 (song; Armand Silvestre)

Ballade for Piano and Orchestra, Op. 19
Poème d'un jour, Op. 21 (songs; Charles Grandmougin)
      Rencontre, Op. 21, No. 1
      Toujours, Op. 21, No. 2
      Adieu, Op. 21, No. 3
Le Ruisseau, Op. 22 (two-part women's chorus; Anon.)

Les Berceaux, Op. 23, No. 1 (song; Armand Sully-Pru-dhomme)
Notre amour, Op. 23, No. 2 (song; Armand Silvestre)
Le Secret, Op. 23, No. 3 (song; Armand Silvestre)
Romance for Violin and Orchestra, Op. 28

La Naissance du Vénus, Op. 29 (soloists, chorus and orchestra; Paul Collin)

1883

Élégie, Op. 24 (cello and piano)
Impromptu No. 1 in E flat Major, Op. 25 (piano)
Barcarolle No. 1 in A Minor, Op. 26 (piano)
Chanson d'amour, Op. 27, No. 1 (song; Armand Silvestre)
La Fée aux chansons, Op. 27, No. 2 (song; Armand Silvestre)
Valse-Caprice No. 1 in A Major, Op. 30 (piano)
Impromptu No. 2 in F Minor, Op. 31 (piano)
Mazurka in B flat Major, Op. 32 (piano)
Trois Nocturnes, Op. 33 (piano)
      Nocturne No. 1 in E flat Minor, Op. 33, No. 1
      Nocturne No. 2 in B Major, Op. 33, No. 2
      Nocturne No. 3 in A flat Major, Op. 33, No. 3
Impromptu No. 3 in A flat Major, Op. 34 (piano)

1884 (?)

Tu es Petrus, no opus number (soloists and chorus)

1884

Madrigal, Op. 35 (soprano, alto, tenor and bass soloists or four-part chorus and orchestra; Armand Silvestre)
Nocturne No. 4 in E flat Major, Op. 36 (piano)
Nocturne No. 5 in B flat Major, Op. 37 (piano)
Valse-Caprice No. 2 in D flat Major, Op. 38 (piano)
Aurore, Op. 39, No. 1 (song; Armand Silvestre)
Fleur jetée, Op. 39, No. 2 (song; Armand Silvestre)
Le Pays des rêves, Op. 39, No. 3 (song; Armand Silvestre)
Les Roses d'Ispahan, Op. 39, No. 4 (song; Leconte de Lisle)
Symphony in D Minor, Op. 40

Barcarolle No. 2 in G Major, Op. 41 (piano)
Barcarolle No. 3 in G flat Major, Op. 42 (piano)

Noël, Op. 43, No. 1 (song; Victor Wilder)
Nocturne, Op. 43, No. 2 (song; Villiers de l'Isle-Adam)
Barcarolle No. 4 in A flat Major, Op. 44 (piano)
Piano Quartet No. 2 in G Minor, Op. 45

Les Présents, Op. 46, No. 1 (song; Villiers de l'Isle-Adam)
Clair de lune, Op. 46, No. 2 (song; Paul Verlaine)
Two offertories, Op. 47
        O salutaris, Op. 47, No. 1 (voice and organ)
            Maria, Mater gratiae, Op. 47, No. 2 (two voices and
                organ)
Messe de Requiem, Op. 48 (soprano, baritone, chorus, or-
    chestra and organ)
Pavane, Op. 50 (chorus and orchestra; Anon.)

Caligula, Op. 52—incidental music to the play by Alexandre
    Dumas fils.

Larmes, Op. 51, No. 1 (song; Jean Richepin)
Au cimetière, Op. 51, No. 2 (song; Jean Richepin)
Spleen, Op. 51, No. 3 (song; Paul Verlaine)
La Rose, Op. 51, No. 4 (song; Leconte de Lisle)

Petite Pièce, Op. 49 (cello and piano)
Shylock, Op. 57—incidental music to the play by Edmond
    Haraucourt after Shakespeare (orchestra)

c. 1890

Ecce fidelus servus, Op. 54 (soprano, tenor, baritone, organ
    and double-bass)
Tantum ergo, Op. 55 (soloist and chorus)

1890

Cinq Mélodies, Op. 58 (songs; Paul Verlaine)
    Mandoline, Op. 58, No. 1
    En sourdine, Op. 58, No. 2
    Green, Op. 58, No. 3
    A Clymène, Op. 58, No. 4
    C'est l'extase, Op. 58, No. 5
En prière, no opus number (song; Stéphane Bordèse)
La Passion, no opus number (chorus and orchestra; Edmond
    Haraucourt)

1891

Valse-Caprice No. 3 in G flat Major, Op. 59 (piano)

1892

La Bonne Chanson, Op. 61 (song; Paul Verlaine)
    Une Sainte en son auréole, Op. 61, No. 1
    Puisque l'aube grandit, Op. 61, No. 2
    La lune blanche luit dans les bois, Op. 61, No. 3
    J'allais par des chemins perfides, Op. 61, No. 4
    J'ai presque peur, en verité, Op. 61, No. 5

Avant que tu ne t'en ailles, Op. 61, No. 6
Donc, ce sera par un clair jour d'été, Op. 61, No. 7
N'est-ce pas?, Op. 61, No. 8
L'hiver a cessé, Op. 61, No. 9

c. 1894

Nocturne No. 6 in D flat Major, Op. 63 (piano)
Two Offertories, Op. 65
    Ave, verum corpus, Op. 65, No. 1 (two women's voices
      or women's chorus)
    Tantum ergo, Op. 65, No. 2 (three-part women's chorus)

1894

Hymne à Appolo, Op. 63a (harmonization of 2nd Century B.C.
    melody restored by Theodore Reinach, words restored
    by H. Weil)
Valse-Caprice No. 4 in A flat Major, Op. 62 (piano)

c. 1895

Barcarolle No. 5 in F sharp Minor, Op. 66 (piano)
Two Offertories, Op. 67 (voice and organ)
    Salve regina, Op. 67, No. 1
    Ave Maria, Op. 67, No. 2
Romance in A Major, Op. 69 (cello and piano)

c. 1896

Pleurs d'or, Op. 72 (mezzo-soprano and baritone; Albert
    Samain)

1896

Barcarolle No. 6 in E flat Major, Op. 70 (piano)
Dolly, Op. 56 (suite for piano four hands; later orchestrated
    by Henri Rabaud)

Thème et variations in C sharp Minor, Op. 73 (piano)

Nocturne No. 7 in C sharp Minor, Op. 74 (piano)
Andante, Op. 75 (violin and piano)
Le Parfum impérissable, Op. 76, No. 1 (song; Leconte de Lisle)
Arpège, Op. 76, No. 2 (song; Albert Samain)
Papillon, Op. 77 (cello and piano)
Sicilienne, Op. 78 (cello and piano)
Fantaisie, Op. 79 (flute and piano)
Pelléas et Mélisande, Op. 80—incidental music to the play by Maurice Maeterlinck (orchestra)

Prométhée, Op. 82 (opera; Jean Lorrain and F. A. Hérold)
Prison, Op. 83, No. 1 (song; Paul Verlaine)
Soir, Op. 83, No. 2 (song; Albert Samain)

Le Voile du Bonheur, Op. 88—incidental music to the play by Georges Clemenceau (orchestra)

Huit Pièces brèves, Op. 84 (piano; begun in 1898)
    Capriccio in E flat Major, Op. 84, No. 1
    Fantaisie in A flat Major, Op. 84, No. 2
    Fugue in A Minor, Op. 84, No. 3
    Adagietto in E Minor, Op. 84, No. 4
    Improvisation in C sharp Minor, Op. 84, No. 5

Fugue in E Minor, Op. 84, No. 6
Allégresse in C Major, Op. 84, No. 7
Nocturne No. 8 in D flat Major, Op. 84, No. 8

1903

Dans le forêt de septembre, Op. 85, No. 1 (song; Catulle Mendès)
La Fleur qui va sur l'eau, Op. 85, No. 2 (song; Catulle Mendès)
Accompagnement, Op. 85, No. 3 (song; Albert Samain)

1904

Impromptu, Op. 86 (harp)
Le Plus doux chemin, Op. 87, No. 1 (song; Armand Silvestre)
Le Ramier, Op. 87, No. 2 (song; Armand Silvestre)

1905 (?)

Tantum ergo, no opus number (soprano, tenor and chorus)

1906

Piano Quintet No. 1 in D Minor, Op. 89
Barcarolle No. 7 in D Minor, Op. 90 (piano)
Impromptu No. 4 in D flat—C sharp Major, Op. 91 (piano)
Le Don silencieux, Op. 92 (song; Jean Dominique)
Ave Maria, Op. 93 (two voices and organ)

1907

Chanson, Op. 94 (song; Henri de Régnier)
Vocalise, no opus number (song; no words)

Barcarolle No. 8 in D flat Major, Op. 96 (piano)
Nocturne No. 9 in B Minor-Major, Op. 97 (piano)
Sérénade, Op. 98 (cello and piano)

1909

Nocturne No. 10 in E Minor, Op. 99 (piano)

1910

Barcarolle No. 9 in A Minor, Op. 101 (piano)
Impromptu No. 5 in F sharp Minor, Op. 102 (piano)
La Chanson d'Ève, Op. 95 (songs; Charles van Lerberghe)
>   *Paradis, Op. 95, No. 1*
>   *Prima verba, Op. 95, No. 2*
>   *Roses ardentes, Op. 95, No. 3*
>   *Comme Dieu rayonne, Op. 95, No. 4*
>   *L'Aube blanche, Op. 95, No. 5*
>   *Eau vivante, Op. 95, No. 6*
>   *Veilles-tu, ma senteur de soleil?, Op. 95, No. 7*
>   *Dans un parfum de roses blanches, Op. 95, No. 8*
>   *Crépuscule, Op. 95, No. 9*
>   *O Mort, poussière d'étoiles, Op. 95, No. 10*

1911

Neuf Préludes, Op. 103 (piano; begun in 1910)

1913

Nocturne No. 11 in F sharp Minor, Op. 104, No. 1 (piano)
Barcarolle No. 10 in A Minor, Op. 104, No. 2 (piano)
Impromptu No. 6 in D flat Major, Op. 86b (piano; transcribed
>   from harp solo, Op. 68)
Pénélope, no opus number (opera; René Fauchois)

Barcarolle No. 11 in G Minor, Op. 105, No. 1 (piano)

Barcarolle No. 12 in E flat Major, Op. 105, No. 2 (piano)
Nocturne No. 12 in E Minor, Op. 107 (piano)

Sonata No. 2 for Violin and Piano in E Minor, Op. 108

Sonata No. 1 for Cello and Piano in D Minor, Op. 109
Une Châtelaine en sa tour, Op. 110 (harp)
Le Jardin clos, Op. 106 (songs; Charles van Lerberghe)
    Exaucement, Op. 106, No. 1
    Quand tu plonges tes yeux dans mes yeux, Op. 106, No. 2
    La Messagère, Op. 106, No. 3
    Je me poserai sur ton coeur, Op. 106, No. 4
    Dans la nymphée, Op. 106, No. 5
    Dans la pénombre, Op. 106, No. 6
    Il m'est cher, Amour, Op. 106, No. 7
    Inscription sur le sable, Op. 106, No. 8

Fantaisie in G Major, Op. 111 (piano and orchestra)
Mirages, Op. 113 (songs; Baronne de Brimont)
    Cygne sur l'eau, Op. 113, No. 1
    Reflets dans l'eau, Op. 113, No. 2
    Jardin nocturne, Op. 113, No. 3
    Danseuse, Op. 113, No. 4

Masques et bergamasques, Op. 112—incidental music to the play by René Fauchois; also an orchestral suite (orchestra)

C'est la paix, Op. 114 (song; begun in 1919; Georgette Debladis)

Piano Quintet No. 2 in C Minor, Op. 115
Barcarolle No. 13 in C Major, Op. 116 (piano)
Chant funérarie, no opus number (military band)

Sonata No. 2 for Cello and Piano in G Minor, Op. 117
L'Horizon chimérique, Op. 118 (songs; Jean de la Ville de Mirmont)
    La Mer est infinie, Op. 118, No. 1
    Je me suis embarqué, Op. 118, No. 2
    Diane, Séléné, Op. 118, No. 3
    Vaisseaux, nous vous aurons aimés, Op. 118, No. 4
Nocturne No. 13 in B Minor, Op. 119

Trio in D Minor, Op. 120 (violin, cello and piano)

String Quartet in E Minor, Op. 121

Messe basse, no opus number, is believed to be an early composition (three women's voices and organ)

Discography

by Steven Smolian

It was not always possible to give complete information on certain records as the catalogues and, even more surprisingly, the records themselves do not always list the names of all performers.

I received invaluable assistance from a number of persons in compiling this discography. Particular thanks are due David Hall, Marion Grady and Jeff Cobb of the Rodgers and Hammerstein Archive of the New York Public Library, Jerrold Moore and Richard Warren of the Historical Sound Recordings Collection at Yale University and James Smart at the Library of Congress. Mary Alice Wotring of Columbia Records and Scott Mampie of Mercury-Phillips were helpful in gathering information from their respective companies. Gregor Benko and Albert Petrak of the International Piano Library supplied much data, particularly concerning piano rolls. Finally, I am beholden to Thomas Clear for granting me access to his superb record collection. They have helped me fill many gaps and correct errors. Those which remain are mine.

STEVEN SMOLIAN
New York City
1969

USING THIS DISCOGRAPHY

Every composition by Fauré is listed in this discography. The arrangement is by type of composition and the categories are: *Orchestral Works, Stage Works, Instrumental and Chamber Music, Piano Music, Songs* and *Vocal Ensembles and Choral Music.*

Each composition is listed by its full title together with the name of poets and/or librettists where applicable and the date of composition. In compositions for solo instrument and accompaniment, the soloist is named first. Works for voice(s) and orchestra differ only in that the conductor is the first named.

This discography also indicates the date the recording was released to the public.

ABBREVIATIONS

Performer(s) column

arr.	arrangement
(b)	baritone
(bs)	bass
cho.	chorus
cond.	conductor
(m-s)	mezzo-soprano
O.	orchestra (if not preceded by a name, ensemble is otherwise unidentified)
orch.	orchestration

org.	organ
p.	piano or pianist
Phil.	Philharmonic
(s)	soprano
S.O.	Symphony Orchestra
unid.	unidentified
vclo.	cello
vla.	viola
vln.	violin

Record label column

Academy	Academy (United States)
ACol	Columbia (United States)
ADec	Decca (United States)
AeolMet	Aeolian Metrostyle (United States)
Allegro	Allegro (United States)
Alpha	Alpha (France)
Ampico	Ampico (United States)
Ang	Angel (United States)
APhil	Philips (United States)
ArcP	Archive of Piano Music (United States)
Argo	Argo (Great Britain)
ATel	Telefunken (Austria)
Atl	Atlantic (United States)
AVox	Vox (United States)
BàM	Boîte à Musique (France)
Baroque	Baroque (United States)
Boston	Boston (United States)
Camb	Cambridge (United States)
Carillon	Carillon (United States)
Cap	Capitol (United States)
CBS	C.B.S. (Europe)

CCol	Columbia (Continental Europe)
CdM	Chant du Monde (France)
CHMV	H.M.V. (Continental Europe)
Clc	Classic (France)
ClubND	Club National du Disque (France)
COLC COLH	These are designations for certain Gramophone Company releases, usually reissues, intended for collectors. The final letter of the four indicates the original source of the material—COLC (Columbia) or COLH (H.M.V.)
Comm	Command (United States)
ConH	Concert Hall (United States)
CVic	R.C.A. Victor (Canada)
Dam	Damon (United States)
Dec	Decca (European)

DGG	Deutsche Grammophon (The same catalog number was used on a number of labels—Grammophon, Polydor, Musica, Siemen's Speziale, etc.)	Lon	London (United States)
		LonInt	London International (United States)
		Lumen	Lumen (France)
		McInt	McIntosh (United States)
		Merc	Mercury (United States)
DucTh	Ducretet-Thomson (France)	Metr	Metronome (Denmark)
		MGM	M.G.M. (United States)
Duo-Art	Duo-Art (United States)	MK	Mezhdunarodnaya Kniga (Soviet Union)
ECol	Columbia (Great Britain)		
Edison	Edison (United States)	Monitor	Monitor (United States)
EHMV	H.M.V. (Great Britain)	MusL	Music Library (United States)
EJS	E.J.S. Golden Age of Opera (United States) (Private distribution)		
		Nixa	Nixa (Great Britain)
		None	Nonesuch (United States)
Elec	Electrola (West Germany)	Oce	Oceanic (United States)
EPhil	Philips (Great Britain)	Od	Odeon (Europe)
Epic	Epic (United States)	OL	L'Oiseau Lyre (France)
Erato	Erato (France)	Orph	Orphee (France)
Euro	Euro-Cord (France)	Oryx	Oryx (Great Britain)
Ever	Everest (United States)	Pacific	Pacific (France)
FCol	Columbia (France)	Parl	Parlophone (Europe)
FDec	Decca (France)	Pathé	Pathé (France)
FDGG	Deutsche Grammophon (France)	Per	Period (United States)
		Phil	Philips (European)
Fest	Festival (United States)	Plé	Pléiade (France)
FEY	Foundation Eugene Ysaye (Belgium)	Polym	Polymusic (United States)
		Pro	Pro Musica (France)
FFest	Festival (France)	Pye	Pye (Great Britain)
FHMV	H.M.V. (France)	Qual	Qualitone (Hungary)
Folk	Folkways (United States)	Radio	Radiola (Hungary)
Fono	Fonotipia (Italy)	RCA	R.C.A. (Europe)
FParl	Parlophone (France)	Rem	Remington (United States)
FPhil	Philips (France)		
FRCA	R.C.A. (France)	Royale	Royale (United States)
GColos	Colloseum (Germany)	Saga	Saga (Great Britain)
GHMV	H.M.V. (Germany)	Saturn	Saturn (France)
GoCr	Golden Crest (United States)	Schirmer	Schirmer (United States)
		Selmer	Selmer (France)
HMundi	Harmonia Mundi (West Germany)	Silv	Silvertone (United States)
		SM	Studio Musical (France)
H.M.V.	H.M.V. (International)	Strad	Stradivarius (United States)
Iramac	Iramac (France)		
IRCC	International Record Collectors' Club (United States)	Sup	Supraphone (Czechoslovakia)
		SwHMV	H.M.V. (Switzerland)
JCol	Columbia (Japan)	Tech	Technichord (United States)
JVic	Victor (Japan)		

176

Tele	Telefunken (Germany)	Vega	Véga (France)
Tri-Erg	Tri-Ergon (Germany)	Vic	R.C.A. Victor (United States)
Turn	Turnabout (United States)	Vox	Vox (International)
Ult	Ultraphone (France)	Welte	Welte (Germany)
Uran	Urania (United States)	West	Westminster (United States)
Valois	Valois (France)	Zodiak	Zodiak (United States)
Vang	Vanguard (United States)		

Date column

RR	Re-recording; electrically transferred from one disc to another.		from master tapes, issued at more than one speed or on more than one size.
RI	Reissue from the original master. Includes copies		

Size and Speed column

LP	Long play, 33⅓ rpm record	45	45 rpm record
S	Stereo, 33⅓ rpm record	PR	piano roll
78	78 rpm record	C	cylinder
78a	78 rpm record, acoustic process	V	vertical cut "hill-and-dale" disc

177

ORCHESTRAL WORKS

Allegro symphonique, Op. 68 (1875) (No. 1 of *Suite, Op. 20*, otherwise unpublished)
No recordings traced

Ballade in F sharp Minor for Piano and Orchestra, Op. 19 (1881)

COMPOSITION AND PERFORMER(S)	RECORD LABEL AND NUMBER	DATE	SPEED
G. Bachauer, A. Sherman, London O.	EHMV CLP-1089	1956	12" LP
G. Casadesus, M. Rosenthal, Lamoureux O.	FDGG 566.278/9	1949	12" 78
	Vox set 645		
	Vox PL-6450		
R. Casadesus, L. Bernstein, New York Phil.	ACol ML 5777, CBS BRG-72015	1962	12" LP
	ACol MS-6377, CBS SBRG-72015	1962	12" S
V. Devetzi, S. Baudo, Paris Conservatoire O.	None 71178	1966	12" S
G. Doyen, J. Fournet, Lamoureux O.	Phil N-00704L	1956	10" LP
	Epic LC-3057	1956	12" LP
G. Farago, J. Ferencsik, Budapest Phil. O.	Radio SP-8011/2	1947	12" 78
G. Johannesen, W. Goehr, Netherlands Phil. O.	ConH CHS-1181	1954	12" LP
K. Long, B. Neel, New S.O.	Dec K-1130/1	1945	12" 78
K. Long, J. Martinon, London Phil. O.	Lon LL-1058, Dec LXT-2963	1954	12" LP
M. Long, P. Gaubert, O.	ACol 68618/9 in set X-62, FCol LFX-54/5	1930	12" 78
M. Long, A. Cluytens, Paris Conservatoire O.	FCol LX-8953/4	1952	12" 78
	FCol 30354, Ang 35013, FCol FCX-169	RI	12" LP
M. Tagliafero, P. Coppola, O.	FHMV W-894/5	1931	12" 78

Composition and Performer(s)	Record Label and Number	Date	Speed
Chant funéraire for military band (1921) (no opus number)			
J. Maillot, Musique des Équipages	DucTh 225-C-072	1959	10" LP
Concerto for Violin and Orchestra, Op. 14 (1878) (incomplete work)			
No recordings traced			
Fantaisie in G Major for Piano and Orchestra, Op. 111 (1919)			
F. Blumenthal, R. Schwarz, Philharmonia O.	FCol FC-1072	1952	10" LP
G. Casadesus, E. Bigot, Pro Musica O.	Vox PL-1780	1950	10" LP
G. Doyen, J. Fournet, Lamoureux O.	HMV DB-1233/4	1949	12" 78
G. Johannesen, E. Goosens, London S.O.	Cap G-7132, EHMV CLP-1255	1959	12" LP
Masques et bergamasques, Op. 112 (suite) (1920) : *1. Overture, 2. Minuet, 3. Gavotte, 4. Pastorale*			
—Complete suite			
E. Ansermet, Suisse Romande O.	Lond 9289, Dec LXT-5667	1962	12" LP
	Lond 6227, Dec SXL-2303	1962	12" S
M. Gaillard, O.	Od 188.929/30	1947	10" 78
W. Goehr, Netherlands Phil. O.	ConH G-9, RG-119	1953	12" LP
H. Tomassi, Lamoureux O.	Pathé PD-120/1	1950	10" 78
G. Tzipine, Paris Opéra-Comique O.	Ang 35311, CCol 33CX-1577	1957	12" LP
A. Winograd, Hamburg Phil. O.	MGM E-3434, E-3518	1957	12" LP
—*No. 1. Overture*			
A. Bernard, London Chamber O.	EHMV B-10562	1953	10" 78
D. Inghelbrecht, Pasdeloup O.	EHMV 7EP-7001	1953	7" 45
	Pathé X-5534	1931	10" 78

179

Composition and Performer(s)	Record Label and Number	Date	Speed
No. 3. Gavotte			
D. Inghelbrecht, Pasdeloup O.	Pathé X-5534	1931	10" 78
Pavane, Op. 50 for chorus and orchestra ad. lib. (1887)			
R. Agoult, New S.O. (no cho.)	Vic LM-2326, RCA RD-27156	1959	12" LP
	Vic LSC-2326, RCA SB-5054	1959	12" S
T. Beecham, French National Radio O. (no cho.)	Ang Sera 60000, HMV ALP-1968	1963	12" LP
	Ang Sera S-60000, HMV ASD-518	1963	12" S
A. Bernard, London Chamber O. & Cho.	EHMV C-4197	1952	12" 78
	EHMV 7EP-7001	1952	7" 45
W. Damrosch, National S.O. (no cho.)	Vic 7323	1930	12" 78
E. Kurtz, Houston S.O. (no cho.)	ACol 13073-D in set MX-336	1950	12" 78
J. Martinon, Lamoureux O. (no cho.)	Epic LC-3058	1955	12" LP
	Phil A-00175L	1955	10" LP
C. Munch, Paris Conservatoire O. (no cho.)	Dec K-1644	1947	12" 78
P. Paray, Detroit S.O. (no cho.)	Merc MG-50029	1954	12" LP
M. Sargent, Philharmonia O. & Cho.	ACol 72707-D, ECol DX-1369	1947	12" 78
D. Willcocks, New Philharmonia O. & Cho.	EHMV ASD-2358	1967	12" S
—arr. Piano (Fauré)			
G. Fauré	AeolMet 65303	pre-1905	PR
G. Fauré	Welte 2772	1913	PR
—arr. Two Guitars			
Pompino-Zarate	Vic LM-2717	1965	12" LP
	Vic LSC-2717	1965	12" S

Composition and Performer(s)	Record Label and Number	Date	Speed

Romance for Violin and Orchestra, Op. 28 (1882)
No recordings traced

Suite for Orchestra, Op. 20 (1875)
Unpublished (see *Allegro symphonique, Op. 68*)

Symphony in D Minor, Op. 40 (1884)
Unpublished

STAGE WORKS

Caligula, Op. 52. Incidental music for the tragedy of Alexandre
Dumas, *fils* (1888)
No recordings traced

Masques et bergamasques, Op. 112. A stage entertainment (opera)
by René Fauchois (1919)
No recordings traced

La Passion. Prologue to the drama of Edmond Haraucourt for
chorus and orchestra (1890)
Unpublished

Pelléas et Mélisande, Op. 80. Incidental music to the drama of
Maurice Maeterlinck (1898)
1. *Prélude,* 2. *Fileuses,* 3. *Sicilienne,* 4. *Molto adagio* (No. 3
is the *Sicilienne for Cello and Piano, Op. 78,* orchestrated by
Charles Koechlin for insertion herein)

181

Composition and Performer(s)	Record Label and Number	Date	Speed
—Complete suite			
E. Ansermet, Suisse Romande O.	Lon 9289, Dec LXT-5567	1962	12" LP
	Lon 6227, Dec SXL-2303	1962	12" S
J. Barbirolli, Hallé O.	CHMV ALP-1244	1955	12" LP
S. Baudo, Paris Conservatoire O.	None 71178, CdM LDX-8330	1964	12" LP
	None 71178, CdM LDX-48330	1964	12" S
P. le Conte, Paris Opéra O.	Cap P-8311,	1955	12" LP
J. Fournet, Lamoureux O.	Epic LC-3165	1956	12" LP
	Phil N-00737R	1956	10" LP
J. Giardino, Concerts Colonne O.	Pathé PAT-153/4	1940	12" 78
D. Inghelbrecht, Champs Elysées O.	DucTh 270-C-082	1956	12" LP
S. Koussevitzky, Boston S.O. (no *Sicilienne*)	Vic 11-8345/6 in set M-941,		
	HMV ED-340/1	1943	12" 78
	Vic LCT-1152	RR	12" LP
C. Munch, London Phil. O.	Dec AK-1740/1 in set EDA-58	1948	12" 78
C. Munch, Philadelphia O.	ACol ML-5923	1964	12" LP
	ACol MS-6523	1964	12" S
P. Paray, Detroit S.O.	Merc 50035, 14009	1954	12" LP
	Merc 18009,	1954	12" S
G. Poulet, London S.O.	MGM E-3116, E-3518,		
	Parl PMC-1016	1954	12" LP
G. Sebastian, Concerts Colonne O.	Uran 7097, Nixa ULP-9097	1953	12" LP
G. Tzipine, Paris Opéra-Comique O.	Ang 35311, CCol 33CX-1577	1959	12" LP
—No. 1. *Prélude*			
A. Wolff, Berlin Phil. O.	DGG 66725, FDGG 516.648,		
	Dec CA-8229	1928	12" 78

Composition and Performer(s)	Record Label and Number	Date	Speed
——arr. Band Garde Républicaine Band	FHMV W-297	1922	12″ 78
—No. 2. *Fileuses* G. Enesco, O.	Silvertone 47 Merc MG-10021	1947 RR	12″ 78 12″ LP
A. Wolff, Berlin Phil. O.	DGG 66725, FDGG 516.648, Dec CA-8229	1928	12″ 78
——arr. Band Garde Républicaine Band	FHMV W-297	1922	12″ 78
——arr. Violin and Piano R. Bas, pianist unid.	Parl 22.730	1930	10″ 78
——arr. Cello and Piano P. Fournier, E. Lush J. Serres, A. Leyvastre	Lon LL-700, Dec LXT-2766 Saturn MSA-5003	1952 1951	12″ LP 10″ LP
—No. 3. *Sicilienne* D. Defauw, Chicago S.O. P. Gaubert, Paris Conservatoire O.	Vic 11-9447 ACol 67577-D in set M-113, FCol 15052	1947 1929	12″ 78 12″ 78
A. Wolff, Berlin Phil. O.	DGG 66726, DGG 66727, FDGG 516.649, Dec CA-8230	1928	12″ 78
Pénélope. Lyric Drama in Three Acts by René Fauchois (1913) No recording of complete opera traced			
—Excerpts (c. one hour) D. Inghelbrecht, R. Crespin (s), R. Jobin (t), C. Gayraud (m-s), French National Radio O. & Cho.	EJS-324 (private issue)	1965	12″ LP

Composition and Performer(s)	Record Label and Number	Date	Speed
—Prélude			
E. Ansermet, Suisse Romande O.	Lon 9289, Dec LXT-5567	1962	12" LP
	Lon 6227, Dec SXL-2303	1962	12" S
J. Fournet, Concerts Colonne O.	Pathé PDT-185	1947	12" 78
—*Je l'attends, Minerva le protége* (I, iv)			
G. Cernay (m-s), G. Cloez, O.	Od 188.619	1930	10" 78
—*Danse* (I, iv)			
G. Cloez, O.	ADec 25815, Od 123.590	1930	12" 78
—*Vous m'avez fait qu'eveiller* (I, iv)			
G. Cernay (m-s), G. Cloez, O.	ADec 25815, Od 123.590	1930	12" 78
—*C'est sur ce banc* (II, ii)			
G. Cernay (m-s), G. Cloez, O.	Od 188.619	1930	10" 78
Prométhée, Op. 82. Lyric Tragedy by Jean Lorrain and F. A. Hérold (1900)			
No recording traced			
Shylock, Op. 57. Incidental music to the drama by Edmond Haraucourt after Shakespeare (1889)			
—Complete, Nos. 1-6			
M. Levine, Y. Duval (t), Strasbourg Festival O.	Saga XID-5104	1961	12" LP
H. Steinke, F. Widemann (t), Hamburg Phil.O.	MGM E-3520	1958	12" LP
—*Orchestra suite* (Nos. 2, 4, 5, 6)			
P. Coppola, Paris Conservatoire O.	FHMV DA-4823/4	1932	10" 78

Composition and Performer(s)	Record Label and Number	Date	Speed
—No. 1. Chanson, *Oh! les filles!* J. Dutey (t), T. Janapoulo, p.	West XWN-18213 in set 5502, Plé P-3062 DucTh 270-C-082 BaM-31 Col DF-2542 Od 188.558	1956 1956 1940 1937 1931	12″ LP 12″ LP 12″ 78 10″ 78 10″ 78
H. Legay (t), D. Inghelbrecht, Champs Elysées O. Y. le Marc' Hadour (b), Mme. le Marc' Hadour, p. P. de Seyguières (t), J. Witkowsky, O. M. Villabella (t), G. Cloez, O.			
—No. 2. *Entr'acte* Not individually recorded			
—No. 3. Madrigal, *Celle que j'aime a de beauté* J. Dutey (t), T. Janopoulo, p.	West XWN-18213 in set 5502 Plé P-3062	1956	12″ LP
H. Legay (t), D. Inghelbrecht, Champs Elysées O. P. de Seyguières (t), J. Witkowsky, O. G. Souzay (b), D. Baldwin, p.	DucTh 270-C-082 Col DF-2542 EPhil. AL-3505, FPhil. L-2405L EPhil. SAL-3505, FPhil. 835.286LY	1956 1937 1966 1966	12″ LP 10″ 78 12″ LP 12″ S
—arr. Chorus and Orchestra R. Ducasse, French Teachers Cho., O.	Pathé X-3461	1930	10″ 78
—No 4. *Epithalame* Not individually recorded			
—No. 5. *Nocturne* J. Barbirolli, Hallé O. P. Gaubert, Paris Conservatoire O.	HMV B-9567, HMV AA-371 ACol 68960-D in set X-75 ECol LX-654, FCol LFX-465	1947 1936 1936	10″ 78 12″ 78 12″ 78

Composition and Performer(s)	Record Label and Number	Date	Speed
T. Schippers, Columbia S.O.	ACol ML-5664 ACol MS-6164	1960 1960	12" LP 12" S
—arr. Cello ond Piano P. Fournier, T. Janopoulo J. Witkowsky, E. Cornette, org.	FHMV DA-4957 FCol DF-714	1941 1933	10" 78 10" 78
—arr. Two Pianos (Gearhardt) V. Morley, L. Gearhardt	ACol ML-2197	1951	10" LP
—arr. Organ V. Fox	Comm 11025 Comm S-11025	1967 1967	12" LP 12" S
—No. 6. Finale Not individually recorded			
—Unid. excerpt: Marche R. Irving, London S.O.	HMV CLP-1571 HMV CSD-1444	1964 1964	12" LP 12" S

Le Voile du Bonheur, Op. 88. Incidental music to a play by Georges Clemenceau (1901)
No recordings traced

INSTRUMENTAL AND CHAMBER MUSIC

Composition and Performer(s)	Record Label and Number	Date	Speed
Andante for Violin and Piano, Op. 75 (1898) D. Soriano, M. Tagliafero Unid. violinist, G. Thyssens-Valentin	Pathé PAT-10 CdM CL-12	1934 1966	12" 78 12" S

Composition and Performer(s)	Record Label and Number	Date	Speed
Berceuse for Violin and Piano, Op. 16 (1880)			
G. Alès, F. Cebron, O.	Lumen 2.08.003, Lumen 30104	1937	10" 78
E. Bastide, Y. Lévy	Tri-Erg 10305	1930	12" 78
L. Bobesco, Guttman	Alpha DB-32	1960	12" LP
M. Boussinot, Defresne	FFest FLD-84	1958	12" LP
H. Bress, C. Reiner	Folk 3353	1962	12" LP
M. Chauveton, B. Anderson	Lumen LD-1.426	1958	7" 45
Y. Curti, G. Andolfi	Pathé X 9751	1929	10" 78
	Pathé 9751	1929	10" V
Y. Curti, pianist unid.	Pathé PA-283	1934	10" 78
M. Elman, J. Seiger	Vang 1173	1968	12" LP
	Vang 71173	1968	12" S
C. Fabrizzio, pianist unid.	Edison 80550	1920	10" Va
C. Ferras, P. Barbizet	Dec GAG-15099	1952	12" 78
C. Flesch, I. Strasfogel	GHMV EW-68	1929	10" 78
J. Gautier, pianist unid.	Od 166.039	1930	10" 78
A. Grumiaux, Hajdo	Phil A-02294L	1963	10" LP
Jarry, Klauffer	ClubND 40	1965	12" LP
J. Levey, pianist unid.	ECol 3163	1923	10" 78a
E. Mendels, accompanist unid.	Pathé 9501	1916	10" Va
I. Menges, E. Beatti	EHMV D-861, FHMV W-735	1925	12" 78a
H. Merkel, P. Coppola, Pasdeloup O.	FHMV L-1015	1932	12" 78
D. Nadien, D. Hancock	Monitor 2017	1961	12" LP
	Monitor S-2017	1961	12" S
L. Schwartz, L. Petijean	FHMV L-881	1930	12" 78
D. Soriano, M. Tagliafero	Pathé PAT-155	1936	12" 78
S. Swaap, accompanist unid.	HMV B-4852	1934	10" 78

Composition and Performer(s)	Record Label and Number	Date	Speed
J. Thibaud, A. Cortot	Vic 8244 in set M-165,	1932	12" 78
	HMV DB-1653	RR	12" LP
	COLH 313	1922	12" 78a
G. Tinlot, accompanist unid.	FHMV L-283	1913	12" 78a
E. Ysaÿe, C. Decreus	ACol 36519, CCol 7112	RI	12" LP
	FEY 3002	1936	10" 78
L. Zighéra, pianist unid.	Dec M-163		
——arr. Cello and Piano (possibly by Fauré)			
R. Bas, pianist unid.	Parl 22.730	1930	10" 78
W. Evans, pianist unid.	FHMV W-292	1919	12" 78a
P. Fournier, E. Lush	HMV DA-2028	1952	10" 78
	Vic EHA-20	RI	7" 45
	Vic LHMV-1043	RI	12" LP
P. Fournier, G. Moore	Ang 35599, CCol 33CX-1606	1958	12" LP
F. Salmond, pianist unid.	ACol 169-M	1927	10" 78
J. Serres, A. Leyvastre	Saturn MSA-5003	1951	10" LP
——arr. Flute and Piano			
J.-P. Rampal, A. D'Arco	Epic LC-3917	1966	12" LP
	Epic BC-1317	1966	12" S
——arr. Piano			
M. Brard	Welte C-7004	1922	PR
Une Châtelaine en sa tour, Op. 110 for Harp (1918)			
M. Jamet	HMundi 30.542	1958	12" LP
McDonald	BaM LD-92	1957	12" LP

Composition and Performer(s)	Record Label and Number	Date	Speed
N. Zabaleta	Per 745	1958	12" LP
	Per S-745	1958	12" S
N. Zabaleta	DGG 18890	1965	12" LP
	DGG 138.890	1965	12" S
Élégie for Cello and Piano or Orchestra, Op. 24 (1883)			
J. Bedetti, S. Koussevitzky, Boston S.O.	Vic 14577, HMV DB-3210	1937	12" 78
R. Boulmé, pianist unid.	Pathé X-9803	1927	10" 78
	Pathé 9803	1927	10" V
P. Casals, cello and cond. Lamoureux O.	Phil. L-77.408 L	1956	12" LP
P. Casals cond., P. Bazelaire, M. Maréchal, G. Cassadò, R. van Tobel, E. Pasquier, A. Lévy, G. Marchesini, G. Fallot, C. Bartsch, J. Vaugeois, cellos, Lamoureux O.	Phil. L-77.408 L	1956	12" LP
G. Cassadò, R. Moralt, Vienna Pro Musica O.	Vox 10920	1960	12" LP
	Vox 510.920	1960	12" S
P. Fournier, E. Lush	HMV DB-21333	1952	12" 78
	Vic EHA-20	RI	7" 45
	Vic LHMV-1043	RI	12" LP
P. Fournier, G. Moore	CCol 33CX-1644	1959	12" LP
H. Honegger, E. Møller	Metr MCEP-3027	1957	7" 45
A. Lévy, pianist unid.	Od 166.051	1931	10" 78
Lieberman, pianist unid.	FParl 22.044	1927	10" 78
M. Khomitser, pianist unid.	MK 3224/5	1957	10" LP
M. Marcelli-Herson, pianist unid.	FHMV L-776	1930	12" 78
M. Maréchal, M. Fauré	ECol DX-49, FCol D-15176	1931	12" 78
S. Mayes, E. Leinsdorf, Boston S.O.	Vic LM-2703, RCA RB-6581	1964	12" LP
	Vic LSC-2703, RCA SB-6581	1964	12" S

Composition and Performer(s)	Record Label and Number	Date	Speed
B. Michelin, P. Hupperts, Haarlem S.O.	ConH CHS-1162, Clc 6245	1953	12" LP
L. Monroe, E. Ormandy, Philadelphia O.	ACol ML-6191	1966	12" LP
	ACol MS-6791	1966	12" LP
A. Navarra, Clavius-Marius	Od 188.939	1947	12" 78
J. Neliz, A. Collard	Pathé PDT-252	1935	12" 78
G. Piatigorsky, R. Berkowitz	ACol 72767-D in set MM-808	1946	12" 78
	ACol ML-4215	RI	12" LP
M. Rostropovich, pianist unid.	MK-00326	1953	7" 45
Salles, G. Thyssens-Valentin	CdM CL-11	1964	12" LP
J. Serres, A. Leyvastre	Saturn MSA-5003	1951	10" LP
J. Starker, W. Susskind, Philharmonia O.	Ang 35417, CCol 33CX-1477	1957	12" LP
	Ang S-35417, CCol SAX-2263	1957	12" S
G. Suggia, R. Paul	HMV DA-1176	1931	10" 78
P. Tortelier, H. Menges, Philharmonia O.	EHMV ALP-1336, FHMV FALP-461	1956	12" LP
P. Tortelier, J. Hubeau	Erato LDE-3193	1960	12" LP
	Erato STE-50.101	1960	12" S
M. Villerouche, pianist unid.	MK D-1001/2	1964	10" LP
L. Yevgrafor, G. Miklos	Qual LP-1168/71	1965	12" LP
Fantaisie for Flute and Piano, Op. 86 (1898)			
J.-P. Rampal, A. D'Arco	Phil A5584L	1959	12" LP
Impromptu, Op. 86 for Harp (1904)			
A. Challan	Ang 36290, CCol SX-1768	1965	12" LP
	Ang S-36290, CCol SCX-3568	1965	12" S
M. Jamet	ClubND-1016	1964	12" LP
L. Laskine	Vic 12005, FHMV L-993	1931	12" 78

COMPOSITION AND PERFORMER(S)	RECORD LABEL AND NUMBER	DATE	SPEED
L. Laskine	Erato LDE-3232	1963	12" LP
	Erato STE-50132	1963	12" S
M. Robles	Argo 458	1966	12" LP
	Argo 5458	1966	12" S
E. Vito	Strad 1007, Per 721	1950	12" LP
	Per 2727	RR	12" S
E. Vito (diff. version?)	Saga XID-5240	1965	12" LP
—arr. Piano (Fauré)			
—See PIANO: Impromptu in D flat Major, Op. 86b			
Papillon for Cello and Piano, Op. 77 (1898)			
G. Cassadó, G. Mendelssohn-Gordigiani	DGG 95028	1926	12" 78
J. Decroos, D. Duchenne	Iramac 6.513	1967	12" LP
P. Fournier, T. Janopoulo	FHMV DA-4957	1941	10" 78
P. Fournier, G. Moore	CCol 33CX-1644	1959	12" LP
B. Michelin, T. Janopoulo	FCol LF-241	1936	10" 78
A. Navarra, Clavius-Marius	Od 188.931	1947	10" 78
J. Serres, A. Leyvastre	Saturn MSA-5003	1951	10" LP
W. Squire, pianist unid.	ECol L-1977	1928	12" 78
J. Starker, L. Pommers	Per SP-708	1958	12" LP
Petite Pièce for Cello and Piano, Op. 49 (1889)			
Unpublished			
Piano Quartet No. 1 in C Minor, Op. 15 (1879)			
R. Anderson, R. Masters, N. Jamieson, M. Taylor (as Robert Masters Piano Quartet)	West XWN-18093, Argo RG-55	1955	12" LP
G. Casadesus, Guilet Trio	Polym 1007, Nixa QLP-4007	1951	12" LP

Composition and Performer(s)	Record Label and Number	Date	Speed
R. Casadesus, J. Calvet, L. Pascal, P. Mas	ACol 68524/7-D in set M-255	1936	12" 78
	FCol LFX-380/3	1942	12" 78
J. Chailley-Richez, M. Ihos, M. Chailley-Guiard, A. Gelu (as Chailley-Richez Quartet)	FCol LFX-637/40	1942	12" 78
L. Crowson, K. Sillito, C. Aronowitz, T. Weil (as Pro Arte Piano Quartet)	OL 289	1966	12" LP
	OL S-289	1966	12" S
E. Gilels, L. Kogan, R. Barshai, M. Rostropovich	MK D-4572/3	1960	10" LP
M. Gazelle, M. Raskin, L. Ardenois, R. Soiron (as London Belgian Quartet)	ECol DX-8163/6	1953	12" 78
E. Gröschel, W. Klepper, H. Blendinger, H. Meltzer	GColos CoM-602	1966	12" S
C. Heffler, C. Tessier, P. Ladhuie, R. Albin	ClubND-8	1965	12" S
B. Henett Quartet (abridged)	FHMV W-528/9	1927	12" 78
M. Horszowski, A. Schneider, M. Katims, F. Miller	ACol ML-5343	1963	12" LP
M. Long, Pasquier Trio	FCol FC-1057	1957	10" LP
	FCol FCX-681, FCol 30293	RI	12" LP
L. Pennario, E. Shapiro, S. Schoenbach, V. Gottlieb	Cap P-8558	1961	12" LP
	Cap SP-8558	1961	12" S
A. Rubinstein, Paganini Quartet members	Vic LM-52, EHMV BLP-1010	1951	10" LP
	Vic WDM-1493	1951	7" 45
E. Zurfluh-Tenroc, H. Merkel, A. Merkel, G. Marchesini	Vic 12481/4 in set M-594, EHMV D-2106/9 in set M-210, FHMV L-973/6	1933	12" 78

Piano Quartet No. 2 in G Minor, Op. 45 (1886)

Composition and Performer(s)	Record Label and Number	Date	Speed
K. Anderson, R. Masters, N. Jamieson, M. Taylor (as Robert Masters Piano Quartet)	West XWN-18093, Argo RG-56	1955	12" LP

Composition and Performer(s)	Record Label and Number	Date	Speed
V. Babin, S. Goldberg, W. Primrose, N. Graudin (as Festival Quartet)	Vic LM-2735	1965	12" LP
	Vic LSC-2735	1965	12" S
G. Casadesus, Guilet Trio	MGM E-3166	1954	12" LP
J. Doyen, Pasquier Trio	Erato LDE-3064		12" LP
J. Françaix, Pasquier Trio	Selmer LPG-8004	1958	12" LP
M. Gazelle, M. Raskin, L. Ardenois, R. Soiron (as London Belgian Piano Quartet)	Dec AK-1183/6 in set EDA-74	1946	12" 78
R. Lev, Pascal Trio	ConH 1093, Cle 6232, Nixa CLP-1093	1951	12" LP
M. Long, J. Thibaud, M. Vieux, P. Fournier	FHMV DB-5103/6	c.1951	12" 78
	COLC 76	RR	12" LP
Piano Quintet No. 1 in D Minor, Op. 89 (1906)			
E. Boynet, Gordon Quartet	Schirmer set 9	1940	12" 78
Piano Quintet No. 2 in C Minor, Op. 115 (1921)			
R. Lev, Pascal Quartet	ConH CHS-1093, Nixa CLP-1093, Cle 6232	1951	12" LP
G. Thyssens-Valentin, French Radio O. Quartet	CdM CL-11	1966	12" S
Romance in A Major for Cello and Piano, Op. 69 (c. 1895)			
G. Fallot, M. Fallot	DucTh 450-C-085	1958	7" 45
P. Fournier, B. Léonet	FHMV DB-11144	1948	12" 78
—arr. Violin and Piano			
G. Poulet, Lacoref	Deva 45az	1960	7" 45
Sérénade for Cello and Piano, Op. 98 (1908)			
No recordings traced			

193

COMPOSITION AND PERFORMER(S)	RECORD LABEL AND NUMBER	DATE	SPEED
Sicilienne for Cello and Piano, Op. 78 (1898)			
U. Benidetti, pianist unid.	FHMV L-664	1928	12" 78
C. Boomkamp, G. Hengeveld	Phil A-1033	1947	12" 78
R. Boulmé, Gaveau	Pathé X-9741	1930	10" 78
	Pathé 9741	1930	10" V
A. Földesey, W. van Vultée	DGG 24416, DGG 10794	1932	10" 78
P. Fournier, G. Moore	CCol 33 CX-1644	1959	12" LP
H. Honeger, E. Møller	Metr MCEP-3027	1954	7" 45
W. Squire, pianist unid.	ECol L-1759	1927	12" 78
G. Suggia, R. Paul	HMV DB-1476	1930	12" 78
—arr. Piano (Fauré)			
G. Fauré	Welte 2777	1913	PR
—arr. Guitar and Piano			
L. Almeida, M. Ruderman	Cap P-8406	1959	12" LP
—arr. Orchestra (Koechlin)			
—See STAGE WORKS: *Pélleas et Mélisande, Op. 80*			
Sonata No. 1 for Violin and Piano in A Major, Op. 13 (1876)			
L. Bobesco, J. Genty	Lon LS-327, Dec LX-3057	1951	10" LP
	Lon LL-1549	RI	12" LP
M. Chauveton, B. Smith	Alleg ALG-3032	1951	12" LP
P. Doukin, T. Cochet	Erato LDE-3061	1957	12" LP
M. Elman, L. Mittman	Vic 18351/3 in M-859 set	1942	12" 78
M. Elman, J. Seiger	Lon LL-1628	1957	12" LP
C. Ferras, P. Barbizet	EHMV ALP-1666, FHMV FALP-420	1958	12" LP

Composition and Performer(s)	Record Label and Number	Date	Speed
J. Fournier, G. Doyen	West WL-5156, XWN-18576, 9072	1952	12" LP
Z. Francescatti, R. Casadesus	ACol ML-5047, Phil L-01.268	1956	12" LP
J. Fuchs, A. Balsam	ADec DL-9716	1954	12" LP
A. Grumiaux, Hajdu	Phil A-02264-L	1961	12" LP
S. Harth, A. Loesser	Iramac 6.523	1967	12" LP
J. Heifetz, E. Bay	Vic 14195/7 in set M-328, HMV DB-3176/8	1937	12" 78
J. Heifetz, B. Smith	Vic LM-2074, RCA 630.509	1957	12" LP
B. Senofsky, G. Grafman	Vic LM-2488	1961	12" LP
	Vic LSC-2488	1961	12" S
D. Soriano, M. Tagliaferro	Pathé PAT-3/5	1934	12" 78
J. Thibaud, A. Cortot	Vic 8086/8, HMV DB-1080/2	1927	12" 78
	COLH 74	RR	12" LP
J. Tomasow, F. Holetschek	Vang VRS-464	1955	12" LP
—First movement: *Allegro molto*			
Y. Menuhin, M. Gazelle	Vic LM-6153	1962	12" LP
Sonata No. 2 for Violin and Piano in E Minor, Op. 108 (1917)			
P. Doukan, T. Cochet	Erato LDE-3061	1957	12" LP
C. Ferras, P. Barbizet	Lon LL-909, Dec LXT-2180	1954	12" LP
	Everest 6140	RI	12" LP
	Everest 3140	RR	12" S
J. Fournier, G. Doyen	West WL-5156, XWN-18576, 9072	1952	12" LP
Z. Francescatti, R. Casadesus	Col ML-5049, Phil L-01.268	1956	12" LP
D. Guilet, G. Casadesus	Polym 1008, Nixa QLP-4008	1952	12" LP

Composition and Performer(s)	Record Label and Number	Date	Speed
Mandel, Koenig	Baroque 1845	1965	12" LP
	Baroque 2845	1965	12" S
R. Posselt, J. Rezits	Festival 70-203	1952	12" LP
Sonata No. 1 for Cello and Piano in D Minor, Op. 109 (1918)			
G. Fallot, M. Fallot	DucTh DTL-93050,	1956	12" LP
	Tele TW-30035		
P. Tortelier, J. Hubeau	Erato LDE-3193	1964	12" LP
	Erato STE-50101	1964	12" S
Sonata No. 2 for Cello and Piano in G Minor, Op. 117 (1922)			
R. Albin, C. Helffer	ClubFD 8	1965	12" LP
J. Decross, D. Duchenne	Iramac 6.513	1967	12" S
G. Fallot, M. Fallot	DucTh DTL-93050,	1956	12" LP
	Tele TW-30035	1945	12" 78
M. Gendron, M. Haas	Dec K-1374/6	1967	12" LP
M. Gendron, J. Françaix	Phil L2.446L	1967	12" S
	Phil 835.316LY	1946	12" LP
A. Navarra, A. D'Arco	FCol LFX-897/8	1952	12" LP
D. Soyer, L. Mittman	Polym 1007, Nixa QLP-4007	1964	12" LP
P. Tortelier, J. Hubeau	Erato LDE-3193	1964	12" S
	Erato STE-50101		
String Quartet in E Minor, Op. 121 (1924)			
Guilet Quartet	Polym 1008, Nixa QLP-4008	1952	12" LP
Krettley Quartet	FCol D-15218/20, JCol 7907/9	1930	12" 78
Loewenguth Quartet	Vox VBX-70, Turn 4014	1965	12" LP
	Vox SVBX-70, Turn 34014	1965	12" S

Composition and Performer(s)	Record Label and Number	Date	Speed
Pascal Quartet	FCol LFX-926/8	1948	12" 78
Pro Arte Quartet	Vic 14456 in set M-372, HMV DB-2763/6	1936	12" 78
Trio for Piano and Strings in D Minor, Op. 120 (1923)			
L. Crowson, K. Sillito, T. Weil (as members of Pro Arte Piano Quartet)	OL 289	1966	12" LP
	OL S-289	1966	12" LP
J. Doyen, J. Pasquier, E. Pasquier	Erato LDE-3064	1961	12" LP
E. Itor-Kahn, G. Ciompi, B. Heifetz (as Albeneri Trio)	Merc MG-10089, Clc 6259	1951	12" LP
G. Joy, J. Gautier, A. Lévy	Pra CL-8001	1957	12" LP
M. Pressler, C. Guilet, B. Greenhouse (as Beaux Arts Trio)	MGM E-3455, Parl PMC-1035	1951	12" LP
A. Previn, F. Roth, J. Schuster	ACol ML-5863	1963	12" LP
	ACol MS-6463	1963	12" S

PIANO MUSIC

Adagietto in A Minor, Op. 84, No. 4
—See *Huit Pièces brèves, Op. 84*

Allégresse in C Major, Op. 84, No. 7
—See *Huit Pièces brèves, Op. 84*

Barcarolles

Composition and Performer(s)	Record Label and Number	Date	Speed
—*Nos. 1–13, complete*			
E. Crochet	Vox SVBX-5423	1963	12" S
G. Johannesen	GoCr 4030; 4046; 4048	1961/3	12" LP
G. Thyssens-Valentin	DucTh 300-C-022	1958	12" LP

197

Composition and Performer(s)	Record Label and Number	Date	Speed
—No. 1 in A Minor, Op. 26 (1883)			
E. Boynet	Vox PL-6910	1951	12" LP
J. Charloff	Ampico 63453	1924	PR
G. Fauré	Welte 2773	1913	PR
	ACol ML-4291, Tele 98	RR	12" LP
K. Long	Lon LS-260, Dec LM-4528	1950	10" LP
	Lon LL-887	RI	12" LP
P. Loyonnet	ConH CHS-16	1950	12" LP
—No. 2 in G Major, Op. 41 (1885)			
E. Boynet	Vox PL-6910	1951	12" LP
G. Doyen	Ult FP-1441	1935	12" 78
J. Eymar	CdM LDM-8168	1958	10" LP
K. Long	Dec M-575	1946	10" 78
K. Long (diff. version?)	Lon LS-246, Dec LM-4523	1950	10" LP
	Lon LL-887	RI	12" LP
M. Long	FCol FCX-30293	1965	12" LP
Mme. Panzéra-Baillot	Merc MG-10097, Clc 6269	1951	12" LP
—No. 3 in G Flat Major, Op. 42 (1885)			
E. Boynet	Vox PL-6910	1951	12" LP
G. Doyen	Phil 641.100	1958	12" LP
M. Fourneau	FCol LF-231	1936	10" 78
M. Fourneau	Pacific LDP-F-168	1959	12" LP
G. Fauré	AeolMet 65841	pre-1905	PR
G. Thyssens-Valentin	DucTh 270-C-086	1956	10" LP
J. Verd	Zodiak 1003	1956	12" LP

Composition and Performer(s)	Record Label and Number	Date	Speed
—No. 4 in A flat Major, Op. 44 (1886)			
E. Boynet	Vox PL-6910	1951	12" LP
J. Damase	Dec FST-133.062,	1955	12" LP
	LonInt TW-91065	1948	12" 78
B. Léonet	FHMV SL-126		
—No. 5 in F sharp Minor, Op. 66 (c. 1895)			
E. Boynet	Vic 4415 in set M-549	1939	10" 78
E. Boynet	Vox PL-6910	1951	12" LP
R. Casadesus	ACol ML-2205	1951	10" LP
B. Léonet	FHMV SL-177	1948	12" 78
—No. 6 in E flat Major, Op. 70 (1896)			
E. Boynet	Vox PL-6910	1951	12" LP
J. Demus	West XWN-18118	1958	12" LP
C. Guilbert	Pathé X-9982	1931	10" 78
C. Guilbert (diff. version?)	Pathé X-98135	1934	10" 78
M. Long	Welte 2860	1913	PR
M. Long	ACol 69063-D, FCol LFX-567	1937	12" 78
M. Long	FCol FCX-30293	1965	12" LP
—No. 7 in D Minor, Op. 90 (1906)			
F. Petit	Erato LDE-1046	1956	7" 45
—No. 8 in D flat Major, Op. 96 (1908)			
M. Fourneau	Pacific LDP-F-168	1959	12" LP
—No. 9 in A Minor, Op. 101 (1910)			
M. Long	Welte 2864	1913	PR

Composition and Performer(s)	Record Label and Number	Date	Speed
—No. 10 in A Minor, Op. 104, No. 2 (1913) Not individually recorded			
—No. 11 in G Minor, Op. 105, No. 1 (1914) Not individually recorded			
—No. 12 in E flat Major, Op. 105, No. 2 (1916)			
J. Damase	Dec 163.709	1956	12" LP
G. Doyen	Phil 641.100	1958	12" LP
—No. 13 in C Major, Op. 116 (1921)			
B. Léonet	FHMV SL-126	1948	12" 78
Capriccio in E flat Major, Op. 84, No. 1			
—See *Huit Pièces brèves, Op. 84*			
Dolly, Op. 56. Suite for Piano, four hands (1893–6) 1. *Berceuse*, 2. *Mi-a-ou*, 3. *Le Jardin de Dolly*, 4. *Kitty valse*, 5. *Tendresse*, 6. *Le Pas Espagnol*			
—Complete suite			
J. Bonneau, G. Joy	Pathé DT-1027	1956	10" LP
J. Bonneau, G. Joy	Erato LDE-3254	1963	12" LP
	Erato STE-50154	1963	12" S
R. Casadesus, G. Casadesus	ACol ML-2205	1951	10" LP
R. Casadesus, G. Casadesus	ACol ML-5723, CBS BRG-72050	1962	12" LP
	ACol MS-5723, CBS SBRG-72050	1962	12" S
W. Klein, B. Klein	Vox 12590	1964	12" LP
	Vox 512.590, Turn 34234	1964	12" S
I. Marika, G. Smadja	Phil N-00637R	1954	10" LP

Composition and Performer(s)	Record Label and Number	Date	Speed
A. Siegel, B. Léonet (child pupils of M. Long)	ACol 4120-M & 9103-M		10" &
	FCol DF-1665 & DFX-193	1936	12" 78
Complete, arr. Piano Solo (A. Cortot) K. Yasukawa	JVic NH-2015/6	1952	12" 78
Complete, Orchestrated (Henri Rabaud)			
T. Beecham, French National Radio O.	HMV ALP-1843	1961	12" LP
A. Fistoulari, London Phil. O.	MGM E-3098, Parl PMC-1004	1954	12" LP
J. Fournet, Concerts Colonne O.	Pathé PDT-186/7	1947	12" 78
G. Tzipine, Paris Opéra-Comique O.	Ang 35311, CCol 33CX-1577	1959	12" LP
No. 1, *Berceuse*			
arr. Piano solo (Alfred Cortot) de Brunhoff	Pathé DTX-316	1960	12" LP
	Pathé ASTX-129	1960	12" S
A. Cortot	Duo-Art 6241	1920	PR
	ArcP X-908	RR	12" PR
R. Lev	Pathé DTX-269	1959	12" LP
arr. Piano, Three Hands			
P. Sellick, C. Smith	EHMV CLP-1666	1963	12" LP
	EHMV CSD-1506	1963	12" S
arr. Violin and Piano			
R. Chemet, pianist unid.	HMV DA-532	1927	10" 78
J. Thibaud, T. Janopoulo	FHMV DA-4999	1941	10" 78
arr. Cello and Piano			
P. Barbezat, pianist unid.	FHMV K-747	1940	10" 78

201

Composition and Performer(s)	Record Label and Number	Date	Speed
—arr. Voice and Piano (Hamille) N. Vallin(s), P. Darck	Od 166.805, ADec 20324	1934	10″ 78
Fantaisie in A flat Major, Op. 84, No. 2			
—See *Huit Pièces brèves, Op. 84*			
Fugue in A Minor, Op. 84, No. 3			
—See *Huit Pièces brèves, Op. 84*			
Fugue in E Minor, Op. 84, No. 6			
—See *Huit Pièces brèves, Op. 84*			
Huit Pièces brèves, Op. 84 (1898–1902)			
—Complete, Nos. 1–8			
E. Crochet	Vox SVBX-5423	1964	12″ LP
G. Johannesen	GoCr 4030	1961	12″ LP
G. Thyssens-Valentin	DucTh 300-C-086	1960	12″ LP
—No. 1. *Capriccio in E flat Major* J. Verd	Zodiak 1003	1956	12″ LP
—No. 2. *Fantaisie in A flat Major* Not individually recorded			
—No. 3. *Fugue in A Minor* Not individually recorded			
—No. 4. *Adagietto in E Minor* Not individually recorded			

Composition and Performer(s)	Record Label and Number	Date	Speed
—No. 5. *Improvisation in C sharp Minor* E. Boynet	Vox PL-6910	1951	12" LP
—No. 6. *Fugue in E Minor* Not individually recorded			
—No. 7. *Allégresse in C Major* Not individually recorded			
—No. 8. *Nocturne No. 8 in D flat Major* (Included in all complete sets of *Nocturnes*) K. Long	Lon LL-1058, Dec LXT-2963, Dec ACL-257	1954	12" LP
Impromptus —Complete, Nos. 1–5 E. Crochet G. Johannesen G. Thyssens-Valentin	Vox SVBX-5424 GoCr 4030 DucTh 300-C-085	1964 1961 1960	12" S 12" LP 12" LP
—*No. 1 in E flat Major, Op. 25* (1883) J. Demus G. Doyen B. Léonet Peters F. Petit	West XWN-18118 Phil 641.100 FHMV SL-113 Pathé DTX-318 Erato LDE-1046	1958 1960 1948 1959 1956	12" LP 12" LP 12" 78 12" LP 7" 45

COMPOSITION AND PERFORMER(S)	RECORD LABEL AND NUMBER	DATE	SPEED
—*Impromptu No. 2 in F Minor, Op. 31* (1883)			
E. Boynet	Pathé PG-3	1934	10" 78
A. Brailowsky	Vic 12-0794	1949	12" 78
G. Casadesus	Vox 16003 in set 163	1948	10" 78
J. Demus	West XWN-18118	1958	12" LP
J. Eymar	CdM LDM-8168	1957	10" LP
S. François	FCol FC-1045	1957	10" LP
C. Guilbert	Pathé X-9895	1930	10" 78
E. Joyce	Parl E-11372, Od 123.833	1937	12" 78
	ADec DL-9528	RR	12" LP
E. Joyce (diff. version?)	Saga XID-5007	1959	12" LP
C. Kahn	Dec 154.010	1959	10" LP
K. Long	Lon LS-246, Dec DM-4523	1950	10" LP
	Lon LL-887	RI	12" LP
M. Long	FCol LF-126	1933	10" 78
M. Long	FCol FCX-681, FCX-30293	1960	12" LP
R. Lortat	Duo-Art 5923	1917	PR
N. Mariño	Vic 11-8589	1944	12" 78
M. Munz	Ampico 67703	1925	PR
C. Overstreet	Welte 6300	1913	PR
F. Petit	Erato LDE-1016	1956	7" 45
O. Samaroff	Welte 1481	1906	PR
M. Tagliafero	Ult BP-757	1930	10" 78
J. Whittaker	Ampico 52174	1921	PR
K. Yasukawa	JVic NH-2017	1952	12" 78
—*Impromptu No. 3 in A flat Major, Op. 34* (1883)			
J. Damase	Dec FST-133.062, Tele TW-91035	1955	12" LP

Composition and Performer(s)	Record Label and Number	Date	Speed
J. Demus	West XWN-18118	1958	12" LP
G. Doyen	Phil 641.100	1960	12" LP
A. Iturbi	Vic 49-3309	1948	7" 45
G. Johannesen	ConH CHS-1181, Nixa CLP-1181	1954	12" LP
L. Kartun	ADec 25944, Od 171.095	1930	12" 78
B. Léonet	FHMV SL-113	1948	12" 78
F. Petit	Erato LDE-1046	1956	7" 45
D. Schafer	Welte 3957	1914	PR
B. Simonds	Carillon P4RM-4372/3	1954	12" LP
M. Tagliafero	FHMV W-985	1929	12" 78
G. Thyssens-Valentin	DucTh 270-C-086	1956	10" LP
K. Yasukawa	JVic NH-2017	1952	12" 78

—*Impromptu No. 4 in D flat-C sharp Major, Op. 91* (1906)

J. Demus	West XWN-18118	1958	12" LP
G. Doyen	Phil 641.100	1960	12" LP

—*Impromptu No. 5 in F sharp Minor, Op. 102* (1910)

R. Casadesus	ACol 68853-D, FCol LFX-401	1936	12" 78
R. Casadesus	ACol ML-2205	1951	10" LP
J. Demus	West XWN-18118	1958	12" LP
J. Eymar	CdM LDM-8168	1957	10" LP
M. Long	FCol LF-126, JCol J-5476	1933	10" 78
	COLC-76	RR	12" LP
G. Johannesen	HMV CLP-1069	1956	12" LP
F. Petit	Erato LDE-1016	1956	7" 45

Composition and Performer(s)	Record Label and Number	Date	Speed
—*Impromptu in D flat Major, Op. 86b* (1913) (Transcription by Fauré of *Impromptu, Op. 86* for harp)			
G. Thyssens-Valentin	DucTh 300-C-085	1959	12" LP
Improvisation in C sharp Minor, Op. 84, No. 5			
—See *Huit Pièces brèves, Op. 84*			
Mazurka in B flat Major, Op. 32 (1833)			
E. Crochet	Vox SVBX-5924	1964	12" S
G. Johannesen	GoCr 4046	1962	12" LP
Neuf Préludes, Op. 103 (1910–11)			
—Complete, Nos. 1–9			
E. Crochet	Vox SVBX-5424	1964	12" LP
J. Damase	Selmer LPG-8006	1951	12" LP
G. Johannesen	GoCr 4030	1961	12" LP
G. Thyssens-Valentin	DucTh 300-C-085	1959	12" LP
—*No. 1 in D flat Major, Op. 103, No. 1*			
R. Casadesus	ACol ML-5777	1962	12" LP
	ACol MS-6377	1962	12" S
—*No. 2 in C sharp Minor, Op. 103, No. 2*			
Not individually recorded			
—*No. 3 in G Minor, Op. 103, No. 3*			
R. Casadesus	ACol ML-5777	1962	12" LP
	ACol MS-6377	1962	12" S
G. Fauré	Welte 2774	1913	PR

Composition and Performer(s)	Record Label and Number	Date	Speed
—*No. 4 in F Major, Op. 103, No. 4*			
Not individually recorded			
—*No. 5 in D Minor, Op. 103, No. 5*			
R. Casadesus	FCol LFX-401	1935	12″ 78
R. Casadesus	ACol ML-5777	1962	12″ LP
	ACol MS-6377	1962	12″ S
—*No. 6 in E flat Minor, Op. 103, No. 6*			
Not individually recorded			
—*No. 7 in A Major, Op. 103, No. 7*			
Not individually recorded			
—*No. 8 in C Minor, Op. 103, No. 8*			
Not individually recorded			
—*No. 9 in E Minor, Op. 103, No. 9*			
Not individually recorded			
Nocturnes			
—Complete, Nos. 1–13			
E. Crochet	Vox SVBX-5924	1964	12″ S
J. Damase	FDec 163.752 & 163.762	1958	12″ LP
E. Heidsieck	FHMV FALP-800/1	1966	12″ LP
	FHMV ADSF-800/1	1966	12″ S
G. Johannesen	GoCr 4030; 4046; 4048	1961-3	12″ LP
G. Thyssens-Valentin	DucTh 320-C-112/3	1958	12″ LP

Composition and Performer(s)	Record Label and Number	Date	Speed
—*No. 1 in E flat Minor, Op. 33, No. 1 (1883)*			
E. Boynet	Vox PL-7520	1952	12" LP
M. Brard	Welte C-7057	1923	PR
J. Eymar	CdM LDM-8168	1957	10" LP
B. Léonet	FHMV SK-118	1948	10" 78
—*No. 2 in B Major, Op. 33, No. 2 (1883)*			
E. Boynet	Vox PL-7520	1952	12" LP
S. François	FCol FC-1045	1957	10" LP
K. Long	Lon LL-1058, Dec LXT-2963	1954	12" LP
F. Petit	Erato LDE-1046	1956	7" 45
—*No. 3 in A flat Major, Op. 33, No. 3 (1883)*			
E. Boynet	Vox PL-7520	1952	12" LP
L. Cimaglia	Vic 11-8588	1944	12" 78
G. Fauré	Welte 2775	1913	PR
C. Guilbert	ACol 69797-D in set X-156, Pathé PAT-114	1939	12" 78
N. Mariño	Vic 11-8589	1944	12" 78
T. van der Pas	Phil A-1041, Dec X-10040	1947	12" 78
A. Rubinstein	Vic 15660, HMV DB-3718, HMV DB-6467	1939	12" 78
A. Rubinstein	Vic LM-2751, RCA RB-6603	1964	12" LP
	Vic LSC-2751	1964	12" S
M. Schwalb	Academy 310	1953	12" LP
B. Simonds	Carillon P4RM-9200/1	1954	12" LP
R. Trouard	Od 123.907	1945	12" 78
K. Yasukawa	JVic NH-2016	1952	12" 78

Composition and Performer(s)	Record Label and Number	Date	Speed
—No. 4 in E flat Major, Op. 36 (1884)			
E. Boynet	Pathé PG-2	1934	10″ 78
E. Boynet	Vox PL-7520	1952	12″ LP
M. Brard	Duo-Art 6148, Welte 7076	1921	PR
S. François	FCol FC-1045	1957	10″ LP
J. Laforge	Pacific LDPC-112	1956	12″ LP
K. Long	Dec M-655	1949	10″ 78
K. Long (diff. version?)	Lon LS-260, Dec LM-4528	1950	10″ LP
	Lon LL-887	RI	12″ LP
M. Long	Welte 2859	1913	PR
M. Long	ACol 69063-D, FCol LFX-567	1937	12″ 78
	COLC 76	RR	12″ LP
R. Pugno	Welte 539	1904	PR
G. Thyssens-Valentin	DucTh 270-C-086	1956	10″ LP
—No. 5 in B flat Major, Op. 37 (1884)			
K. Long	Lon LL-1058, Dec LXT-2963		
	Dec ACL-257	1954	12″ LP
—No. 6 in D flat Major, Op. 63 (c. 1894)			
E. Boynet	Vox PL-7520	1952	12″ LP
J. Demus	West XWN-18118	1958	12″ LP
G. Doyen	FHMV DB-5029	1937	12″ 78
J. Eymer	CdM LDM-8168	1957	10″ LP
C. Guilbert	Pathé PAT-55, JCol JW-523	1936	12″ 78
S. Gyr	SwHMV DB-10079	1946	12″ 78
G. Johannesen	HMV CLP-1069	1956	12″ LP
M. Katz	Pye CCL-30111	1958	12″ LP

209

Composition and Performer(s)	Record Label and Number	Date	Speed
J. Laforge	Pacific LDPC-112	1956	10" LP
K. Long	Dec M-574	1945	10" 78
K. Long (diff. version?)	Lon LS-246, Dec LM-4523	1950	10" LP
	Lon LL-887	RI	12" LP
M. Long	ACol 68935-D, FCol LFX-437	1936	12" 78
	COLC-76	RR	12" LP
G. Thyssens-Valentin	DucTh LAP-1009	1955	7" 45
—arr. Soprano, Flute and Guitar S. Terri, M. Ruderman, L. Almeida			
No. 7 in C sharp Minor, Op. 74 (1898)	Cap P-8461	1960	12" LP
E. Boynet	Vox PL-7520	1952	12" LP
R. Casadesus	ACol ML-2205	1951	10" LP
J. Février	FCol LFX-562	1937	12" 78
K. Long	Lon LL-1058, Dec LXT-2963, Dec ACL-257	1957	12" LP
P. Loyonnet	ConH CHS-16	1950	12" LP
G. Thyssens-Valentin	DucTh AP-1009	1955	7" 45
No. 8 in D flat Major, Op. 84, No. 8			
—*See Huit Pièces brèves, Op. 84*			
No. 9 in B Minor-B Major, Op. 97 (1908) Not individually recorded			
No. 10 in E Minor, Op. 99 (1909) Not individually recorded			

Composition and Performer(s)	Record Label and Number	Date	Speed
—No. 11 in F sharp Minor, Op. 104, No. 1 (1913)			
Not individually recorded			
—No. 12 in E Minor, Op. 107 (1916)			
J. Damase	Dec FST-133.062, Tele TW-91035	1955	12" LP
K. Long	Lon LL-1058, Dec LXT-2963,	1954	12" LP
	Dec ACL-257		
—No. 13 in B Minor, Op. 119 (1922)			
Y. Lefébure	CdM 5008	1949	10" 78
K. Long	Dec M-659	1950	10" 78
K. Long (diff. version?)	Lon LS-246, Dec LM-4523	1950	10" LP
	Lon LL-887	RI	12" LP
K. Long	Lon LL-1058, Dec LXT-2963	1954	12" LP
	Dec ACL-257		
F. Petit	Erato LDE-1016	1956	7" 45
J. Verd	Zodiak 1003	1956	12" LP
Pièces brèves, Op. 84			
—See *Huit Pièces brèves, Op. 84*			
Préludes, Op. 103			
—See *Neuf Préludes, Op. 103*			
Souvenirs de Bayreuth (c. 1880)			
D. Herbrecht, L. Petijean	HMV K-5906	1929	10" 78
F. Petit, A. Beckensteiner	Erato LDE-1017	1956	7" 45
Thème et variations in C sharp Minor, Op. 73 (1897)			
E. Crochet	Vox SVBX-5423	1964	12" S

Composition and Performer(s)	Record Label and Number	Date	Speed
J. Demus	West XWN-18118	1958	12"LP
G. Fauré	AeolMet 63543	pre-1905	PR
C. Guilbert	ACol 69796/7 in set X-156, Pathé PAT-113/4	1939	12" 78
E. Heidsieck	FHMV FALP-801	1966	12" LP
	FHMV ADSF-801	1966	12" S
G. Johannesen	ConH CHS-1181, Nixa CLP-1181	1954	12" LP
G. Johannesen	GoCr 4046	1962	12" LP
J. Laforge	Pacific LDPC-112	1956	10" LP
K. Long	Dec M-547/8	1944	10" 78
K. Long (diff. version?)	Lon LS-260, Dec LM-4528	1950	10" LP
	Lon LL-887	RI	12" LP
M. Long	Welte 2863	1913	PR
P. Loyonnet	ConH CHC-16	1959	12" LP
T. van der Pas	Phil N-00126R	1954	10" LP
G. Thyssens-Valentin	DucTh 270-C-086	1956	12" LP
	DucTh 255-C-122	RI	10" LP
J. Verd	Zodiak 1003	1956	12" LP

Trois Romances sans paroles, Op. 17 (1863?)

—Complete, Nos. 1–3

E. Boynet	Vox PL-6910	1951	12" LP
E. Crochet	Vox SVBX-5424	1964	12" S
G. Johannesen	GoCr 4048	1963	12" LP

—*No. 1 in A flat Major, Op. 17, No. 1*

J. Bergere	Welte 6889	1916	PR

Composition and Performer(s)	Record Label and Number	Date	Speed
C. Kleeberg	Welte 448	1905	PR
(These have not been heard for identification. It is possible they are No. 3)			
—*No. 2 in A Minor, Op. 17, No. 2*			
Not individually recorded			
—*No. 3 in A flat Major, Op. 17, No. 3*			
J. Dennery	ADec 20625, Parl 28.003	1927	10" 78
O. Denton	Duo-Art 6609	1923	PR
F. Ellegaard	DGG 62833, DGG HA-70029	1950	10" 78
G. Fauré	Ampico 66531	1906	PR
	Allegro AL-39	RR	10" LP
	Royale 1402, Royale 1573	RR	12" LP
F. Fox	Ampico 60041	1923	PR
O. Gabrilowitsch	Duo-Art A-5659	1915	PR
—arr. Cello and Piano			
P. Barbezat, pianist unid.	FHMV K-1325	1942	10" 78
H. Britt, J. Adler	ACol 2166-D	1931	10" 78
M. Caponsacchi, pianist unid.	Pathé X-98124	1934	10" 78
J. Hollman, accompanist unid.	Pathé 9508	1916	10" Va
A. Lévy	Od 166.047	1931	10" 78
—arr. Violin and Piano			
Marcelli-Herson, pianist unid.	FHMV K-5140	1927	10" 78
J. Thibaud, accompanist unid.	Pathé 9523	1917	10" Va
Valses-Caprices (1883–1894)			
—Complete, Nos. 1–4			
E. Crochet	Vox SVBX-5423	1964	12" LP

213

Composition and Performer(s)	Record Label and Number	Date	Speed
G. Johannesen	GoCr 4046	1962	12″ LP
G. Thyssens-Valentin	DucTh 300-C-086	1956	12″ LP
—*No. 1 in A Major, Op. 30* (1883)			
G. Fauré	AeolMet 64203	pre-1905	PR
M. Long	Welte 2861	1913	PR
R. Lortat	Duo-Art 6069	1922	PR
—*No. 2 in D flat Major, Op. 38* (1884)			
J. Verd	Zodiak 1003	1956	12″ LP
—*No. 3 in G flat Major, Op. 59* (1891)			
M. Brard	Welte 7060	1923	PR
J. Damase	Dec FST 133.062	1955	12″ LP
G. Doyen	Phil 641.100	1960	12″ LP
G. Fauré	AeolMet 64893	pre-1905	PR
G. Johannesen	HMV CLP-1069	1956	12″ LP
M. Long	Welte 2862	1913	PR
—*No. 4 in A flat Major, Op. 62* (1894)			
G. Fauré	AeolMet 66351	pre-1905	PR

SONGS

Composition and Performer(s)	Record Label and Number	Date	Speed
L'Absent, Op. 5, No. 3 (Hugo) (c. 1865)			
J. Bastard (bs), J. Benvenuti	FCol LFX-599	1939	12″ 78
P. Mollet (b), S. Gouat	West XWN-18211 in set 5502, Plé P-3060	1956	12″ LP
A Clymène, Op. 58, No. 4 (Verlaine) (1890)			
H. Cuénod (t), J. Blancard	Vang VRS-414	1951	12″ LP
B. Kruysen (b), N. Lee	Valois MB-765	1967	12″ S

214

Composition and Performer(s)	Record Label and Number	Date	Speed
C. Maurane (b), L. Bienvenu	Erato LDE-3068	1959	12″ LP
P. Mollet (b), S. Gouat	West XWN-18213 in set 5502, Plé P-3062	1956	12″ LP
G. Souzay (b), D. Baldwin	Phil AL-3505	1963	12″ LP
	APhil 900.191, Phil SAL-3505	1963	12″ S
Accompagnement, Op. 85, No. 3 (Samain) (1903)			
C. Maurane (b), P. Maillard-Verger	Erato EMF-42.079	1964	10″ LP
	Erato STE.60.009	1964	10″ S
P. Mollet (b), S. Gouat	West XWN-18214 in set 5502, Plé P-3064	1956	12″ LP
Adieu, Op. 21, No. 3			
—See *Poème d'un jour, Op. 21*			
Après un rêve, Op. 7, No. 1 (R. Bussine) (c. 1865)			
P. Bernac (b), J. Doyen	Ult BP-1493	1936	10″ 78
P. Bernac (b), F. Poulenc	FHMV DA-4931	1941	10″ 78
A. Collet (b), H. Ebert	HMV X-7550	1948	10″ 78
R. Crespin (s), J. Wustman	Ang 36405	1967	12″ LP
	Ang S-36405	1967	12″ S
C. Croiza (m-s), G. Reeves	FCol LF-63	1932	10″ 78
S. Danco (s), G. Agosti	Dec LW-5229	1955	10″ LP
R. Doria (s), S. Gouat	West XWN-18211 in set 5502, Plé P-3060	1956	12″ LP
K. Fuller (s), pianist unid.	Damon DL-9000	1961	12″ LP
M. Hammel (t), J. Ullern	Lumen 2.00.010, 30125	1938	10″ 78
S. Kowaleska (m-s), pianist unid.	HMV B-4952	1938	10″ 78
M. Marseillac (s), pianist unid.	Od 165.555	1930	10″ 78

Composition and Performer(s)	Record Label and Number	Date	Speed
N. Merriman (m-s), G. Moore	Ang 35217, CCol 33CX-1213	1955	12" LP
E. Noréna (s), orchestra unid.	FHMV DA-4874	1935	10" 78
C. Panzéra (b), pianist unid.	FHMV P-856	1932	10" 78
C. Panzéra (b), Mme. Panzéra-Baillot	FHMV DA-4911	1937	10" 78
	COLH 103	RR	12" LP
L. Pons (s), M. Abravanel, O.	ACol 72050-D in set M-689	1947	12" 78
	ACol ML-4300, ML-5073	RR	12" LP
M. Singher (b), P. Ulanowsky	ACol ML-4258	1950	12" LP
G. Souzay (b), J. Damase	Dec M-604	1948	10" 78
G. Souzay (b), J. Bonneau	Lon LL-245, Dec LXT-2543	1950	12" LP
G. Souzay (b), D. Baldwin	Phil AL-3430	1963	12" LP
	Phil SAL-3480	1963	12" S
M. Teyte (s), accompanist unid.	FDec F-40300	1932	10" 78
M. Teyte (s), R. Mackay	Lon 5889	1937	12" LP
M. Teyte (s), G. Moore	Vic 10-1002 in set M-895, HMV DA-1777	1941	10" 78
	Vic LCT-1133	RR	12" LP
G. Thill (t), M. Fauré	FCol LF-125	1934	10" 78
	Ang, C-3300I, FCol FHX-5012	RR	12" LP
C. Valletti (t), L. Taubman	Vic LM-2787	1965	12" LP
	Vic LSC-2787	1965	12" S
N. Vallin (s), accompanist unid.	Pathé 3222	1922	10" Va
N. Vallin (s), violin, cello, piano unid.	Pathé X-3378	1928	10" 78
	Pathé 3378	1928	10" V
	Pathé X-93081	1933	10" 78
N. Vallin (s), G. Andolfi			
G. Vishnevskaya (s) (in Russian), B. Khaikin, Bolshoi Theatre O.	EHMV ALP-157	1960	12" LP

COMPOSITION AND PERFORMER(S)	RECORD LABEL AND NUMBER	DATE	SPEED
—arr. Violin and Piano or Orch.			
Y. Bratza, pianist unid.	ACol 1857-D	1928	10" 78
M. Elman, L. Mittman	Vic 11-8429 in set M-938	1943	12" 78
G. Knudsen, pianist unid.	HMV AL-2883	1948	10" 78
G. Knudsen, E. Garcia	MusL 5003, MusL 42	1952	10" LP
N. Milstein, A. Fiedler, O.	Vic set DM-1404	1951	12" 78
	Vic ERA-77	1951	7" 45
N. Milstein, accompanist unid.	Cap PBR-8502	1960	12" LP
A. Moguilevsky, accompanist unid.	JCol JD-6028	1933	10" 78
—arr. Viola and Piano (Tertis)			
L. Tertis, pianist unid.	FCol D-1562	1931	10" 78
—arr. Cello and Piano (Casals)			
D. Alexanian, M. Wittels	FHMV K-7173	1934	10" 78
P. Casals, C. Baker	ACol A-6020	1918	12" 78a
P. Casals, N. Mednikoff	Vic 1083, HMV DA-731	1926	10" 78
	Vic LM-2699	RR	12" LP
G. Cassadó, pianist unid.	ACol X-3636, ECol D-1598	1931	10" 78
G. Crépax, accompanist unid.	ACol 5168, ECol D-5831	1931	10" 78
Y. Curti, G. Andolfi	Pathé 9745	1927	10" V
	Pathé X-9745	1927	10" 78
E. Feuermann, F. Rupp	Vic CAL-292	1955	12" LP
M. Gendron, M. Haas	Dec K-1376	1945	12" 78
L. Hoelscher, M. Raucheisen	Tele LGX-66061	1956	12" LP
H. Honegger, E. Møller	Metr MCEP-3027	1957	7" 45
A. Janigro, E. Bagnoli	West XWN-18004	1955	12" LP

Composition and Performer(s)	Record Label and Number	Date	Speed
S. Kates, S. Sanders	Vic LM-2940	1967	12" LP
	Vic LSC-2940	1967	12" S
R. Krotschak, E. Baltzer	ATel M-5004, Euro BM-5004	1947	10" 78
	Euro LPG-631	RR	10" LP
M. Maréchal, M. Fauré	ACol 2446-M, FCol D-13108	1931	10" 78
B. Michelin, T. Janopoulo	FCol LF-241	1935	10" 78
A. Navarra, Clavius-Marius	Od 188.937	1947	10" 78
P. Olevsky, G. Silfies	McInt MM-103	1957	12" LP
L. Radisse, pianist unid.	Od 166.194	1930	10" 78
M. Rostropovich, pianist unid.	MK 23772	1948	10" 78
F. Salmond, pianist unid.	ACol 2045-M	1928	10" 78
C. Sharpe, pianist unid.	EHMV B-2785	1928	10" 78
C. Sharpe, G. Moore	FDec F-7630	1938	10" 78
J. Starker, L. Pommers	Per SPL-708	1953	12" LP
Vectomov, A. Holecek	Sup 20065	1960	10" LP
L. Yevgrafov, G. Miklos	Qual LP-1168/71	1965	12" LP
—arr. String Quartet American Art Quartet	Vic LBC-1086	1955	12" LP
—arr. Horn and Piano J. Stagliano, P. Ulanowsky	Bost 212	1955	12" LP
	Bost S-1009	1955	12" S
—arr. Piano (Maier) G. Maier	Welte X-7795	1925	PR
Arpège, Op. 76, No. 2 (Samain) (1898) R. Doria (s), S. Gouat	West XWN-18214 in set 5502, Plé P-3063	1956	12" LP

Composition and Performer(s)	Record Label and Number	Date	Speed
I. French (s), Doguereau	Tech set 7	1949	12″ 78
G. Souzay (b), D. Baldwin	Dec M-606	1948	10″ 78
G. Souzay (b), J. Bonneau	Lon LL-245, Dec LXT-2543	1951	12″ LP
G. Souzay (b), J. Damase	APhil 500.132, Phil A-02324-L	1963	12″ LP
	APhil 900.132, Phil 835.201AY	1963	12″ S
G. Touraine (s), J. Bonneau	Lumen LD-3-402	1955	12″ LP
Au bord de l'eau, Op. 8, No. 1 (Sully-Prudhomme) (c. 1865)			
G. Bacquier (b), pianist unid.	ClubND 61	1965	12″ LP
R. Crespin (s), J. Wustman	Ang 36405	1967	12″ LP
	Ang S-36405	1967	12″ S
R. Doria (s), S. Gouat	West XWN-18211 in set 5502, Plé P-3060	1956	12″ LP
G. Boué (s), M. Fauré	Uran 7070	1953	12″ LP
G. Guillamat (s), P. Sancan	FCol LF-190	1935	10″ 78
L. Price (s), D. Garvey	Vic LM-2279	1959	12″ LP
	Vic LSC-2279	1959	12″ S
G. Souzay (b), J. Bonneau	Lon LL-245, Dec LXT-2543	1950	12″ LP
N. Vallin (s), G. Andolfi	Pathé X-2622	1929	10″ 78
N. Vallin (s), G. Andolfi	Pathé X-9308l	1933	10″ 78
Au cimetière, Op. 51, No. 2 (Richepin) (c. 1889)			
G. Guillamat (s), P. Sancan	FCol LF-190	1935	10″ 78
B. Kruysen (b), N. Lee	Valois MB-765	1967	12″ S
B. Monmart (s), S. Gouat	West XWN-18213 in set 5502, Plé P-3062	1956	12″ LP

219

COMPOSITION AND PERFORMER(S)	RECORD LABEL AND NUMBER	DATE	SPEED
C. Panzéra (b), Mme. Panzéra-Baillot	Vic 15036 in set M-478,	1933	12" 78
	HMV DB-4906	RR	12" LP
	COLH 103	1959	12" LP
L. Price (s), D. Garvey	Vic LM-2279	1959	12" S
	Vic LSC-2279	1959	12" S
A. Raveau (m-s), G. Andolfi	Pathé X-93077	1933	10" 78
N. Vallin (s), M. Fauré	Pathé PD-66	1944	10" 78
	Vox PL-1730	RR	10" LP
Aubade, Op. 6, No. 1 (Pommey) (c. 1865)			
J. Dutey (t), T. Janopoulo	West XWN-18211 in set 5502,	1956	12" LP
	Plé P-3060		
L'Aube blanche, Op. 95, No. 5			
—See *La Chanson d'Ève, Op. 95*			
Aurore, Op. 39, No. 1 (Silvestre) (1884)			
R. Doria (s), S. Gouat	West XWN-18212 in set 5502,	1956	12" LP
	Plé P-3061	1949	12" 78
I. French (s), P. Doguereau	Tech. set 7	1937	10" 78
G. Guillamat (s), V. Perlemutter	FCol DF-2487	1951	12" LP
P. Mollet (b), P. Maillard-Verger	Selmer LPG-8006	1937	10" 78
C. Panzéra (b), Mme. Panzéra-Baillot	FHMV DA-4913	RR	12" LP
	COLH-103	1961	12" LP
G. Souzay (b), D. Baldwin	Epic LC-3764, Phil A-02059L	1961	12" S
	Epic BC-1122	1944	10" 78
N. Vallin (s), M. Fauré	Pathé PD-46	RR	10" LP
	Vox PL-1730	1944	10" 78
S. Wyss (s), J. St. John	Dec M-553		

COMPOSITION AND PERFORMER(S)	RECORD LABEL AND NUMBER	DATE	SPEED
Automne, Op. 18, No. 3 (Silvestre) (c. 1880)			
G. Bacquier (b), pianist unid.	Club ND 61	1965	12" LP
P. Bernac (b), F. Poulenc	HMV DA-1885	1948	10" 78
A. Endreze (b), A. Krieger	Pathé PA-1986	1941	10" 78
P. Frijsh (s), C. Dougherty	Vic 18053 in set M-789, HMV ED-517	1941	12" 78
A. Gaudin (b), pianist unid.	DGG 561.017	1931	10" 78
G. Guillamat (s), P. Sancan	FCol LF-191	1935	10" 78
I. Kolassi (m-s), J. Bonneau	Lon LS-568, Dec LX-3080	1952	10" LP
B. Kruysen (b), N. Lee	Valois MB-765	1967	12" LP
J. McCormack (t), E. Schneider	HMV DA-1286, HMV VA-72	1932	10" 78
B. Monmarte (s), S. Gouat	West XWN-18212 in set 5502, Plé P-3061	1956	12" LP
C. Panzéra (b), pianist unid.	FHMV P-515	1925	10" 78a
C. Panzéra (b), Mme. Panzéra-Baillot	FHMV DA-4911	1937	10" 78
	COLH-103	RR	12" LP
C. Valletti (t), L. Taubman	Vic LM-2787	1965	12" LP
	Vic LSC-2787	1965	12" S
N. Vallin (s), pianist unid.	ADec 20373, Parl RO-20094, Od 188.578	1930	10" 78
N. Vallin (s), P. Darck	Pathé PG-60	1935	10" 78
Avant que tu ne t'en ailles, Op. 61, No. 6			
—See *La Bonne Chanson, Op. 61*			
Barcarole, Op. 7 No. 3 (Monnier) (c. 1865)			
J. Dutey (t), T. Janapoulo	West XWN-18211 in set 5502, Plé P-3060	1956	12" LP

Composition and Performer(s)	Record Label and Number	Date	Speed
A. Raveau (m-s), G. Andolfi	Pathé X-93078	1933	10" 78
Les Berceaux, Op. 23, No. 1 (Sully-Prudhomme) (1882)			
M. Angelici (s), M. Cébron	Lumen 2.00.005, 33191	1939	10" 78
G. Bacquier (b), Brilli	Orph 51071/2	1963	12" LP
P. Bernac (b), F. Poulenc	HMV DA-1885	1948	10" 78
	FHMV FALP-50036	RI	12" LP
E. Billot (b), pianist unid.	Od 188.814	1931	10" 78
R. Bourdin (b), pianist unid.	Od 188.564	1934	10" 78
S. Brohly (m-s), accompanist unid.	FHMV 33761, P-235, P-394	1912	10" 78a
J. Chalud-ben-Baruch, orchestra unid.	Saturn 1001	1951	10" LP
M. Dens (b), J. Bonneau	Pathé DTX-30	1959	12" LP
	Pathé ASTX-114	1959	12" S
A. Endrèze (b), A. Krieger	Pathé PA-1986	1941	10" 78
F. Litvinne (s), A. Cortot	FHMV G-C-33159 (matrix 1359-F-1)	1903	10" 78a
F. Litvinne (s), pianist unid.	FHMV G-C-33159 (matrix 2256-c.s.1)	1903	10" 78a
C. Maurane (b), L. Bienvenu	Pathé PD-136	1950	10" 78
A. Mestral (b), I. Aitoff	Phil N432.012E,	1962	7" 45
	Phil M.A.77501S	1962	7" S
P. Mollet (b), P. Maillard-Verger	Selmer LPG-8006	1951	12" LP
B. Monmart (s), S. Gouat	West XWN-18212 in set 5502, Plé P-3061	1956	12" LP
L. Nucelly (b), pianist unid.	FHMV K-2305	1943	10" 78
C. Panzéra (b), Mme. Panzéra-Baillot	FHMV P-724, EHMV E-602	1928	10" 78

Composition and Performer(s)	Record Label and Number	Date	Speed
C. Panzéra (b), Mme. Panzéra-Baillot	FHMV DA-4909	1937	10" 78
	COLH 103	RR	12" LP
	Atl 1207	1952	12" LP
M. Powers (m-s), F. La Forge	Pathé 3490	1930	10" V
A. Raveau (m-s), G. Andolfi	Pathé X-3490	1930	10" 78
A. Raveau (m-s), G. Andolfi (different vers.?)	Pathé X.93120	1933	10" 78
M. Sibelle (s), accompanist unid.	Pathé 3410	1929	10" V
G. Souzay (b), D. Baldwin	Epic LC-3764, Phil A-02059L	1961	12" LP
	Epic BC-1122	1961	12" S
J. Tourel (m-s), G. Reeves	ECol LX-1306	1951	12" 78
N. Vallin (s), M. Long	FCol LF-125	1933	10" 78
J. Vieuille (b), pianist unid.	Parl 28.518	1931	10" 78
L. Warren (b), W. Sektberg	Vic LM-2266	1958	12" LP
S. Wyss (s), J. St. John	Dec M-529	1943	10" 78

La Bonne Chanson, Op. 61 (Verlaine) (1891–2) (Cycle of 9 songs)

Composition and Performer(s)	Record Label and Number	Date	Speed
—Complete cycle			
J. Brainerd (s), J. Paull	ConH CHC-49	1950	12" LP
H. Cuénod (t), F. Hollechek	West WL-5278, XWN-18707	1955	12" LP
S. Danco (s), G. Agosti	Lon LS-589, Dec LX-3111	1953	10" LP
	Lon LL-1324	RI	12" LP
P. Derenne (t), Houdy	CdM CL-2	1964	12" S
D. Fischer-Dieskau (b), G. Moore	EHMV BLP-1106, Elec 70370	1959	10" LP
C. Maurane (b), L. Bienvenu	Erato LDE-3068	1959	12" LP
C. Maurane (b), P. Maillard-Verger	Erato EMF-42.079	1964	10" LP
	Erato STE-60.009	1964	10" S

Composition and Performer(s)	Record Label and Number	Date	Speed
P. Mollet (b), S. Gouat	West XWN-18213 in set 5502,	1956	12" LP
	Plé P-3062	1954	12" LP
V. Osborne (s), R. Cumming	MusL 7044		
C. Panzéra (b), Mme. Panzéra-Baillot	Vic 15033/5 in set M-478,	1939	12" 78
	FHMV DB-5020/2	RR	12" LP
M. Singher (b), Tree (vln), Nugele (vln), Molieu (vla), Grebanier (vc), R. Goode (p)	FHMV FALP-50008	1961	12" LP
G. Souzay (b), D. Baldwin	ACol ML-5644	1961	12" S
	ACol MS-6244	1961	12" LP
S. Stappen (s), P. Coppola, O. (orch. by Le Boucher)	Epic LC-3764, Phil A-02059L	1961	12" S
Sussman, P. Maillard-Verger	Epic BC-1122		
S. Wyss (s), K. Long	FHMV K-7327;7368;7458/60	1935	10" 78
	ClubND 10	1965	12" LP
	FDec AF-9414/8	1946	10" 78
—No. 1. *Une Sainte en son auréole* Not individually recorded			
—No. 2. *Puisque l'aube grandit* Not individually recorded			
—No. 3. *La lune blanche luit dans les bois* M. Teyte (s), G. Moore	HMV GSC-22 in set GS-3	1947	12" 78
—No. 4. *J'allais par des chemins perfides* Not individually recorded			
—No. 5. *J'ai presque peur* M. Teyte (s), G. Moore	HMV GSC-22 in set GS-3	1947	12" 78

Composition and Performer(s)	Record Label and Number	Date	Speed
—No. 6. *Avant que tu ne t'en ailles* Not individually recorded			
—No. 7. *Donc ce sera par un clair jour d'été* Not individually recorded			
—No. 8. *N'est-ce pas?* Not individually recorded			
—No. 9. *L'hiver a cessé* M. Teyte (s), G. Moore	HMV DA-1893	1948	10" 78
C'est l'extase, Op. 58, No. 5 (Verlaine) (1890)			
H. Cuénod (t), J. Blancard	Vang VRS-414	1951	12" LP
P. Curtin (s), R. Edwards	Camb 706	1965	12" LP
	Camb 1706	1965	12" S
	Valois MB-765	1967	12" S
B. Kruysen (b), N. Lee	Erato LDE-3068	1958	12" LP
C. Maurane (b), L. Bienvenu	West XWN-18213 in set 5502,		
P. Mollet (b), S. Gouat	Plé P-3062	1956	12" LP
C. Panzéra (b), Mme. Panzéra-Baillot	FHMV DA-4913	1937	10" 78
	COLH 103	RR	12" LP
G. Souzay (b), J. Bonneau	Lon LD-9023, Dec LX-3149	1956	10" LP
G. Souzay (b), D. Baldwin	EPhil AL-3505, FPhil. L-2405L	1966	12" LP
	APhil 900.191, EPhil SAL-3505,		
	FPhil 835.286LY	1966	12" S
C'est la paix, Op. 114 (Debladis) (1919–20)			
R. Doria (s), S. Gouat	West XWN-18215 in set 5502,		
	Plé P-3064	1956	12" LP

225

Composition and Performer(s)	Record Label and Number	Date	Speed
Chanson, Op. 94 (de Régnier) (1907)			
R. Doria (s), S. Gouat	West XWN-18214 in set 5502,		
	Plé P-3063	1956	12" LP
Chanson d'amour, Op, 27, No. 1 (Silvestre) (1883)			
V. de los Angeles (s), G. Moore	Ang 35971, HMV ALP-1838	1961	12" LP
	Ang S-35971	1961	12" S
B. Kruysen (b), N. Lee	Valois MB-765	1967	12" S
P. Mollet (b), S. Gouat	West XWN-18212 in set 5502,		
	Plé P-3061	1956	12" LP
La Chanson d'Ève, Op. 95 (van Lerberghe) (1907–10) (cycle of 10 songs)			
—Complete cycle			
P. Curtin (s), R. Edwards	Camb 706	1965	12" LP
	Camb 1706	1965	12" S
R. Doria (s), S. Gouat	West XWN-18214 in set 5502,		
	Plé P-3063	1956	12" LP
I. Kolassi (m-s), A. Collard	Lon LL-919, Dec LXT-2897	1954	12" LP
—1. *Paradis*			
Not individually recorded			
—2. *Prima verba*			
Not individually recorded			
—3. *Roses ardentes*			
Not individually recorded			

Composition and Performer(s)	Record Label and Number	Date	Speed
—4. *Comme Dieu rayonne* Not individually recorded			
—5. *L'Aube blanche* Not individually recorded			
—6. *Eau vivante* G. Souzay (b), D. Baldwin	Phil AL-3505, A-02405L APhil 900.191, EPhil SAL-3505, FPhil 835.286LY	1965 1965	12" LP 12" S
—No. 7. *Veilles-tu, ma senteur de soleil?* Not individually recorded			
—No. 8. *Dans un parfum de roses blanches* Not individually recorded			
—No. 9. *Crépuscule* Not individually recorded			
—No. 10. *O Mort, poussière d'étoiles* G. Souzay (b), D. Baldwin	EPhil AL-3505, FPhil A-2405L APhil 900.191, EPhil SAL-3505, FPhil 835.286LY	1965 1965	12" LP 12" S
Chanson du pêcheur, Op. 4, No. 1 (Gautier) (c. 1865) G. Bacquier (b), Laforge R. Bourdin (b), E. Nerini D. Devriès (t), G. Cloez, O. P. Mollet (b), S. Gouat	Vega L30-PO-357 FDGG 590.112 Od 188.792 West XWN-18211 in set 5502, Plé P-3060	1966 1930 1931 1956	12" LP 10" 78 10" 78 12" LP

Composition and Performer(s)	Record Label and Number	Date	Speed
P. Mollet (b), P. Maillard-Verger	Selmer LPG-8006	1951	12" LP
C. Panzéra (b), P. Coppola, O. (mislabeled "Lamento")	FHMV P-739	1930	10" 78
C. Panzéra (b), Blondel String Quartet	FHMV DA-4873	1935	10" 78
C. Panzéra (b), Mme. Panzéra-Baillot	FHMV DA-4909	1937	10" 78
	COLH 103, FCol 50028	RR	12" LP
C. Panzéra (b), Mme. Panzéra-Baillot	Merc MG-10097	1951	12" LP
G. Souzay (b), D. Baldwin	Epic LC-3764, Phil A-02059L	1961	12" LP
	Epic BC-1122	1961	12" S
Chant d'automne, Op. 5, No. 1 (Baudelaire) (c. 1865)			
B. Monmart (s), S. Gouat	West XWN-18211 in set 5502, Plé P-3060	1956	12" LP
P. de Seyguières (t), Y. Vallier	FCol DFX-220	1938	12" 78
Cinq Mélodies, Op. 58 (Verlaine) (1890)			
—See *Mandoline, En sourdine, Green, A Clymène, C'est l'extase.*			
Claire de lune, Op. 46, No. 2 (Verlaine) (1887)			
V. de los Angeles (s), G. Moore	Ang 35971, HMV ALP-1838	1961	12" LP
	Ang S-35971	1961	12" S
G. Bacquier (b), Laforge	Vega L-30-PO-357	1966	12" LP
J. Bathori (s), self-accompanied	FCol D-13097	1931	10" 78
	FCol 50030	RR	12" LP
E. Clément (t), pianist unid.	Pathé 3165	1919	10" Va
R. Crespin (s), J. Wustman	Ang 36405	1967	12" LP
	Ang S-36405	1967	12" S
C. Croiza (m-s), F. Poulenc	FCol D-13033	1931	10" 78

Composition and Performer(s)	Record Label and Number	Date	Speed
H. Cuénod (t), J. Blancard	Vang VRS-414	1951	12" LP
P. Curtin (s), R. Edwards	Camb 706	1965	12" LP
	Camb 1706	1965	12" S
M. Dobbs (s), G. Moore	Ang 35094, CCol 33CX-1154	1954	12" LP
R. Doria, S. Gouat	West XWN-18212 in set 5502, Plé P-3061	1956	12" LP
E. Farrell (s), G. Trovillo	ACol ML-5924	1964	12" LP
	ACol MS-6524	1964	12" S
	Uran 7070	1953	12" LP
G. Boué (s), M. Fauré	Pathé X-3419	1929	10" 78
G. Gills (s), M. Franck	Pathé 3419	1929	10" V
	FCol LF-191	1935	10" 78
G. Guillamat (s), P. Sancan	Lumen 2.00.010, 30125	1938	10" 78
M. Hamel (t), J. Ullern	Valois MB-765	1967	12" S
B. Kruysen (b), N. Lee	FHMV 33753, P-232	1912	10" 78a
J. Lindsay (s), accompanist unid.	Pathé 3175	1921	10" Va
J. Marny (t), accompanist unid.	Erato LDE-3068	1959	12" LP
C. Maurane (b), L. Bienvenu	Phil N-432.012E	1962	7" 45
A. Mestral (b), I. Aïtoff	Phil M.A.77.501S	1962	7" S
P. Mollet (b), P. Maillard-Verger	Selmer LPG-8006	1951	12" LP
M. Nespoulous (m-s), M. van Parys	FCol D-12028	1928	10" 78
E. Noréna (s), accompanist unid.	FHM DA-4874	1935	10" 78
V. Osborne (s), R. Cummings	MusL 7044	1954	12" LP
C. Panzéra (b), accompanist unid.	FHMV P-489	1925	10" 78a
C. Panzéra (b), P. Coppola, O.	FHMV P-739, EHMV E-519	1930	10" 78
C. Panzéra (b), Mme. Panzéra-Baillot	FHMV DB-4887	1935	10" 78
	COLH 103	RR	12" LP

Composition and Performer(s)	Record Label and Number	Speed	Date
M. Pechenart (s), accompanist unid.	FCol LF-167	10" 78	1936
L. Price (s), D. Garvey	Vic LM-2279	12" LP	1959
	Vic LSC-2279	12" S	1959
A. Raveau (m-s), G. Andolfi	Pathé 7222	10" V	1930
	Pathé X-34902	10" 78	1930
A. Raveau (m-s), G. Andolfi (diff. version?)	Pathé X-93120	10" 78	1933
Schmidt, Brilli	Orph 51071/2	12" LP	1964
L. ben Sedira (s), pianist unid.	Ult BP-1578	10" 78	1936
G. Souzay (b), J. Damase	Dec M-606	10" 78	1947
G. Souzay (b), J. Bonneau	Lon LL-245, Dec LXT-2543	12" LP	1950
M. Teyte (s), G. Moore	HMV DA-1876	10" 78	1948
G. Thill (t), M. Fauré	ACol 4164, FCol LF-154	10" 78	1936
A. Thursfield (s), I. Newton	EHMV E-452	10" 78	1927
C. Valletti (t), L. Taubman	Vic LM-2787	12" LP	1965
	Vic LSC-2787	12" S	1965
N. Vallin (s), G. Andolfi	Pathé X-3465	10" 78	1930
N. Vallin (s), P. Darck	Pathé PG-101	10" 78	1940
N. Vallin (s), pianist unid.	ADec 20323, Parl RO-20094, Od 188.578	10" 78	1930
—arr. Piano			
E. Boynet	Vox PL-6910	12" LP	1951
M. Volvay	Welte B-6917	PR	1917

Comme Dieu rayonne, Op. 95, No. 4

—See *La Chanson d'Ève, Op. 95*

Crépuscule, Op. 95, No. 9

Composition and Performer(s)	Record Label and Number	Date	Speed
—See *La Chanson d'Ève, Op. 95*			
Cygne sur l'eau, Op. 113, No. 1			
—See *Mirages, Op. 113*			
Dans le forêt de septembre, Op. 85, No. 1 (Mendès) (1903)			
B. Monmart (s), S. Gouat	West XWN-18214 in set 5502,		
	Plé P-3063	1956	12" LP
	FHMV DA-5008	1941	10" 78
N. Pérrugia (s), I. Aitoff	EPhil AL-3505, FPhil L-2405L	1963	12" LP
G. Souzay (b), D. Baldwin	APhil 900.191, EPhil SAL-3505,		
	FPhil 835.286LY	1963	12" S
Dans la nymphée, Op. 106, No. 5			
—See *Le Jardin clos, Op. 106*			
Dans la pénombre, Op. 106, No. 6			
—See *Le Jardin clos, Op. 106*			
Dans un parfum de roses blanches, Op. 95, No. 8			
—See *La Chanson d'Ève, Op. 95*			
Dans les ruines d'une abbaye, Op. 2, No. 1 (Hugo) (c. 1865)			
R. Doria (s), S. Gouat	West XWN-18211 in set 5502,		
	Plé P-3060	1956	12" LP
P. Frijsh (s), E. Nielsen	Vic 1653, HMV DA-1324	1934	10" 78
M. Marcelin (t), pianist unid.	FHMV P-838	1929	10" 78
	EPhil AL-3505, FPhil L-2405L	1963	12" LP
G. Souzay (b), D. Baldwin	APhil 900.191, EPhil SAL-3505,		
	FPhil 835.286	1963	12" S

231

Composition and Performer(s)	Record Label and Number	Date	Speed
M. Teyte (s), G. Moore	HMV DA-1810	1942	10" 78
C. Valletti (t), L. Taubman	Vic LM-2787	1965	12" LP
	Vic LSC-2787	1965	12" S
Danseuse, Op. 113, No. 4			
—See *Mirages, Op. 113*			
Diane, Séléné, Op. 118, No. 3			
—See *L'Horizon chimérique, Op. 118*			
Le Don silencieux, Op. 92 (Dominique) (1906)			
R. Doria (s), S. Gouat	West XWN-18214 in set 5502,		
	Plé P-3063	1956	12" LP
I. Kolassi (m-s), pianist unid.	Lumen LD-2.406	1957	10" LP
C. Maurane (b), L. Bienvenu	Erato LDE-3068	1959	12" LP
S. Metcalf-Casals (s), G. Moore	EHMV JG-22	1938	12" 78
N. Pérrugia (s), I. Aïtoff	FHMV DA-5008	1941	10" 78
G. Souzay (b), D. Baldwin	Epic LC-3764, Phil A-02059L	1961	12" LP
	Epic BC-1122	1961	12" S
Donc ce sera par un clair jour d'été, Op. 61, No. 7			
—See *La Bonne Chanson, Op. 61*			
En prière (Bordèse) (1890)			
C. Butt (m-s), accompanist unid.	HMV a-033099	?	12" 78a
G. Cernay (m-s), F. Cebron, O.	Lumen 2.20.014, 30085	1937	10" 78
G. Guillamat (s), V. Perlemutter	FCol DF-2486	1937	10" 78

COMPOSITION AND PERFORMER(s)	RECORD LABEL AND NUMBER	DATE	SPEED
C. Maurane (b), P. Maillard-Verger	Erato EFM-42.079	1964	10″ LP
	Erato STE-60.009	1964	10″ S
	FCol DF-2260	1936	10″ 78
J. Micheau (s), Cariven, O.	West XWN-18214 in set 5502,		
P. Mollet (b), S. Gouat	Plé P-3063	1956	12″ LP
V. Osborne (s), R. Cumming	MusL 7044	1954	12″ LP
C. Panzéra (b), Mme. Panzéra-Baillot	FHMV DA-4887	1936	10″ 78
G. Thill (t), M. Fauré	ACol 4218-M, FCol LF-152, LB-42	1936	10″ 78
Eau vivante, Op. 95, No. 6			
See *La Chanson d'Ève, Op. 95*			
En sourdine, Op. 58, No. 2 (Verlaine) (1890)			
H. Cuénod (t), J. Blancard	Vang VRS-414	1951	12″ LP
P. Curtin (s), R. Edwards	Camb 706	1965	12″ LP
	Camb 1706	1965	12″ S
R. Doria (s), S. Gouat	West XWN-18213 in set 5502,		
	Plé P-3062	1956	12″ LP
G. Guillamat (s), V. Perlemutter	FCol DF-2485	1934	10″ 78
B. Kruysen (b), N. Lee	Valois MA-765	1967	12″ S
C. Maurane (b), L. Bienvenu	Erato LDE-3068	1959	12″ LP
P. Mollet (b), P. Maillard-Verger	Selmer LPG-8006	1951	10″ LP
C. Panzéra (b), Mme. Panzéra-Baillot	Vic 15036 in set M-478, FHMV		
	DB-4903	1933	12″ 78
	COLH 103	RR	12″ LP
G. Souzay (b), J. Damase	Dec M-604	1946	10″ 78
G. Souzay (b), J. Bonneau	Lon LL-245, Dec LXT-2543	1951	12″ LP

233

Composition and Performer(s)	Record Label and Number	Date	Speed
G. Souzay (b), D. Baldwin	EPhil AL-3505, FPhil L-2405L APhil 900.191, EPhil SAL-3505, FPhil 835.286LY	1963	12″ LP
N. Vallin (s), P. Darck	Pathé PG-102	1963 1940	12″ S 10″ 78
N. Vallin (s), M. Fauré	Pathé PD-46 AVox PL-1730	1944 RR	10″ 78 10″ LP
Exaucement, Op. 106, No. 1			
—See *Le Jardin clos, Op. 106*			
La Fée aux chansons, Op. 27, No. 2 (Silvestre) (1883)			
R. Doria (s), S. Gouat	West XWN-18212 in set 5502, Plé P-3061	1956	12″ LP
B. Kruysen (b), N. Lee	Valois MB-765	1965	12″ S
M. Marcelin (t), pianist unid.	FHMV P-838	1929	10″ 78
N. Mathot (s), Jacque-Dupont	FRCA F-230.005	1956	10″ LP
L. ben Sedira (s), pianist unid.	Ult BP-1578	1936	10″ 78
Fleur jetée, Op. 39, No. 2 (Silvestre) (1884)			
M. Harrell (b), B. Smith	Rem 199-140	1953	12″ LP
F. Jagel (t), R. Hill	IRCC 3064	1953	10″ 78
P. Mollet (b), S. Gouat	West XWN-18212 in set 5502, Plé P-3061	1956	12″ LP
V. Osborne (s), R. Cumming	MusL 7044	1954	12″ LP
G. Souzay (b), D. Baldwin	Epic LC-3764, Phil A-02057L	1961	12″ LP
	Epic BC-1122	1961	12″ S
G. Thill (t), M. Fauré	FCol LF-157	1934	10″ 78

Composition and Performer(s)	Record Label and Number	Date	Speed
La Fleur qui va sur l'eau, Op. 85, No. 2 (Mendès) (1903)			
B. Monmart (s), S. Gouat	West XWN-18214 in set 5502, Plé P-3063	1956	12" LP
	EPhil AL-3505, FPhil L-2405L	1963	12" LP
G. Souzay (b), D. Baldwin	APhil 900.191, EPhil SAL-3505, FPhil 835.286LY	1963	12" S
Green, Op. 58, No. 3 (Verlaine) (1890)			
H. Cuénod (t), J. Blancard	Vang VRS-414	1951	12" LP
P. Curtin (s), R. Edwards	Camb 706	1965	12" LP
	Camb 1706	1965	12" S
B. Kruysen (b), N. Lee	Valois MB-765	1967	12" S
C. Maurane (b), L. Bienvenu	Erato LDE-3068	1959	12" LP
P. Mollet (b), S. Gouat	West XWN-18213 in set 5502, Plé P-3062	1956	12" LP
G. Souzay (b), J. Bonneau	Lon LD-9023, Dec LX-3149	1956	10" LP
G. Souzay (b), D. Baldwin	EPhil AL-3505, FPhil L-2405L	1963	12" LP
	APhil 900.191, EPhil SAL-3505, FPhil 835.286LY	1963	12" S
L'hiver a cessé, Op. 61, No. 9			
—See *La Bonne Chanson, Op. 61*			
L'Horizon chimérique, Op. 118 (de la Ville de Mirmont) (1922) (cycle of 4 songs)			
—Complete cycle			
B. Kruysen (b), N. Lee	Valois MB-765	1967	12" S
C. Maurane (b), L. Bienvenu	Erato LDE-3068	1959	12" LP

Composition and Performer(s)	Record Label and Number	Date	Speed
P. Mollet (b), S. Gouat	West XWN-18215 in set 5502,	1956	12" LP
	Plé P-3064		
C. Panzéra (b), Mme. Panzéra-Baillot	FHMV DB-4972	1935	12" 78
C. Panzéra (b), Mme. Panzéra-Baillot	FHMV DB-5009, Vic 15037 in set M-478	1936	12" 78
C. Panzéra (b), Mme. Panzéra-Baillot (Note: This work was dedicated to Charles Panzéra)	COLH 103	RR	12" LP
	Merc MG-10097	1951	12" LP
G. Souzay (b), J. Damase	Dec K-1693	1948	12" 78
G. Souzay (b), J. Bonneau	Lon LL-245, Dec LXT-2543	1951	12" LP
G. Souzay (b), D. Baldwin	EPhil AL-3505, FPhil L-2405L	1963	12" LP
	APhil 900.191, EPhil SAL-3505, FPhil 835.286	1963	12" S
—No. 1. *La Mer est infinie*			
Not individually recorded			
—No. 2. *Je me suis embarqué*			
C. Panzéra (b), pianist unid.	FHMV P-519	1925	10" 78a
—No. 3. *Diane, Séléné*			
O. di Napoli (m-s), P. Doguereau	Tech set T-7	1949	12" 78
C. Panzéra (b), pianist unid.	FHMV P-519	1925	12" 78a
—No. 4. *Vaisseaux, nous vous aurons aimés*			
Not individually recorded			
Hymne, Op. 7, No. 2 (Baudelaire) (c. 1865) J. Dutey (t), T. Janopoulo	West XWN-18211 in set 5502,	1956	12" LP
	Plé P-3060		

Composition and Performer(s)	Record Label and Number	Date	Speed
Hymne à Apollo, Op. 63a (harmonization of 2nd century B.C. melody restored by Theodore Reinach, words restored by H. Weil) (1894)			
R. Doria (s), S. Gouat	West XWN-18215 in set 5502, Plé P.3064	1956	12″ LP
Ici-bas, Op. 8, No. 3 (Sully-Prudhomme) (c. 1865)			
R. Doria (s), S. Gouat	West XWN-18211 in set 5502, Plé P.3060	1956	12″ LP
N. Merriman (m-s), G. Moore	Ang 35217, CCol 33CX-1213	1955	12″ LP
M. Teyte (s), G. Moore	HMV DA-1830	1943	10″ 78
Il m'est cher, Amour, Op. 106, No. 7			
—See *Le Jardin clos, Op. 106*			
Inscription sur le sable, Op. 106, No. 8			
—See *Le Jardin clos, Op. 106*			
J'ai presque peur, Op. 61, No. 5			
—See *La Bonne Chanson, Op. 61*			
J'allais par des chemins perfides, Op. 61, No. 4			
—See *La Bonne Chanson, Op. 61*			
Le Jardin clos, Op. 106 (van Lerberghe) (1915–18) (cycle of 8 songs)			
—Complete cycle C. Maurane (b), L. Bienvenu	Erato LDE-3068	1959	12″ LP

Composition and Performer(s)	Record Label and Number	Date	Speed
B. Monmart (s), S. Gouat	West XWN-18215 in set 5502, Plé P-3064	1956	12" LP
N. Perrugia (s), J. Benvenuti	FHMV DB-5157/8	1951	12" 78
—No. 1. *Exaucement* G. Souzay (b), D. Baldwin	EPhil AL-3505, FPhil L-2405L APhil 900.191, EPhil CAL-3505, FPhil 835.286	1963 1963	12" LP 12" S
—No. 2. *Quand tu plonges tes yeux dans mes yeux* Not individually recorded			
—No. 3. *La Messagère* Not individually recorded			
—No. 4. *Je me poserai sur ton coeur* G. Souzay (b), D. Baldwin	EPhil AL-3505, FPhil L-2405 APhil 900.191, EPhil SAL-3505, FPhil 835.286LY	1963 1963	12" LP 12" S
—No. 5. *Dans la nymphée* Not individually recorded			
—No. 6. *Dans la pénombre* Not individually recorded			
—No. 7. *Il m'est cher, Amour* Not individually recorded			
—No. 8. *Inscription sur le sable* Not individually recorded			

Composition and Performer(s)	Record Label and Number	Date	Speed
Je me poserai sur ton coeur, Op. 106, No. 4			
—See *Le Jardin clos, Op. 106*			
Je me suis embarqué, Op. 118, No. 2			
—See *L'Horizon chimérique, Op. 118*			
Jardin nocturne, Op. 113, No. 3			
—See *Mirages, Op. 113*			
Larmes, Op. 51, No. 1 (Richepin) (c. 1889)			
B. Kruysen (b), N. Lee	Valois MB-765	1967	12″ S
B. Monmart (s), S. Gouat	West XWN-18212 in set 5502,	1956	12″ LP
O. di Napoli (m-s), P. Doguereau	Plé P-3061	1949	12″ 78
	Tech set T-7		
La lune blanche luit dans les bois, Op. 61, No. 3			
—See *La Bonne Chanson, Op. 61*			
Lydia, Op. 4, No. 2 (de Lisle) (c. 1865)			
P. Bernac (b), F. Poulenc	FHMV DA-4931	1940	10″ 78
	FHMV FALP-50036	RR	12″ LP
R. Bourdin (b), pianist unid.	Od 188.634	1931	10″ 78
R. Doria (s), S. Gouat	West XWN-18211 in set 5502,	1956	12″ LP
	Plé P-3060	1949	12″ 78
I. French (s), P. Doguereau	Tech set T-7	1956	10″ LP
N. Mathot (s), Jacque-Dupont	FRCA F-230.005	1935	10″ 78
C. Panzéra (b), Mme. Panzéra-Baillot	Vic 1897, FHMV DA-4878	RR	12″ LP
	COLH 103		

239

Composition and Performer(s)	Record Label and Number	Date	Speed
C. Panzéra (b), Mme. Panzéra-Baillot	Merc ML-10097	1951	12" LP
C. Rouselière (t), orchestra unid.	FDGG 561.022, 524.058	1931	10" LP
M. Teyte (s), G. Moore	HMV DA-1831	1943	10" 78
G. Touraine (s), J. Bonneau	Lumen LD-3-402	1956	12" LP
Mai, Op. 1, No. 2 (Hugo) (c. 1865)			
J. Dutey (t), T. Janopoulo	West XWN-18211 in set 5502, Plé P-3060	1956	12" LP
Mandoline, Op. 58, No. 1 (Verlaine) (1890)			
H. Cuénod (t), J. Blancard	Vang VRS-414	1951	12" LP
P. Curtin (s), R. Edwards	Camb 706	1965	12" LP
	Camb 1706	1965	12" S
I. French (s), P. Doguereau	Tech set T-7	1949	12" 78
I. Kolassi (m-s), J. Bonneau	Lon LS-568, Dec LX-3080	1952	10" LP
B. Kruysen (b), N. Lee	Valois MB-765	1967	12" S
C. Maurane (b), L. Bienvenu	Erato LDE-3068	1959	12" LP
P. Mollet (b), P. Maillard-Verger	Selmer LPG-8006	1951	12" LP
B. Monmart (s), S. Gouat	West XWN-18213 in set 5502, Plé P-3062	1956	12" LP
L. Price (s), D. Garvey	Vic LM-2279	1959	12" LP
	Vic LSC-2279	1959	12" S
G. Souzay (b), J. Bonneau	Lon LD-9023, Dec LX-3149	1956	10" LP
G. Souzay (b), D. Baldwin	EPhil AL-3505, FPhil L-2405L	1963	12" LP
	APhil 900.191, EPhil SAL-3505, FPhil 835.286LY	1963	12" S
Les Matelots, Op. 2, No. 2 (Gautier) (c. 1865)			
P. Mollet (b), S. Gouat	West XWN-18211 in set 5502, Plé P-3060	1956	12" LP

Composition and Performer(s)	Record Label and Number	Date	Speed
Les Mélodies de Vénise, Op. 58 (Verlaine) (1890)			
—See *Mandoline, En sourdine, Green, A Clymène, C'est l'extase.*			
La Mer est infinie, Op. 118, No. 1			
—See *L'Horizon chimérique, Op. 118*			
La Messagère, Op. 106, No. 3			
—See *Le Jardin clos, Op. 106*			
Mirages, Op. 113 (de Brimont) (1919) (cycle of 4 songs)			
—Complete cycle			
L. Daniels (s), J. Benvenuti	OL 27/28	1938	10″ & 12″ 78
P. Derenne (t), H. Cox	West XWN-18215 in set 5502,	1956	12″ LP
	Plé P-3064	1955	10″ LP
I. Kolassi (m-s), pianist unid.	Lumen LD-2.406	1959	12″ LP
C. Maurane (b), L. Bienvenu	Erato LDE-3068	1963	12″ LP
G. Souzay (b), D. Baldwin	EPhil AL-3505, FPhil L-2405L		
	APhil 900.191, EPhil SAL-3505,		
	FPhil 835.286LY	1963	12″ S
—No. 1. *Cygne sur l'eau*			
Y. le Marc' Hadour (b), Mme. le Marc' Hadour	BaM 31	1940	12″ 78
—No. 2. *Reflets dans l'eau*			
Not individually recorded			

Composition and Performer(s)	Record Label and Number	Date	Speed
—No. 3. *Jardin nocturne*			
P. Bernac (b), F. Poulenc	FHMV DA-4889	1936	10" 78
	FHMV FALP-50036	RR	12" LP
—No. 4. *Danseuse*			
O. di Napoli (m-s), P. Doguereau	Tech set T-7	1949	12" 78
Nell, Op. 18, No. 1 (de Lisle) (c. 1880)			
R. Doria (s), S. Gouat	West XWN-18212 in set 5502,		
	Plé P-3060	1956	12" LP
E. Farrell (s), G. Trovillo	ACol ML-5924	1964	12" LP
	ACol MS-6524	1964	12" S
P. Frijsh (s), C. Dougherty	Vic 2078 in set M-668	1939	10" 78
G. Guillamat (s), P. Sancan	FCol LF-192	1935	10" 78
J. Harsanyi (s), O. Herz	Per SPL-581	1954	12" LP
B. Kruysen (b), N. Lee	Valois MB-765	1967	12" S
S. Metcalf-Casals (s), G. Moore	HMV JG-22	1938	12" 78
P. Mollet (b), P. Maillard-Verger	Selmer LPG-8006	1951	12" LP
O. di Napoli (m-s), P. Doguereau	Tech set T-7	1949	12" 78
M. Singher (b), P. Ulanowsky	ACol ML-4258	1950	12" LP
M. Teyte (s), G. Moore	HMV DA-1831	1943	10" 78
N. Vallin (s), P. Darck	Pathé PG-102	1940	10" 78
N. Vallin (s), M. Fauré	Pathé PD-51	1944	10" 78
	AVox PL-1730	RR	10" LP
—arr. Piano (Grainger)			
P. Grainger	Duo-Art 6931	1924	PR

Composition and Performer(s)	Record Label and Number	Date	Speed
N'est-ce pas?, Op. 61, No. 8			
—See *La Bonne Chanson, Op. 61*			
Nocturne, Op. 43, No. 2 (de l'Isle-Adam) (1886)			
J. Bastard (bs), J. Benvenuti	FCol LFX-599	1939	12" 78
C. Maurane (b), P. Maillard-Verger	Erato EFM-42.079	1964	10" LP
	Erato STE-60.009	1964	10" S
P. Mollet (b), S. Gouat	West XWN-18212 in set 5502,	1956	12" LP
	Plé P-3061		
C. Panzéra (b), Mme. Panzéra-Baillot	FHMV DA-4905	1937	10" 78
	COLH 103	RR	12" LP
Nöel, Op. 43, No. 1 (Wilder) (1886)			
R. Doria (s), S. Gouat	West XWN-18212 in set 5502,	1956	12" LP
	Plé P-3061		
E. Farrell (s), G. Trovillo	ACol ML-5924	1964	12" LP
	ACol MS-6524	1964	12" S
G. Thill (t), M. Fauré	ACol 4218-M, FCol LF-152, FCol		
	LB-42	1936	10" 78
	FCol FH-504	RR	10" LP
J. Wilson (s), G. Trovillo	ADec DL-9554	1952	12" LP
Notre amour, Op. 23, No. 2 (Silvestre) (1882)			
M. Dobbs (s), G. Moore	Ang 35094, CCol 33CX-1154	1954	12" LP
R. Doria (s), S. Gouat	West XWN-18212 in set 5502,	1956	12" LP
	Plé P-3061		
L. Price (s), D. Garvey	Vic LM-2279	1959	12" LP
	Vic LSC-2279	1959	12" S

Composition and Performer(s)	Record Label and Number	Date	Speed
Paradis, Op. 95, No. 1			
—See *La Chanson d'Ève, Op. 95*			
Le Papillon et la fleur, Op. 1, No. 1 (Hugo) (1860)			
R. Doria (s), S. Gouat	West XWN-18211 in set 5502,	1956	12" LP
	Plé P-3060	1957	10" LP
N. Oboukhova (m-s), pianist unid.	MK D-2404/5	1958	10" LP
A. Solenkova (s), pianist unid.	MK D-3344/5	RI	12" LP
	MK D-012353/4		
O Mort, poussière d'étoiles, Op. 95, No. 10			
—See *La Chanson d'Ève, Op. 95*			
Le Parfum impérissable, Op. 76, No. 1 (de Lisle) (1897)			
G. Cernay (m-s), G. Cloez	Od 188.764	1934	10" 78
G. Guillamat (s), V. Perlemutter	FCol DF-2484	1937	10" 78
R. Hahn (b), self-accompanied	FCol D-2029	1931	10" 78
P. Mollet (b), P. Maillard-Verger	Selmer LPG-8006	1951	12" LP
B. Monnart (s), S. Gouat	West XWN-18214 in set 5502,	1956	12" LP
	Plé P-3063	1935	10" 78
C. Panzéra (b), Mme. Panzéra-Baillot	Vic 1897, FHMV DA-4878	RR	12" LP
	COLH 103, FHMV FALP-50028		
P. de Seyguières (t), J. Witkowsky, O.	F Col DF-2452	1937	10" 78
G. Souzay (b), D. Baldwin	Epic LC-3764, Phil A-02059L	1961	12" LP
	Epic BC-1122	1961	12" S
N. Vallin (s), M. Fauré	Pathé PD-51	1944	10" 78
	Vox PL-1730	RR	10" LP

Composition and Performer(s)	Record Label and Number	Date	Speed
Le Pays des rêves, Op. 39, No. 3 (Silvestre) (1884)			
B. Monmart (s), S. Gouat	West XWN-18212 in set 5502, Plé P-3061	1956	12" LP
Le Plus doux chemin, Op. 87, No. 1 (Silvestre) (1904)			
J. Dutey (t), T. Janopoulo	West XWN-18214 in set 5502, Plé P-3063	1956	12" LP
I. French (s), P. Doguereau	Tech set T-7	1949	12" 78
Poème d'un jour, Op. 21 (Grandmougin) (1881) (cycle of 3 songs) (orch. by A. Martz)			
—Complete cycle			
C. Maurane (b), L. Bienvenu	Pathé PD-137	1950	10" 78
P. Mollet (b), S. Gouat	West XWN-18212 in set 5502, Plé P-3061	1956	12" LP
E. Noréna (s), Coppola, O.	FHMV K-7202	1934	10" 78
C. Panzéra (b), pianist unid.	FHMV P-765	1928	10" 78
G. Sciutti (s), J. Bonneau	Phil A-76.705R	1954	10" LP
G. Souzay (b), D. Baldwin	Epic LC-3764, Phil A-02059L	1961	12" LP
	Epic BC-1122	1961	12" S
G. Thill (t), M. Fauré	ACol 17157-D, FCol LF-157	1937	10" 78
J. Tourel (m-s), G. Reeves	ACol ML-4158	1949	12" LP
N. Vallin (s), P. Darck	Pathé PG-61	1935	10" 78
—No. 1. *Rencontre*			
A. Gaudin (b), accompanist unid.	FDCG 561.017	1931	10" 78
J. Harsanyi (s), O. Herz	Per SPL-581	1954	12" LP
Mellot-Joubert (s), Le Boucher	FCol D-12030	1931	10" 78

245

Composition and Performer(s)	Record Label and Number	Date	Speed
C. Panzéra (b), pianist unid.	FHMV P-497	1925	10" 78a
M. Sibelle (s), pianist unid.	Pathé 3410	1929	10" V
M. Villabella (t), G. Cloez, O.	Od 123.517	1931	12" 78
——Accompaniment only			
M. Fauré	FCol DF-1105	1933	10" 78
—No. 2. *Toujours*			
V. de los Angeles (s), G. Soriano	HMV ALP-2287	1967	12" LP
	HMV ASD-2287	1967	12" S
——Accompaniment only			
M. Fauré	FCol DF-1105	1933	10" 78
—No. 3. *Adieu*			
E. Clément (t), pianist unid.	Pathé 3319	1926	10" V
C. Panzéra (b), Mme. Panzéra-Baillot	Merc MG-10097	1951	12" LP
Les Présents, Op. 46, No. 1 (de l'Isle-Adam) (1887)			
B. Kruysen (b), N. Lee	Valois MB-765	1967	12" LP
F. Mertens (t), E. Lush	Vic LM-6153, HMV HLPS-25	1960	12" LP
B. Monmart (s), S. Gouat	West XWN-18212 in set 5502, Plé P-3061	1956	12" LP
Prima verba, Op. 95, No. 2			
—See *La Chanson d'Ève, Op. 95*			
Prison, Op. 83, No. 1 (Verlaine) (1900)			
P. Bernac (b), F. Poulenc	FHMV DA-4889	1937	10" 78
C. Croiza (m-s), F. Poulenc	FCol D-13033	1931	10" 78

Composition and Performer(s)	Record Label and Number	Date	Speed
G. Guillamat (s), V. Perlemutter	FCol DF-2487	1937	10" 78
B. Kruysen (b), N. Lee	Valois MB-765	1967	12" S
Y. le Marc' Hadour (b), Mme. le Marc' Hadour	BaM 31	1940	12" 78
P. Mollet (b), S. Gouat	West XWN-18214 in set 5502,	1956	12" LP
	Plé P-3063		
O. di Napoli (m-s), P. Doguereau	Tech set T-7	1949	12" 78
G. Souzay (b), J. Bonneau	Lon LD-9023, Dec LX-3149	1956	10" LP
G. Souzay (b), D. Baldwin	Phil AL-3480, CPhil A-02324-L	1963	12" LP
	Phil SAL-3480, CPhil 835201AY	1963	12" S
Puisque l'aube grandit, Op. 61, No. 2			
—See *La Bonne Chanson, Op. 61*			
Quand tu plonges tes yeux dans mes yeux, Op. 106, No. 2			
—See *Le Jardin clos, Op. 106*			
Le Ramier, Op. 87, No. 2 (Silvestre) (1904)			
J. Dutey (t), T. Janopoulo	West XWN-18214 in set 5502,	1956	12" LP
	Plé P-3063		
La Rançon, Op. 8, No. 2 (Baudelaire) (c. 1865)			
B. Monmart (s), S. Gouat	West XWN-18211 in set 5502,	1956	12" LP
	Plé P-3060		
Rêve d'amour, Op. 5, No. 2 (Hugo) (c. 1885)			
J. Dutey (t), T. Janopoulo	West XWN-18211 in set 5502,	1956	12" LP
	Plé P-3060		

247

Composition and Performer(s)	Record Label and Number	Date	Speed
La Rose, Op. 51, No. 4 (de Lisle) (c. 1889)			
R. Doria (s), S. Gouat	West XWN-18213 in set 5502,		
	Plé P-3062	1956	12" LP
G. Souzay (b), D. Baldwin	EPhil AL-3505, FPhil L-2405L	1963	12" LP
	APhil 900.191, EPhil SAL-3505,		
N. Vallin (s), P. Darck	FPhil 835.286LY	1963	12" S
	Pathé PG-60	1935	10" 78
Reflets dans l'eau, Op. 113, No. 2			
—See *Mirages, Op. 113*			
Rencontre, Op. 21, No. 1			
—See *Poème d'un jour, Op. 21*			
Roses ardentes, Op. 95, No. 3			
—See *La Chanson d'Ève, Op. 95*			
Les Roses d'Ispahan, Op. 39, No. 4 (de Lisle) (1884)			
V. de los Angeles (s), G. Soriano	HMV ALP-2287	1967	12" LP
	HMV ASD-2287	1967	12" S
G. Auzeneau (bs), A. Collard	FCol LF-251	1936	10" 78
E. Billot (b), accompanist unid.	Od 123.779	1934	12" 78
R. Bourdin (b), pianist unid.	Od 188.634	1933	10" 78
D. Devriès (t), G. Cloez, O.	Od 123.553	1931	12" 78
R. Doria (s), S. Gouat	West XWN-18212 in set 5502,		
	Plé P-3061	1956	12" LP
E. van Dyck (t), pianist unid.	Fono 39226	1905	10" 78a
G. Boué (s), M. Fauré	Uran 7070	1953	12" LP

Composition and Performer(s)	Record Label and Number	Date	Speed
G. Guillamat (s), P. Sancan	FCol LF-192	1934	10″ 78
B. Kruysen (s), N. Lee	Valois MB-765	1967	12″ S
G. Martinelli (s), accompanist unid.	FDGG 566.170	1935	12″ 78
N. Mathot (s), Jacque-Dupont	FRCA F-230.005	1956	10″ LP
J. Micheau (s), H. Greenslade	Dec M-630	1949	10″ 78
C. Panzéra (b), pianist unid.	FHMV P-852	1931	10″ 78
L. Pons (s), F. La Forge	Vic 1997 in set M-599, HMV DA-1727		
L. Pons (s), M. Abravanel, O.	ACol 72048-D in set M-689	1939	10″ 78
	ACol ML-4300	1947	12″ 78
M. Sauvageot (b), accompanist unid.	FHMV P-372	RR	12″ LP
Schmidt, Brilli	Orph 51071/2	1923	10″ 78a
M. Sénéchal (t), J. Bonneau	Phil N-00681R	1964	12″ LP
S. Stappen (s), P. Coppola, O.	FHMV K-7460	1956	10″ LP
M. Teyte (s), G. Moore	HMV DA-1819	1935	10″ 78
N. Vallin (s), G. Andolfi	Pathé X-3465	1942	10″ 78
N. Vallin (s), M. Fauré	Pathé PD-66	1930	10″ 78
	Vox PL-1730	1944	10″ 78
S. Wyss (s), J. St. John	Dec M-533	RR	10″ LP
		1943	10″ 78

Une Sainte en son auréole, Op. 61, No. 1

—See *La Bonne Chanson, Op. 61*

Le Secret, Op. 23, No. 3 (Silvestre) (1882)

Composition and Performer(s)	Record Label and Number	Date	Speed
G. Bacquier (b), J. Laforge	Vega L-30-PO-357	1967	12″ LP
P. Bernac (b), F. Poulenc	HMV DA-1884	1948	10″ 78
R. Crespin, J. Wustman	Ang 36405	1967	12″ LP
	Ang S-36405	1967	12″ S

Composition and Performer(s)	Record Label and Number	Date	Speed
M. Dens (b), J. Bonneau	Pathé DTX-306	1959	12" LP
	Pathé ASTX-114	1959	12" S
P. Frijsh (s), D. Dougherty	Vic 2078 in set M-668	1939	10" 78
J. Lindsay (s), accompanist unid.	FHMV 33754, P-232	1912	10" 78
C. Maurane (b), L. Bienvenu	Pathé PD-136	1950	10" 78
S. Metcalf-Casals (s), G. Moore	HMV JG-22	1938	12" 78
B. Monnart (s), S. Gouat	West XWN-18212 in set 5502, Plé P-3061	1956	12" LP
C. Panzéra (b), Mme. Panzéra-Baillot	Merc MG-10097	1951	12" LP
A. Raveau (m-s), G. Andolfi	Pathé X-93077	1933	10" 78
M. Sauvageot (b), accompanist unid.	FHMV P-378	1923	10" 78
Schmidt, Brilli	Orph 51071/2	1964	12" LP
G. Souzay (b), D. Baldwin	Epic LC-3764, Phil A-2059L	1961	12" LP
	Epic BC-1122	1961	12" S
M. Teyte (s), G. Moore	HMV DA-1876	1948	10" 78
C. Valletti (t), L. Taubman	Vic LM-2787	1965	12" LP
	Vic LSC-2787	1965	12" S
N. Vallin (s), M. Fauré	Pathé PD-45	1944	10" 78
	Vox PL-1730	RR	10" LP
Vanni-Marcoux (bs), accompanist unid.	FHMV DA-4814	1932	10" 78

Sérénade toscane, Op. 3, No. 2 (Bussine) (c. 1865)

Composition and Performer(s)	Record Label and Number	Date	Speed
R. Doria (s), S. Gouat	West XWN-18211 in set 5502, Plé P-3060	1956	12" LP
G. Thill (t), M. Fauré	ACol 4164-M, FCol LF-154	1936	10" 78

Seule!, Op. 3, No. 1 (Gautier) (c. 1865)

Composition and Performer(s)	Record Label and Number	Date	Speed
B. Monnart (s), S. Gouat	West XWN-18211 in set 5502, Plé P-3060	1956	12" LP

Composition and Performer(s)	Record Label and Number	Date	Speed
Soir, Op. 83, No. 2 (Samain) (1900)			
P. Bernac (b), J. Doyen	Ult BP-1493	1936	10" 78
P. Bernac (b), F. Poulenc	HMV DA-1884, DA-1907	1948	10" 78
C. Boons (s), accompanist unid.	DGG 561.073	1932	10" 78
R. Crespin (s), J. Wustman	Ang 36405	1967	12" LP
	Ang S-36405	1967	12" S
C. Croiza (m-s), G. Reeves	FCol LF-63	1931	10" 78
M. Dens (b), J. Bonneau	Pathé DTX-306	1959	12" LP
	Pathé ASTX-114	1959	12" S
R. Doria (s), S. Gouat	West XWN-18214 in set 5502,	1956	12" LP
	Plé P-3063		
G. Gills (s), M. Frank	Pathé 3419	1929	10" V
G. Guillamat (s), V. Perlemutter	FCol DF-2484	1937	10" 78
I. Kolassi (m-s), J. Bonneau	Lon LS-568, Dec LX-3080	1952	10" LP
B. Kruysen (b), N. Lee	Valois MB-765	1967	12" S
M. Marseillac (s), pianist unid.	Od 165.555	1930	10" 78
N. Mathot (s), Jacque-Dupont	FRCA F-230.005	1956	10" LP
S. Metcalf-Casals (s), G. Moore	HMV JG-22	1938	12" 78
P. Mollet (b), P. Maillot-Verger	Selmer LPG-8006	1951	12" LP
O. di Napoli (m-s), P. Doguereau	Tech set T-7	1949	12" 78
C. Panzéra (b), pianist unid.	FHMV P-852	1930	10" 78
C. Panzéra (b), Mme. Panzéra-Baillot	FHMV DB-4971	1935	12" 78
	COLH 103, FHMV 50028	RR	12" LP
G. Souzay (b), D. Baldwin	Epic LC-3764, Phil A-2059L	1961	12" LP
	Epic BC-1122	1961	12" S
M. Teyte (s), G. Moore	HMV DA-1819	1942	10" 78
N. Vallin (s), P. Darck	Pathé PG-101	1940	10" 78

Composition and Performer(s)	Record Label and Number	Date	Speed
N. Vallin (s), M. Fauré	Pathé PD-45	1944	10" 78
	Vox PL-1730	RR	10" LP
—Accompaniment only M. Fauré	FCol DF-1105	1933	10" 78
Spleen, Op. 51, No. 3 (Verlaine) (c. 1889)			
H. Cuénod (t), J. Blancard	Vang VRS-414	1951	12" LP
P. Curtin (s), R. Edwards	Camb 706	1965	12" LP
	Camb 1706	1965	12" S
R. Doria (s), S. Gouat	West XWN-18212 in set 5502, Plé P-3061	1956	12" LP
I. French (s), P. Doguereau	Tech set T-7	1949	12" 78
G. Guillamat (s), V. Perlemutter	FCol DF-2486	1937	10" 78
B. Kruysen (b), N. Lee	Valois MB-765	1967	12" S
C. Panzéra (b), Mme. Panzéra-Baillot	COLH 103, FHMV 50028 (no 78 rpm issue traced)	c. 1937	12" LP
G. Souzay (b), J. Bonneau	Lon LD-9023, Dec LX-3149	1956	10" LP
Sylvie, Op. 6, No. 3 (de Choudens) (c. 1865)			
J. Dutey (t), T. Janopoulo	West XWN-18211 in set 5502, Plé P-3060	1956	12" LP
Toujours, Op. 21, No. 2			
—See *Poème d'un jour, Op. 21*			
Tristesse, Op. 6, No. 2 (Gautier) (c. 1865)			
V. de los Angeles (s), G. Soriano	HMV ALP-2287	1967	12" LP
	HMV ASD-2287	1967	12" S

Composition and Performer(s)	Record Label and Number	Date	Speed
G. Guillamat (s), V. Perlemutter	FCol DF-2485	1937	10" 78
B. Monmart (s), S. Gouat	West XWN-18211 in set 5502, Plé P-3060	1956	12" LP
N. Perrugia (s), J. Benvenuti	FHMV DB-5178	1951	12" 78
G. Souzay (b), J. Bonneau	Lon LL-245, Dec LXT-2543	1950	12" LP
Vaisseaux, nous vous aurons aimés, Op. 118, No. 4			
—See *L'Horizon chimérique, Op. 118*			
Veilles-tu, ma senteur de soleil?, Op. 95, No. 7			
—See *La Chanson d'Ève, Op. 95*			
Vocalise (1907) (no words)			
R. Doria (s), S. Gouat	West XWN-18214 in set 5502, Plé P-3063	1956	12" LP
E. Farrell (s), G. Trovillo	ACol ML-5924	1964	12" LP
	ACol MS-6524	1964	12" S
—arr. Oboe and Piano (Doney)			
L. Goossens, C. Raybould	ECol DB-691, FCol DF-794	1934	10" 78
—arr. Bass Clarinet and Piano (Doney and Sargent)			
W. Lear, M. Sargent	EHMV C-3621	1947	12" 78
Le Voyageur, Op. 18, No. 2 (Silvestre) (c. 1880)			
B. Kruysen (b), N. Lee	Valois MB-765	1967	12" S
P. Mollet (b), S. Gouat	West XWN-18212 in set 5502, Plé P-3061	1956	12" LP
A. Raveau (m-s), G. Andolfi	Pathé X-93078	1933	10" 78
M. Sauvageot (b), accompanist unid.	FHMV P-378	1923	10" 78a

Composition and Performer(s)	Record Label and Number	Date	Speed
VOCAL ENSEMBLES AND CHORAL MUSIC			
Ave Maria, no opus number, for three male voices (c. 1871) Unpublished			
Ave Maria, Op. 67, No. 2, for voice and organ (c. 1895) M. Singher (b), cello and piano unid.	ACol 72901-D in set MM-878 ACol ML-4258	1952 RR	12″ 78 12″ LP
Ave Maria, Op. 93, for two voices and organ (1906) No recordings traced			
Ave, verum corpus, Op. 65, No. 1, for two female voices, solo or chorus (c. 1894) M. Angelici (s), A. Fauré-Esperal (m-s), J. Ullern, p.	Lumen 2.22.007, 30107	1938	10″ 78
Cantique de Jean Racine, Op. 11, for mixed chorus, harmonium and string quartet or orchestra (c. 1873) L. Frémaux, Caillard Cho., Monte Carlo Opera O.	Epic LC-3885, Erato LDE-3228 Epic BC-1285, Erato STE-50128	1965 1965	12″ LP 12″ S
D. Inghelbrecht, French Radio Cho., Champs-Elysées O.	DucTh DTL-93083	1956	12″ LP
—arr. Solo voices, Organ and Orchestra F. Cébron cond., M. Angelici (s), G. Cernay (m-s), J. Giovanetti (t), P. Gianotti (b), N. Pierront, org., O.	Lumen 2.22.010, 33080	1937	10″ 78
Les Djinns, Op. 12 for chorus and orchestra (Hugo) (c. 1875) No recordings traced			
Ecce fidelus servus, Op. 54 for soprano, tenor, bass, organ and string bass (c. 1890) No recordings traced			

254

Composition and Performer(s)	Record Label and Number	Date	Speed
Madrigal, Op. 35 for four solo voices or mixed chorus and orchestra (Silvestre) (1884)			
N. Boulanger cond., unid. solo voices and O.	BaM 79	1947	12" 78
N. Boulanger, G. Peyron (s), M. Holley (m-s), P. Derenne (t)	Vox PL-6380	1950	12" S
D. Conrad (b), unid. instrumental ens. (different version?)	DucTh 93083	1956	12" LP
D. Inghelbrecht cond. French Radio Cho., Champs-Elysées O.	Pathé X-0462, X-3461	1936?	10" 78
Conductor unid., Paris Teachers' Cho.			
Maria, Mater gratiae Op. 47, No. 2 for two female voices and organ (c. 1887)			
M. Angelici (s), A. Fauré-Esperal (m-s), J. Ullern, p.	Lumen 2.22.007, 30107	1938	10" 78
Doniau-Blanc (s), Franck (m-s), Pascal Quartet	Lumen 2.22.007, 30009	1933	10" 78
Messe basse, no opus number, for soprano solo, three part women's chorus and organ or harmonium (early)			
Collinico cond. unnamed soloist, Chanteurs Côte d'Azur	SM 45-16	1958	7" 45
J. Jouineau cond. unnamed soloist, RTF Children's Chorus	Pathé DTX-247	1955	12" LP
K. Kreuder cond. Gagnard (s), unid. vocal ensemble and organ	Erato EFM-42.017	1958	10" LP
La Naissance de Vénus, Op. 29, for solo voices, chorus and orchestra (Collin) (1882)			
No recordings traced			
Noël—"Il est né le divin Enfant". No opus number, no date, no poet identified.			
—arr. Andolfi			
G. Andolfi, S. Laydecker (s), J. Renault (a), unid. O. and organ	Pathé PA-987	1936	10" 78

255

Composition and Performer(s)	Record Label and Number	Date	Speed
G. Andolfi, unid. soloists, orchestra and organ	Pathé X-3413	1930	10" 78
O salutaris Op. 47, No. 1 for voice and organ (c. 1887)			
C. Maurane (b), M. LeClair Alain, organ	Erato LPEV-477	1964	7" 45
Pleurs d'or, Op. 72 for mezzo-soprano and baritone (Samain) (c. 1896)			
V. de los Angeles (s), D. Fischer-Dieskau (b), G. Moore, p.	Ang 35936, HMV ALP-1891	1962	12" LP
	Ang S-35936, HMV ASD-459	1962	12" S
G. Cernay (m-s), R. Tabla (t), pianist unid.	FCol BF-22	1934	10" 78
R. Doria (s), P. Mollet (b), S. Gouat, p.	West XWN-18214 in set 5502, Plé P-3063	1956	12" LP
Puisqu'ici-bas, Op. 10, No. 1, for two sopranos or soprano & tenor (Hugo) (c. 1870)			
R. Doria (s), B. Monmart (s), S. Gouat, p.	West XWN-18212 in set 5502, Plé P-3061	1956	12" LP
Requiem, Op. 48, for soprano, baritone, mixed chorus, orchestra and organ (1887)			
E. Ansermet, S. Danco (s), G. Souzay (b), Tour de Peliz Cho., Suisse Romande O., E. Schmidt, org.	Lon 5221, Dec LXT-5158	1956	12" LP
	Dec SXL-2211	1960	12" S
E. Bourmack, S. Dupont (s), M. Didier (b), Les Chanteurs de Lyons, Trigintour Instrumental Lyonnais, E. Cornette, org.	ACol 69423/7 in set M-354, ECol LX-773/7, FCol RFX-63/7	1939	12" 78
	ACol ML-4529	RR	12" LP
G. Bret, M. Malnory-Marseillac (s), L. Morturier (b), Bach Society Cho., Bach Society O., A. Cellier, org.	Vic 11154/8, EHMV D-2101/5, FHMV W-1154/8	1931	12" 78

Composition and Performer(s)	Record Label and Number	Date	Speed
A. Cluytens, V. de los Angeles (s), D. Fischer-Dieskau (b), E. Brasseur Cho., Paris Conservatoire O., H. Puig-Roget, org.	Ang 35974, HMV AN-107 Ang S-35974, HMV SAN-107	1963 1963	12" LP 12" S
Erlandson, soprano, baritone, chorus, organist unid. San Jose State College O. and Cho.	MusL 7103	issued?	12" LP
J. Fournet, P. Alarie (s), C. Maurane (b), E. Brasseur Cho., Lamoureux O., M. Duruflé, org.	Epic LC-3044 Phil A-00669R, Phil ABR-4012, Phil G-5373R	1953 1953	12" LP 10" LP
L. Frémaux, D. Thilliez (boy s), B. Kruysen (b), P. Gallard Cho., Monte Carlo Opera O., H. Carol, org.	Epic LC-3885, Erato LDE-3228 Epic BC-1285, Erato STE-50128	1965 1965	12" LP 12" S
D. Inghelbrecht, F. Ogéas (s), B. Demigny (b), RTF Cho., Champs Elysées O., J. Baudry-Goddard, org.	DucTh DTL-93083	1956	12" LP
R. Liebowitz, N. Sautereau (s), B. Demigny (b), Paris Phil. Cho., Paris Phil. O., org. unid.	Oce OCS-26	1950	12" LP
L. Martini, J. Chamonin (s), G. Abdoun (b), Jeunesse Musicale Cho., Colonne Concert O., organist unid.	Turn 34147	1967	12" S
W. Pelletier, M. Denya (s), M. Harrell (b), Disciples of Massenet Cho., Montreal Festival O., R. Roy, org.	Vic 18296/300 in set M-844, HMV ED-364/8 CVic LCT-7003	1943 RR	12" 78 12" LP
R. Wagner, P. Beems (s), T. Uppman (b), R. Wagner Chorale, Concert Arts O., organist unid.	Cap P-8241	1953	12" LP
R. Wagner, M. Gibson (s), M. Roux (b), R. Wagner Chorale, Paris Conservatoire O., organist unid.	Cap P-8586 Cap SP-8586	1962 1962	12" LP 12" S
—Pie Jesu D. Devries (t), G. Cloez cond. O.	Od 188.782	1931	10" 78

Composition and Performer(s)	Record Label and Number	Date	Speed
Doniau-Blanc (s), Lepage cond. O.	Lumen 2.20.012, 30003	1933	10" 78
M. Journet (b), orchestra unid.	Vic 64582	1917	10" 78a
J. Laval (s), J. Witkowsky cond. O.	FCol BFX-3	1934	12" 78
H. Ludolph (s), orchestra unid.	HMV C-4876	1946	12" 78
H. St. Cricq (t), orchestra unid.	Pathé X-3424	1929	10" 78
M. Barrow (boy s), C. Dearnely cond. O.	Oryx M-706, Lyr 174	1965	12" LP
	Lyr 7174	1966	12" S
—In paradisum			
Abbé Lepage cond. St. Nicholas Cho., O. unid.	Lumen 2.20.012, 30003	1933	10" 78
Le Ruisseau, Op. 22, for two-part female chorus (Anon.) (1881)			
J. Kreuder, vocal ensemble unid.	Erato EFM-42.017	1958	10" LP
Salve Regina, Op. 67, No. 1, for voice and organ (c. 1895)			
G. Cernay (m-s), unid. organ and orch.	Lumen 2.20.014, 30085	1938	10" 78
Tarentelle, Op. 10, No. 2, for two sopranos and piano (Monnier) (c. 1870)			
G. Cernay (m-s), R. Tabla (t), pianist unid.	FCol BF-22	1934	10" 78
R. Doria (s), B. Monmart (s), S. Gouat, p.	West XWN-18212 in set 5502, Plé P-3061	1956	12" LP
—arr. Cello and Piano			
G. Piatigorsky, V. Pavlovsky	ACol 17308-D in set MM-501	1942	12" 78
Tantum ergo, Op. 65, No. 2, for three-part female chorus (c. 1894)			
Jouineau cond. RTF Children's Chorus, Orch. Nationale	Pathé DTL-247	1959	12" LP

Composition and Performer(s)	Record Label and Number	Date	Speed
Tantum ergo, no opus number, for soprano, tenor and chorus (1905?) No recordings traced			
Tu es Petrus, no opus number, for baritone and chorus (1884?) Delmotte (b), Abbé Lepage, St. Nicholas Cho.	Lumen 2.24.011, 30006	1933	10" 78

259

❧ Index

261

264

℀ Émile Vuillermoz

Émile Vuillermoz, one of France's most influential critics, was born in Lyons in 1878. His father, a banker, destined the young man to a career in law and literature. But it was during his college days that Vuillermoz met Daniel Fleuret, the organist at the Church of the Redemption in Lyons, studied organ and harmony with him, and decided that music was to be his career.

Eventually, his family grudgingly allowed him to enroll in the Paris Conservatoire. There, he studied composition with Gabriel Fauré where his classmates included Maurice Ravel, Georges Enesco, Florent Schmitt and other composers who were to achieve recognition.

Upon the conclusion of his studies, Vuillermoz chose criticism as his primary field. From 1905 until his death in 1960, he contributed articles and critiques to numerous journals and periodicals, including *Le Temps, Excelsior, Candide, L'Eclair, Comoedia, L'Illustration, Le Journal Musical Français, Spectateur, Opéra, La Revue des Deux-Mondes,* and *Paris-Presse-L'Intransigeant.*

In 1910 he was one of the founders of the Société Musicale Indépendante, whose president was Gabriel Fauré. He also served as the editor-in-chief of the society's magazine and was instrumental in assembling a brilliant team of contributors that included Claude Debussy and Vincent d'Indy.

In addition to writing about music, he also contributed many illuminating film critiques. His eclecticism is mirrored in the titles of his books, from serious works on music such as *Gabriel Fauré, Claude Debussy, Ravel par quelques-uns de ses*

familiers, Histoire de la Musique and *Musique d'Aujourd'hui*
to *La Nuit des Dieux,* a book on mythology, and *Le Savoir-
Boire,* a study of French wines.

As a leading figure on the French musical scene and a
known composer of light and serious music, he was one of
the founders of the important Concerts Pasdeloup, he conceived ballet themes, organized festivals, presided over La
Commission de la Musique à la Radio and presented a music
appreciation program on the air.

Émile Vuillermoz was also instrumental in having modern
music accepted in France. Besides championing the compositions of Fauré, Debussy and Ravel, he also fought for Arthur
Honegger, Igor Stravinsky, Florent Schmitt and many other
vital musicians of the twentieth century.

Gabriel Fauré was completed a scant three months before
his death on March 2, 1960.